MARX
IN THE MID-TWENTIETH CENTURY

GAJO PETROVIĆ, associate professor of philosophy at the University of Zagreb, Yugoslavia, is author of *English Empiricist Philosophy, Philosophical Views of G. V. Plekhanov,* and *From Locke to Ayer.* Born in Karlovac, Yugoslavia, in 1927, he studied philosophy in Zagreb, Leningrad, and Moscow, and spent two years studying in Great Britain and the United States.

MARX in the
mid-twentieth century

A YUGOSLAV PHILOSOPHER
CONSIDERS KARL MARX'S WRITINGS

Gajo Petrović

ANCHOR BOOKS
DOUBLEDAY & COMPANY, INC.
GARDEN CITY, NEW YORK

Anchor Books edition: 1967

Preface

The papers published in this book discuss seemingly different and even mutually independent topics. In fact they are all concerned with different aspects of the same basic topic, which is indicated by the title, and they are inspired by the same endeavor: to penetrate to the essence of Marx's original thought and to think further in its spirit about the momentous philosophical questions of the contemporary world and man. Despite certain differences in approach, form and stress, all the papers are imbued with the same guiding ideas.

The first part of the book is concerned with the relationship between philosophy and Marxism, the essence and the development of Marx's thought and the difference between creative and dogmatic Marxism. This is, consequently, a kind of "general" introduction with strong "historico-philosophical" elements. In the second part, man, praxis, freedom, alienation, de-alienation, socialism and humanism are discussed; in traditional terminology this is something like "philosophical anthropology," partly also "ethics," "philosophy of history," "social and political philosophy." The third part would seem to be predominantly "ontological" and "epistemological"; in it, being, truth, knowledge, meaning, logic and mathematics are examined. The last contribution is "terminological" (partly even "philological"); however, as it considers "ontological" terminology (and not merely terminology) it obviously also belongs here. I hope the reader will come to see that the traditional labels can characterize only very inadequately these writings because, for example, those published in the second part are no less "ontological" than those in the third, and those in the third part are no less "anthropological" than those in the second.

All these papers have been written in the last few years. For those who are acquainted with my previous writings it will not be difficult to see both continuity and difference. Nevertheless, there are a few points I would like to mention: the first years of the postwar development of Yugoslav Marxist philosophy were marked by the predominance of imported, Stalinistic conceptions. The emancipation from these conceptions was a long, arduous and contradictory process. I believe that my critique of Rosenthal (published in January 1950) was the first extensive Yugoslav criticism of Stalin and Stalinism in philosophy; and that some of my later writings also represented a contribution to the critical examination of Stalinism. The process of liberation from Stalinism in philosophy, however, neither was nor could be merely a matter of removing Stalinistic additions or "admixtures" from Marxism and "correcting" certain "mistakes" or "shortcomings" of Engels or Lenin. Emancipation was possible only through a renewal and further development of Marx's original thought. The papers in this book differ from the earlier ones especially in that those earlier writings strove for the revival of the most basic conceptions of creative Marxism, whereas I have made an attempt here to realize some of the possibilities offered now that the platform of creative Marxism has been gained. It is, of course, up to the reader to judge whether, or to what extent, the attempt has proved successful.

Zagreb, October 1964   G.P.

Contents

Preface   5

Part I

Marxism versus Stalinism   9
The "young" and the "old" Marx   31
The continuity of Marx's thought   35
Dialectical materialism and the philosophy of
    Karl Marx   52

Part II

Marx's concept of man   67
Man as economic animal and man as praxis   90
What is freedom?   115
Alienation and de-alienation   135
Philosophy and politics in socialism   154

Part III

Praxis and Being   171
Truth and reflection   190
What is meaning?   199
Logic and mathematics   218

Index   231

PART I

Marxism versus Stalinism

What is happening in Yugoslav Marxist[1] philosophy today?

Apparently, unusual discussions have become frequent lately: the "young" and "old" Marx, praxis, subject-object and reflection, humanistic problems of Marxism.[2] Questions are being asked that not long ago were held to be finally settled; contrapositions are being made that seem directly unthinkable. Karl Marx is not only being opposed to Engels and Lenin—his own authority no longer seems sacrosanct.

Is our philosophy turning its back on Marxism, yielding to seductive but precarious currents of bourgeois philosophical thought? Or is it today more than ever before truly Marxist and truly philosophy?

I. *Authentic Marxism*

Some people are inclined to weep for the golden age of our postwar Marxism, when Yugoslav philosophers used to "stand firmly" on the position of Marxism. But if they

[1] There are also non-Marxists among present-day Yugoslav philosophers. But this article (originally published in 1961) is concerned only with the Marxist (prevailing and in the view of the author most interesting) current in contemporary Yugoslav philosophy. The term "Yugoslav Marxist Philosophy" in the text of this article means the same as "Marxist Philosophy in Yugoslavia."

[2] Discussions on the "young" and the "old" Marx (Zagreb, December, 1960) and on the humanistic problems of Marxism (Zagreb, December, 1961) were organized by Croatian Philosophical Society; discussion on praxis, subject-object and reflection (Bled, October, 1961) by Yugoslav Philosophical Association.

wipe the tears from their eyes they will see that the child whose firm standing they lament has meanwhile begun to walk. Did not our philosophy, however, after it started walking, wander away where chance led it?

To the satisfaction of all malicious persons and pessimists we must frankly "confess": during the postwar years Yugoslav Marxist philosophy moved in a certain sense "backward"—from a Stalinistic version of Marxist philosophy, which became predominant in the first years after the war, to the original form of that philosophy as contained in the works of Marx, Engels and Lenin. But this way "backward," from the caricature to the original was, in fact, a way forward—from a dead thought to a live one. The criticism of the Stalinistic conception of philosophy meant not the abandonment but the revival and regeneration of Marxism in philosophy.

I do not wish to suggest that this revival of the creative spirit of Marxism is, or was, making progress only in Yugoslavia or only in the field of philosophy. In different forms and at different rates of speed creative Marxism has been making progress in other fields and other countries as well. The whole Yugoslav theory and practice of revolutionary Marxism came into the conflict with international Stalinism. But during the same period the criticism of Stalinism in philosophy and other fields was going on in many other countries too.

It is not the purpose of this article to give an exhaustive analysis and explanation of all these complex processes inside and outside Yugoslav philosophy, but rather to sketch the essence of processes that were and still are taking place in our philosophy, to draw attention to some of its main achievements and problems.

I do not think that Stalin and Stalinism are exclusively "negative" historical phenomena. But regardless of how history finally weighs all Stalin's political "merits" and "mistakes" one thing is already certain: Stalin's conception of Marxist philosophy differs essentially from Marx's, Engels' and Lenin's. The return from Stalin to Marx, Engels and Lenin was not a return from one completed system of philosophical dogmas to another, but a rediscovery of many important insights, which were distorted or left out by Stalinism, and at the same time a reopening of many problems that were closed by Stalinism. Stalin simplified, distorted and made rigid philosophical views contained in the works of Engels and Lenin, and almost completely ignored Marx's own philosophical inheritance. For that very reason it became more than merely a return. In reviving the real Marx we could not remain with his solutions, we had to try to answer the questions that he left open.

Stalinism as a complete system of established dogmas required its adherents to "stand firmly," always in the same place; Marxism as a theory that contains unsettled questions can be held only through a creative effort and progress.

Without attempting a complete analysis, we will point to some aspects of the return to Marx, Engels and Lenin that have led both to the revival of authentic Marxism in philosophy and to the discovery of open problems that we have to solve by ourselves.

II. *Marxism's Philosophical Inheritance*

Stalinism was, among other things, a strange combination of an extremely dogmatic and an extremely nihilistic attitude toward the philosophical inheritance of Marxism.

Marx, Engels, Lenin and Stalin are, according to Stalinistic doctrine, the "classics of Marxism," the collective discoverers and possessors of absolute truth. They have made a revolution in philosophy, finally settled all basic problems, and created a complete philosophical system in which there are no gaps. They are, to be sure, four, but their teaching is one, absolutely coherent and indivisible. It is unthinkable that one of them could contradict any of the others or himself. In their work there are no "mistakes," therefore no "emendations" are possible. A quotation from the classics is the most cogent argument for a thesis (or against it). Marxist philosophy can and must develop, but its development cannot and need not lead to the negation of any of its essential theses; it can only confirm, specify and "deepen" them. How is a development possible through confirmation only, without any negation? This is already a question that it is not polite to ask.

The other side of the unhistoric dogmatico-apologetic attitude toward the "classics of Marxism" represents a no less nonhistoric nihilism. Stalinism, in fact, acknowledges in Marxist philosophical conception only that which does not contradict its own caricature of these conceptions. There are glasses through which one has to look at the philosophical inheritance of Marxism, glasses through which one sees only what one has to see.

Stalinism declared the so-called early works of Marx immature—still Hegelian, not yet Marxist; Lenin's *Philosophical Notebooks* were written for his personal, private use. In disqualifying the "young" Marx and the "old" Lenin, Stalinism did not hesitate to borrow such quotations from them as were accidentally convenient; and, while declaring itself an adherent of the "mature" Marx and Engels and the "public" Lenin, Stalinists tacitly reject whatever in their "true," "Marxist" works does not serve its own cause.

Marxist philosophical works not written by Marx, Engels or Lenin Stalinism are regarded at best as successful popularizations. Those that deviate in the least from Stalinistic dogmas are automatically classified as revisionist and non-Marxist. According to Stalinism, Plekhanov is partly a good popularizer of Marxist philosophy and partly a revisionist; Lukacs and Bloch, mainly revisionists. In this way Stalinism forbids an open criticism of Marx, Engels and Lenin and at the same time tacitly ignores a great part of Marxist philosophical inheritance. The overcoming of both sides of this double attitude is one of the results of our postwar philosophic development.

Why should we assume that the "classics of Marxism" are the exclusive possessors of philosophic truth? Why should we belittle all other Marxist philosophers? Why should we conceal the differences among Marx, Engels and Lenin that actually exist? Why should we exclude a priori the possibility of errors and contradictions in Engels and Lenin and even in Marx "himself"?

On the other hand, why should any of the Marxist philosophical texts (Marx or Engels, Lukacs or Bloch) be either, a priori, suspect or prohibited? Who is competent to issue such prohibitions? Why should we not study the philosophic inheritance of Marxism in all its integrity and breadth?

The taking off of Stalinistic glasses and the revival of the Marxist attitude toward the theoretic inheritance of Marxism has led to important insights. It has turned out that the ban that Stalinism allegedly put on "some parts" of Marx's philosophic inheritance was really a prohibition upon the fundamental meaning of his philosophy.

The "young" Marx is not a juvenile sin of the "old" genius, who wrote *Capital.* Marx's youth was not merely a passing young-Hegelian episode, but a period in which Marx developed the basic philosophic conceptions to which he remained faithful in his later works. Without the "young" Marx, a full understanding of the "old" is impossible.

The *Philosophical Notebooks* is not a work that may, but need not, be taken into account in the investigation of Lenin's philosophical views. In the *Notebooks* Lenin considers critically philosophical concepts that he himself held earlier. *Materialism and Empirio-Criticism* is not his last word in philosophy.

Lenin was exaggerating a little when he asserted that what Plekhanov wrote on philosophy was the "best in all of international Marxist literature,"[3] but it is true that the philosophical works of Plekhanov bear comparison with those of Engels and Lenin. In their best works Lukacs and Bloch start primarily from the "young" Marx, but they are neither revisionists nor popularizers; they are original Marxist thinkers.

But if surmounting dogmatico-nihilistic attitudes toward

[3] V. I. Lenin, *Sočinenija* (*Works*), 4th ed., vol. 32, pp. 72–73.

the classics of Marxism made possible fruitful work in Marxist analysis and evaluation of the development of Marxist philosophy, it did not settle automatically all the problems that it opened. While it was shown rather convincingly that it is impossible to oppose the "young" and the "old" Marx, that Marx's philosophical work is basically unified, it also became equally clear that Marx's philosophical views changed in many respects and in many other respects remained incomplete and unfinished. We cannot boast that we have exhaustively studied and determined all the stages of Marx's philosophical development, exactly reconstructed and analyzed all of Marx's solutions, difficulties and questions.

It has further become apparent that there are considerable differences between the philosophical views and interests of Marx and those of Engels. In the center of Marx's philosophy is a certain conception of man; Engels' philosophical endeavors were directed more toward the development of a dialectics of nature. The question naturally arises whether Marx's (and Engels') theory of man and Engels' conception of dialectics of nature complement each other or follow logically from each other or, on the contrary, mutually exclude each other. There are differences of opinion on these questions. It has been shown that Engels sometimes contradicts Marx, or at least is not at the same level, but discussions seem to be far from finished.

Plekhanov as well as Marx and Engels had a great influence upon the formation of Lenin's philosophical views, and some think that Boltzmann was the decisive influence on *Materialism and Empirio-Criticism*. The exact measure of all these influences, as well as the extent to which this work is original, is still not definitively established. Some of the main differences between *Materialism and Empirio-Criticism* and the *Philosophical Notebooks* have been clearly displayed. But the relationship between these works has not been explored and determined in detail.

Lukacs's juvenile work *History and Class Consciousness* (1923) is an example of a creative interpretation of

Marx's conception of man. His later works contain much of value, despite sometimes greater and sometimes lesser concessions to Stalinism. What in Lukacs's work is alive and what is dead; what is Marx's, what Lukacs's and what Stalin's?

These are only some of the questions to which Yugo- slav philosophers have been led by the abandonment of the dogmatico-nihilistic attitude toward the philosophic in- heritance of Marxism. We are rather far from their de- finitive settlement. But we are not in the blind alley to which Stalinistic dogmatism wanted to lead us either.

III. *Marxism and Non-Marxist Philosophy*

Marx and Engels were full of respect for Aristotle, Hegel and other great philosophers of the past, which did not prevent them from taking a critical attitude toward their philosophical works. Stalinism, on the other hand, looks with contempt on all pre-Marxist philosophy, regarding it as a mere prehistory, separated by an enormous gap from Marxist, scientific philosophy and of no essential impor- tance for the understanding and further development of Marxism. In comparison with such giants as Marx, Engels and Lenin, Hegel, Feuerbach and other pre-Marxist phi- losophers are mere "predecessors."

In contradistinction to pre-Marxist philosophy, which is only prescientific, all non-Marxist philosophy after Marx, according to Stalinism is directly unscientific, necessarily bourgeois and, as such, socially reactionary. Since it is both unscientific and reactionary, it does not, naturally, contain anything of value. Accordingly, the attitude of Marxist philosophers toward it can be only an attitude of unsparing criticism. If a Marxist agrees partly with a non- Marxist, that is sufficient reason to doubt his Marxism.

In returning to the authentic Marxist attitude toward the non-Marxist philosophy, our postwar philosophical de- velopment has overturned these Stalinistic dogmas.

Lenin thought that "one cannot fully understand Marx's *Capital* and especially its first [distinctly philosophic—G.P.]

chapter if one does not study and understand the *whole* of Hegel's 'Logic.' "[4] Something similar is true of all other, and especially of all philosophic, works of Marx and Engels. Marx is in many respects inconceivable without Hegel, Feuerbach and the whole development of European thought that led to Hegel and Feuerbach. For that reason the study of pre-Marxist philosophy is not merely a special and professional job of philosophic historiography, it is also an essential precondition for a full understanding and further development of Marxist philosophy.

It is also absurd to maintain that all non-Marxist philosophy after Marx must necessarily be "unscientific" and reactionary. Why could not non-Marxists discover a part of philosophical truth? Why should we close our eyes to the fact that most of the important non-Marxist philosophers in the nineteenth and twentieth centuries are not apologists of the bourgeois society but its critics? Why should we be angry if some of them, although they do not start from Marx, come to similar conclusions?

Rejecting a sectarian dogmatico-nihilistic attitude toward non-Marxist philosophy does not, however, solve the problem of a concrete Marxist analysis of all important philosophers and philosophical trends of past and present. Since Stalinism knew in advance that all non-Marxist philosophy was either prescientific or unscientific, either partly progressive or reactionary, and as it reduced the task of the history of philosophy to that of supplying labels, it was not difficult for it to assess all philosophical trends. A really Marxist analysis of non-Marxist philosophy is a much more complicated task.

Many interesting and valuable studies have been published during recent years in Yugoslavia about the great philosophers of the past. But this is just a beginning. We have rejected, for example, the Stalinistic dogma about Hegel's philosophy as an aristocratic reaction to the French revolution. But we cannot quote a single book that con-

[4] V. I. Lenin, *Filosofskie tetradi* (*Philosophical Notebooks*) (Ogiz, 1947), p. 154.

tains detailed elucidation either of Hegel's philosophic work in general or of the relationship of Hegel to Marx.

We have written quite a lot on contemporary non-Marxist philosophy. However . . .

The contemporary philosophy of existentialism is concerned with humanistic problems about which the young Marx wrote but which were neglected by Marxists afterward. Its conception of man is, on the whole, different from the Marxist one, but on some points they come near each other. It was not only a formal compliment when Sartre's teacher Heidegger wrote that the "Marxist conception of history [*Geschichte*] is superior to all other history [*Historie*]" and that "neither phenomenology nor existentialism [he meant Sartre's existentialism; he does not consider himself an existentialist—G.P.] attains that dimension where a productive discourse with Marxism becomes possible."[5] It is not quite a bare contingency that Sartre himself during recent years came to the conclusion that Marxism was the only possible philosophy of our time, and that he himself, at least in his own opinion, has become a Marxist. But although we are today far from both a nihilistic rejection of existentialism and an identification or "fusion" of it with Marxism, we cannot boast that we have sufficiently investigated and assessed its value and its relationship to Marxism.

To the uninformed the pragmatic theory of truth seems identical with Marx's. In order to prevent this confusion some have maintained that pragmatism considers true everything that is useful to somebody, "simply everything that is pleasant and useful from the standpoint of 'business' and the struggle against materialism."[6] Today we have come a great distance from such a rude falsification, and

[5] M. Heidegger, *Platons Lehre von der Wahrheit. Mit einem Brief über den "Humanismus"* (Plato's Teachings on Truth with a Letter on Humanism), Zweite Auflage (Bern, 1954), s. 87.

[6] *Kratkii filosofskii slovar'* (*The Brief Philosophical Dictionary*), edited by M. Rosental and P. Iudin, 3rd ed. (1952), p. 112.

also from the confusion of pragmatism with Marxism. Can we, however, say that we have sufficiently studied and elucidated the relation between Marxism and pragmatism?

The last hundred years have been a time of vigorous development in symbolic logic. Since it developed mostly after Marx and was not inspired by him, it was declared unscientific and reactionary by Stalinism. Even those who were the most dedicated Stalinists have abandoned this position today and some of our Marxists have made valuable attempts at a Marxist analysis of the new logic. But we cannot claim that the question of the value of symbolic logic and its place in philosophy (or outside it) is settled.

IV. *Philosophy and the Transformation of the World*

According to the Stalinist conception, Marxist philosophy is dialectical materialism, and dialectical materialism is "the world outlook of the Marxist-Leninist party."[7] This thesis is usually interpreted in such a way that the deepest meaning and most honorable task of Marxist philosophy are to serve as a tool of the communist party in its practical revolutionary struggle, and that its value is measured by the degree to which it fulfills this function. Accordingly, it is assumed that the party, in the person of its leaders, has the right and duty to improve the tool and to assess its value. Through its leaders and directing bodies the party assigns tasks to philosophy and assesses whether they are successfully accomplished.

The resolution of the Central Committee of the Communist Party of the Soviet Union (Bolsheviks) "On the Review Under the Banner of Marxism" in 1931 and Zhdanov's criticism of Aleksandrov in 1947 were based

[7] *History of the Communist Party of the Soviet Union (Bolsheviks)*, short course, edited by a Commission of the C.C. of the C.P.S.U. (b.), authorized by the C.C. of the C.P.S.U. (b.) 1938, Foreign Languages Publishing House (Moscow, 1952), p. 165.

on this assumption. And it was in accordance with it that Stalin wrote his article "On Dialectical and Historical Materialism" and included it in the *History of C.P.S.U.* (*b.*) in this way attributing to it the character of the official party interpretation of philosophy.

Adherents of the view that philosophy should be subordinated to politics seldom appeal to Marx and Engels because it is too obvious that they cannot find any support for their view there. Instead they quote Lenin as a champion of the principle of the party-character (*partijnost*).

In *Materialism and Empirio-Criticism* Lenin does indeed defend the party-character of philosophy. But what he had in mind was the struggle between the two opposite philosophical "parties," materialism and idealism, in which he claimed it was impossible for philosophy to remain neutral.[8] And whatever one may think of this thesis, it certainly does not mean that the political party of the working class should direct the development of philosophy.

At the time of his fight against empirio-criticism Lenin used to stress that philosophical disagreements cannot be settled by decisions of party bodies but only by free philosophical discussion. Some of his letters to Gorki are good illustrations of this attitude.[9]

Yugoslav Marxists have overcome the Stalinistic dogmas about philosophy as a servant of politics and party as the supreme judge in philosophic disputes, and revived Marx's and Lenin's conception of philosophy as an independent creative activity and free philosophical discussion as a means of settling philosophical disputes. But it would be incorrect to give philosophers all the credit for this. In the struggle to restore a right relationship between philosophy and politics, politicians were equally active, and today we all agree: *philosophy is its own judge.*

This does not mean that philosophy is indifferent to the

[8] V. I. Lenin, *Collected Works, Materialism and Empirio-Criticism,* International Publishers (New York, 1927), vol. XIII, p. 311.

[9] V. I. Lenin, *Sočinenija (Works),* 4th ed., vol. 13, pp. 416–17; vol. 34, pp. 343, 344.

problems of life, but rather that it is fully responsible for itself. Nobody has the right to prescribe either its topics or its conclusions, and for that very reason philosophy has no right to blame anyone else for its failures.

One failure would be for philosophy to remain apart from the vital problems of its time. Hegel taught that philosophy is its own time conceived in thoughts, and Marx reproached philosophers for having merely interpreted the world in various ways, whereas the point is to change it.

Does this mean that philosophy, which has proved capable merely of interpreting the world, must leave the scene, turning over the transformation of the world to others? Or is it Marx's thought that philosophy, which has merely interpreted the world in the past, has to change it in the future?

If philosophy can and ought to change the world, how shall and can this be done?

Some interpret Marx in such a way that philosophers must be not only philosophers but also politicians and social workers. But if philosophers can change the world only by becoming politicians, this means that they cannot change it as philosophers.

Some people think that philosophers can participate in the transformation of the world indirectly, by developing a scientific method that will serve those who change the world directly, that is, scientists and politicians. Philosophy and science do meet in the field of methodology. But the conception that some people only make methods and some only apply them seems dubious.

Perhaps philosophy, however, remaining philosophy, can change the world. Is not every philosophical interpretation necessarily a certain change and even a creation of the world? Does Marx's "the point, however, is to *change* it," mean that the world must be changed in any case, even if purposelessly, partially and in a reactionary direction; that it is important to change something? Or does it perhaps mean that the hour of total revolutionary change has struck? Does Marx's reproach that "philosophers have only *interpreted* the world, in various ways" mean that philosophers should not interpret the world any more? Or that philosophers must interpret (because only they can do it) the essence of the present historic moment, the moment of revolution and human (not only political or economic) emancipation? Perhaps such an interpretation is not merely an interpretation but a decisive act of revolutionary change.

v. *Philosophy and Man*

Marxist philosophy according to the Stalinistic conception is "dialectical materialism," and it has two parts: the dialectical method and the materialist theory. The first part reduces to four and the second to three "principal features." The "dialectical materialism" that is a "world outlook" is closely connected with the "historical materialism" that is "the extension of the principles of dialectical materialism to the study of social life, an application of principles of dialectical materialism to the phenomena of the life of society, to the study of society, and of its history."[10]

Is historical materialism also philosophy, so that the Marxist philosophy can be divided into two main "branches" (dialectical and historical materialism), or is historical materialism a "special science," which is in an exceptional, privileged relation to philosophy? This is a question on which Stalin did not speak out and did not consider it advisable to ask.

Our postwar philosophic development has gone far beyond the limits of this division of philosophy and at the same time has opened a number of questions that are still being discussed.

The term "dialectical materialism" does not appear in Karl Marx at all: is it an adequate name for Marx's philosophy? Engels speaks about dialectical and historical materialism, but to him they are not two different philo-

[10] *History of the Communist Party of the Soviet Union (Bolsheviks)*, p. 165.

sophic branches. According to him modern materialism is
dialectical because it is historical. The separation of the
dialectical method from the materialist theory is not in
accordance with Hegel's, Marx's or Lenin's conception of
method as a form of the internal self-movement of the
content. There is no place for logic in Stalin's conception
of philosophy; logic can be added only from the outside,
as was done later. Ethical and aesthetic problems appear
only inside historical materialism, as a part of the theory
of the primacy of the social Being in relation to social
consciousness. Such a way of looking at ethical and
aesthetic phenomena merely through the prism of their
social (or even economic) determination and the "recip-
rocal influence" on the "foundation" fails to get at their
essential specificity.

We have merely touched upon these important questions in order to stress what is still more important: in the
Stalinistic conception there is no place for man.

In the center of the Stalinistic conception of dialectical
materialism are such concepts as "matter," "nature,"
"mind," "consciousness," "universal connection," "movement," etc. In historical materialism everything turns upon
"society," "conditions of the material life," "productive
forces." Neither dialectical nor historical materialism, as
conceived by Stalinists, contains any word about man as
man.

Some people say that one cannot speak about man as
man, that man as such is an empty abstraction. "Matter,"
"mind," "movement," "quantity," "quality," "society," etc.,
accordingly, are not abstractions! Is only man abstract?

The study of different aspects or forms of man's activity
(economic, political, artistic, scientific) that are *abstracted*
from the whole man Stalinism regards as *concrete*. Only
the *whole* (concrete) man is abstract!

One of the basic achievements of our postwar philosophical development is the discovery that man, who was
excluded from the Stalinistic version of Marxist philosophy
as an abstraction, is in the center of authentic Marxist
philosophic thought. Marx's primary concern in philosophy

is not a definition of matter or mind but the liberation of man, the revolutionary change of a world in which a "general or a banker plays a great part but mere man (man as man), on the other hand, a very shabby part."[11]

Although it explicitly rejects philosophical discussion of man, Stalinism assumes a certain concept of man—man as an economic animal. Such a concept of man was equally strange to the young and the old Marx. In contradistinction to all previous philosophy, Marx holds that man differs from animal not only in a particular property but in the whole nature and structure of his being. Man is neither a "rational animal" nor a "toolmaking animal," he is praxis. And "man is praxis" means man is society, freedom, history and future.

When we say that man is a creator, it does not mean that every man necessarily always creates. But man is really a man when he does not become alienated from his creative essence, when he is open toward the future and when, in realizing his historically given human possibilities, he creates new and higher ones.

In discovering free creativity as man's essential human possibility, Marx at the same time discovered the essence and the main forms of the phenomenon of self-alienation. In showing that contemporary class society was the society of a self-alienated man, Marx's theory of man was simultaneously a demand for a revolutionary change of the world and an act of such a change.

The time that has passed since Marx has not solved but deepened and sharpened the problem that he was the first to see. At a time when inhumanity is practiced in a "civilized" form, and a fantastic progress of science and technique alienated from man brings bigger and bigger troubles and anxieties to mankind, Marx's humanistic thought becomes more and more actual.

[11] K. Marx, *Capital: A Critique of Political Economy*, translated from the third German edition by S. Moore and E. Aveling; edited by Friedrich Engels; revised and amplified according to the fourth German edition by Ernest Untermann; vol. I, p. 51.

Marx's conception of man, even in the form in which it was left by Marx, is superior to other contemporary conceptions of man. But it has its own unsolved problems and difficulties, and new times have brought new problems. In what sense, if any, is it possible to speak about man's essence? What do "praxis," "freedom," "possibility," "future," "alienation," "self-alienation" mean? What do socialism and workers' self-management, hydrogen bombs, peace-hating war-loving coexistence and cosmic flights bring to man? All these are questions that are being much discussed in Yugoslav philosophy.

VI. *Dialectics*

According to the Stalinistic conception, dialectic is a "method" of studying and apprehending natural phenomena, and it is characterized by four principal "features": universal connection, movement and change, passage of quantitative changes into qualitative ones and the struggle of the opposites. This systematization is held to be perfect and exhaustive. It is not possible either to add anything to or to subtract anything from it; it is also impossible to make any changes in the sequence of traits.

The return to Marx, Engels and Lenin revealed that their conception of dialectics is considerably different from Stalin's, who, in fact, borrowed his systematization of dialectical traits from Bukharin. Lenin (like Hegel) does not reduce dialectics to only four traits. In *Philosophical Notebooks*, for example, he at one point enumerates sixteen elements of dialectics. And, the negation of negation, which is for Marx and Engels the essence of dialectics, the idea by which the dialectic concept of development differs most decisively from a mechanistic one, disappeared from Stalin's systematization.

The return to Marx, Engels and Lenin opened at the same time many problems about dialectics. Although all Marx's works are brilliant examples of dialectics, he did not write any special treatise on the subject. In a letter to Engels (January 14, 1858) he speaks about his desire sometime to explain briefly (in two or three author's sheets) "what is rational in the method that Hegel discovered and mystified at the same time."[12] He never fulfilled this wish. Was it because he never could find time or because he came to the conclusion that a general "dialecticizing" has no sense?

Both Engels and Lenin wrote about dialectics in general, and Engels worked intensively on the dialectics of nature. Was their work in the spirit and on the level of Marx?

In Engels general considerations about dialectics are found for the most part in *Anti-Dühring* and *Dialectics of Nature*. In conceiving dialectics as a science of the most general laws of every movement Engels explains and substantiates these most general "dialectical laws" by analyzing freely chosen "examples," often very special and specific, from different fields of nature and society. Plekhanov expounded dialectics in a similar way, a way that Lenin criticizes in *Philosophical Notebooks*.

After he has pointed out that the correctness of the content of dialectics has to be verified by the history of science, Lenin remarks: "Insufficient attention is usually paid to this aspect of dialectics [for example in Plekhanov]: the identity of the contraries is taken as a sum of *examples* ['for example grain'; 'for example the original communism']. The same thing is true of Engels. But this is 'for popularity . . .' and not because it is *law of knowledge* [*and* a law of the objective world]."[13]

In criticizing the tendency to reduce dialectics to a sum of examples, Lenin also opposes the reduction of dialectics to merely a method or a theory of movement. For him dialectics is also a theory of knowledge and logic.

If there is need for a general theory of dialectics, in which way can it develop? It is a rather common view

[12] K. Marx, F. Engels, *Prepiska*, Kultura (Beograd, 1958), Vol. II, p. 303.

[13] Lenin, *Philosophical Notebooks*, p. 327.

that dialectics must be sought primarily in the natural sciences. Natural sciences are like a kind of warehouse of dialectical material; one has simply to come with a truck and cart dialectics home.

Lenin had a somewhat different opinion about the development of dialectics and its relationship to natural sciences. In his philosophical testament, his article "On the Role of Militant Materialism," he advised the contributors to the review *Under the Banner of Marxism* to organize a "systematic study of Hegel's dialectics from a materialist standpoint, that is, of the dialectics that was practically applied by Marx in his *Capital* and in his historical and political works. . . ."[14]

In trying to explain and substantiate this thought Lenin writes: "In learning how Marx applied Hegel's materialistically conceived dialectics we can and must elaborate this dialectics from all sides, we must publish in the review fragments from Hegel's principal works to interpret them materialistically, commenting on them by examples of the application of dialectics in Marx, and also by those examples of dialectics in the field of economic and political relations, which recent history, especially contemporary imperialist war and revolution, provides in large numbers. The editors and the contributors to *Under the Banner of Marxism* must, in my opinion, be a sort of 'society of materialist friends of Hegel's dialectics.' Contemporary natural scientists (if they know how to look and if we can learn to help them) will find in Hegel's dialectics materialistically interpreted a series of answers to those philosophical questions that arise from the revolution in the natural sciences where intellectuals—admirers of the bourgeois fashion—'go astray' to reaction."[15]

Instead of directing us to look for dialectics in nature and in natural sciences, Lenin advises us to start from Hegel, Marx and history. He does not say a word here about philosophers needing to learn from natural sciences.

14 V. I. Lenin, *Sočinenija* (*Works*), 4th ed., vol. 33, p. 207.
15 *Op. cit.*, pp. 207–8.

On the contrary, the naturalists, "if they knew how to look," would learn something from a materialistically interpreted Hegel. To be sure they will not find in dialectics any concrete directions for their work or a solution of their scientific problems, but they will find an answer to those *philosophic* questions that arise from the revolution in the natural sciences.

I do not maintain that in this way Lenin solved the problem of the development of dialectics or the question of the relationship between natural sciences and philosophy. On the contrary he thus opened up another problem —the problem of dialectics in nature.

Holding that "objective dialectics prevails throughout nature"[16] Friedrich Engels for about ten years worked intensively on a book in which he wanted to give a systematic exposition of the dialectics of nature.

In this work, as he himself says, he did not aspire to discover new dialectical laws and to examine their inner interconnection, but only to show that "dialectical laws are the real laws of the development of nature."[17]

But in his unfinished manuscript on the *Dialectics of Nature* he maintains, among other things, that all nature is "in eternal flux and cyclical course,"[18] that there is "an eternal cycle in which matter moves," a cycle wherein nothing is eternal but eternally changing, eternally moving matter and the laws according to which it moves and changes, and this matter in spite of its changeability "remains eternally the same in all its transformations" so that "none of its attributes can ever be lost."[19]

Is this conception of an "eternal circle flux," with a matter whose attributes and laws are always the same, in accordance with the thesis of a dialectical development of nature?

What is Marx's attitude toward the dialectics of nature?

[16] Friedrich Engels, *Dialectics of Nature,* Foreign Languages Publishing House (Moscow, 1954), p. 280.
[17] *Ibid.,* p. 84.
[18] *Ibid.,* p. 43.
[19] *Ibid.,* p. 54.

Here and there Marx used to remark that dialectical laws hold not only for society but also for nature. But he never became so interested in the dialectics of nature as to try to write more about it. The opinion was advanced that Marx's conception of man as a producer of his world excludes the possibility of a dialectics of nature. This thesis, too, of course, can be disputed, but there is no reason to disqualify it in advance as heretical.

VII. *Materialism*

One of the basic characteristics of the Stalinist philosophic concept is the absolute opposition of idealism and materialism. According to this concept, materialism is a scientific and progressive, idealism a reactionary and unscientific world outlook. The history of philosophy is the history of the beginning and development of the scientific, materialist view of the world and of its struggle with the unscientific, idealistic one. Materialism before Marx was inconsistent, only half materialist, and therefore only half progressive and scientific. Marxist materialism which is to the end consistent, scientific and revolutionary, is characterized by three "principal features": the materiality of the world, the primacy of matter and the secondary character of consciousness, the possibility of knowledge of the world.

It is difficult to enumerate all the defects of this conception. In the history of philosophy, idealism is sometimes more "scientific" and progressive than materialism, as Marx and Engels very well knew. The "young" Lenin (in the *Materialism and Empirio-Criticism*) was sometimes inclined to forget it, but the "old" Lenin (in the *Philosophical Notebooks*) corrected his own mistake by pointing out that "an intelligent idealism is closer to an intelligent materialism than is a stupid materialism."[20]

In the "young" Lenin we also find a nondialectical theory of reflection according to which our consciousness is only a reflection of the external world, which exists outside

[20] Lenin, *Philosophical Notebooks*, p. 258.

and independent of it. The "old" Lenin, in his *Philosophical Notebooks*, also corrected this sin of the "young" one. "Man's consciousness not only reflects the objective world, it also creates it."[21]

The problems are not finally settled by these corrections, but some of them are more clearly posed. Some statements in the spirit of the theory of reflection can be found not only in Lenin and Engels but also in Marx. Nevertheless, can even an improved variation of the theory of reflection be brought into harmony with Marx's theory of man as a creative practical being? Does it give a satisfactory explanation of the phenomena of consciousness, truth and knowledge? Or is it a task of Marxist philosophers to develop a Marxist theory of spiritual creativity starting from Marx's theory of man?

Engels, Plekhanov and Lenin used to stress that Marx's materialism is essentially different from all previous materialism, including Feuerbach's. But is Marx's philosophy only an intelligent (dialectical) materialism, or does Marx's theory of praxis supersede the traditional opposition between materialism and idealism?

The "young" Marx writes that in a social condition "spiritualism and materialism, activity and passivity cease to be antinomies and thus cease to exist as such antinomies."[22] Denying such traditional oppositions, he advocates a realized or "consistent naturalism or humanism," which differs "from both idealism and materialism, and at the same time constitutes their unifying truth."[23]

The "old" Marx several times calls himself a materialist. Is he in this way characterizing more precisely his philosophical standpoint, or is he rather belittling the value of what is new in it?

---

21 *Ibid.*, p. 181.

22 E. Fromm, *Marx's Concept of Man*, with a translation of Marx's *Economic and Philosophical Manuscripts* by T. B. Bottomore, Frederick Ungar Publishing Company (New York, 1961), p. 135.

23 *Ibid.*, p. 269.

VIII. *Objections and Replies*

The "strange discussions" that have lately become frequent in Yugoslavia are free philosophical discussions about the open question of Marxist philosophy. The remnants of Stalinism in us (stronger in some, weaker in others) oppose free discussions on philosophy. An internal voice in us (or in some of us) is murmuring discontentedly: "Don't we behave too freely toward our great teachers?"

"First of all," wrote Engels to Plekhanov, "please stop calling me teacher. My name is simply Engels."[24]

"However, should we not be a little more modest?"

"The truth is as little modest as the light," says Marx, "and toward whom should it be? Toward itself? *Verum index sui et falsi.* Accordingly *toward the untruth?*"[25]

"By a free discussion of everything will we not confuse and disorient the masses?" Why should we underestimate the "masses"? Why could not an undogmatic Marxism be at least as conceivable to them as the dogmatic one?

"What are the opponents of Marxism going to say? Will they not feel they have triumphed when they see that we write critically of Marx?" They may. But let us hope that they will soon no longer be able to say: "Jesuits have written more studies about Marx and Marxism than Marxists themselves."

"And what will our Marxist critics, for example the Chinese, say?" Probably the same as the Albanian.

"But will not all these discussions weaken Marxist philosophy in its struggle against non-Marxist philosophy?" Why should a living Marxism be weaker than a dead one?

[24] *Perepiska K. Marksa i F. Engelsa s russkimi političeskimi dejateljami* (Ogiz, 1947), p. 267.

[25] K. Marx and F. Engels, *Werke* (Berlin, 1957), bd. I, s. 6.

The "young" and the "old" Marx

I

If the question about the "real" Marx is to have any sense, it can be neither merely factual and historical nor merely subjective and evaluative. The "real" Marx can be neither a heap of historical "facts" nor a free creation of somebody's imagination. He can be neither an entirely "objective" Marx, which once upon a time existed "in itself," nor a purely "subjective" Marx who somebody finds likeable or useful. It is impossible to expound the first, and the second is more than one man. The "real" Marx is the Marx to whom history owes a debt, and the "real" Marx's philosophy is Marx's contribution to the development of philosophical thought.

II

Stalinists and those who practice Stalinist criticism, while rejecting it in word, oppose the "old" Marx to the "young," maintaining that the "real" Marx is the "old." They find the "young" Marx interesting merely as an historical document, a testimony to Marx's original immaturity and his gradual emancipation from Hegelian and Feuerbachian errors. By their outcry against the "young" Marx they hope to conceal the fact that they have departed equally far from the "old" Marx. Marxism is a philosophy of freedom, and Stalinism a "philosophical" justification of unfreedom.

III

The thesis that the "real" Marx is the "young" one represents the first, ill-considered reaction of awakened Marxist thought against Stalinism. It is a negation of Stalinism that makes concessions to Stalinism. Its supporters accept the opposition between the "young" and the "old" Marx and at the same time magnanimously surrender the "old" Marx to the Stalinists.

IV

The theory of alienation is not only the central theme of Marx's "early" writings; it is also the guiding idea of all his "later" works. The theory of man as a being of praxis is not a discovery of the "old" Marx; we already find it in a developed form in the "young" one. The "young" and the "old" Marx are essentially one and the same: Marx the fighter against self-alienation, dehumanization and exploitation; Marx the combatant for the full humanization of man, for a many-sided development of man's human possibilities, for the abolition of class society and for the realization of an association in which the "free development of every individual is a condition of free development for all."

V

The unity of Marx's essential thought does not preclude its development. Marx's work is an unremitting self-criticism, a continuous revision of his own views. The division into the "young" and the "old" Marx only very incompletely describes this complex process. It is usually held that the "mature" Marx begins with the *Poverty of Philosophy* and the *Manifesto of the Communist Party*. The Marx of the doctoral thesis, the Marx of the *Economic and Philosophical Manuscripts* and the Marx of the *German Ideology* are supposed to be one and the same "young" Marx; the Marx of the *Manifesto* and the Marx of *Capital*, one and the same "old" Marx. On the other hand, Marx in *German Ideology* is considered as quite different from Marx in *Poverty of Philosophy* or the *Manifesto!* But not only is the opposition between the "young" and the "old"

Marx untenable; even the twofold division of Marx's development, which this opposition assumes, is dubious.

VI

The fundamental coherence of Marx's thought does not mean that it is an all-embracing and finished system. The essential truthfulness of Marx's thought does not mean that it is an eternal truth for all time. Marx's work is full of open problems; it contains questions without answers, searches without final results. Some people find definitive solutions in Marx precisely where he himself saw difficulties. But what was merely a question for Marx *cannot* be a ready answer for us; what Marx himself regarded as a solution *may* become a problem for us. Great thinkers cast light far into the future, but every generation has to work out for itself a concrete solution to its own problems.

VII

Some people still think that the "old" Marx definitively parted company with philosophy and philosophical "phraseology." But what kind of "phraseology" is it when Marx in the first volume of *Capital* indicts bourgeois society because in it "a general or a banker plays a great part, but mere man [man as man], on the other hand, a very shabby part"? Or when in the third volume he writes about the conditions of production that are most adequate to the *"human nature"* of the producers. Marx's thought has a philosophical meaning when he, as in *German Ideology*, directly renounces philosophy and also when he, as in *Capital*, maintains that he is only flirting with it.

VIII

Nevertheless, in many respects Marx merely indicated his philosophy. Engels' and Lenin's philosophical works—*Anti-Dühring, Dialectics of Nature, Materialism and Empirio-*

Criticism and *Philosophical Notebooks*—are regarded by some as a worthy supplement to Marx, and by others as a complete failure, inadequate to the basic sense of Marxism. In fact, Engels, Plekhanov and Lenin were right in feeling the need to develop more explicitly and fully the ontological foundations of Marx's philosophy. It is not their fault if they were unable to do it on the level on which it could have been done by Marx himself. Undoubtedly the development of the ontologico-epistemological foundations of Marx's philosophy still needs to be done. It is illusory to think that a "pure" anthropology or an "ontology of man" free from general ontological assumptions is possible. It is a dubious idea also that questions of general ontology are merely a part of an ontology of man.

IX

It is the task of followers of Marx to develop his thought in all directions. One of the aspects of this task is a critical analysis and evaluation of new philosophical trends and phenomena. To be sure, there are some "Marxists" who do not see the difference between a Marxist criticism of non-Marxist philosophy and an inconsistent yielding to it. The only consistent Marxist for them is Comrade Ostrich, who in burying his head in the sand clearly draws the boundaries between himself and "the seemingly new philosophical schools and little schools" (and the external world in general). In his attempt to evade an independent analysis of new phenomena the dogmatist simply labels them old. Creative Marxism has no reason to follow his example.

The continuity of Marx's thought

The question about continuity or discontinuity is one of the most important and most topical in connection with Marx's thought, which is not to say that it is a vital question only in connection with Marx. There is no thinker for whom it is without consequence, because in putting this question we are really asking whether we have to do with one or a number of different thinkers. It has, however, a special significance where Marx is concerned, not only because very different answers to this question have been given and ardently defended in regard to him but also because these diverse "theoretical" answers have been connected with divergent "practical" aims and actions.

The thesis that there is a discontinuity in Marx's thought has mainly appeared, and still appears, in the theory about the fundamental differences between the "young" or "immature" Marx, represented by his works up to 1844–45 (according to others up to 1847–48), and the "old" or "mature" Marx, represented by his later works. This theory has many different variants.

In "Marxism"–Stalinism the theory is concretized into the thesis that the mature Marx, the sober scientist-economist, transcended and made uninteresting the young Marx, the abstract philosopher-dreamer. Criticizing the "young" Marx's philosophical idealism and political liberalism, Stalinists affect being consistent revolutionaries fighting against what is non-Marxist in the young Marx, against the misuse of Marx's juvenile failings and mistakes by the enemies of socialism. However, the question irresistibly imposes itself: is not the alleged purification of the young Marx from "Hegelianism" and "bourgeois liberalism" in fact a "cleansing" of Marx's thought from its humanistic essence, a pragmatic "preparation" for making it serviceable as a theoretical justification of bureaucratic, antisocialist practice?

Among non-Marxists, too, there are adherents of the thesis who hold that the old, "scientific" Marx, and not the young, "confused" one, is the "real" Marx; that although Marx's political economy is relatively the most valuable part of his theoretical work, it is none the less basically wrong, or at least outdated. It is becoming more and more frequent, however, among the critics of Marxism to make this opposition in favor of the "young" Marx, and simultaneously to belittle the thought of the "young" Marx by declaring it an ill-considered synthesis of Hegel and Feuerbach. In both cases the question naturally arises: is not the aim of proclaiming either the "old" or the "young" Marx the only "true" Marx to restrict Marxism to a more narrow field (in which the critic feels more confident), and thus to make criticism of it easier?

The thesis that there is a continuity in Marx's thought has also been interpreted in various ways, and its adherents have been accused of holding that Marx's conceptions never changed at all, but always remained exactly the same. Conceived in this way, the continuity thesis is obviously unfounded and it would be strange for anybody to advocate it, since it implies that Marx was a narrow-minded theoretician incapable of any development. And were anyone to try to defend it, it would be easy to refute him; it is not difficult to show that some of Marx's essential views changed considerably.

Maintaining the continuity of Marx's thought, I do not mean that his views never changed, that he was, so to speak, born with the beard, but rather, that there are not two fundamentally different and mutually unconnected Marxs. From his high school years to his death, Marx's thought was constantly changing, but there were no such turns in this process as would represent a complete break with former ideas and the passage to entirely different or even opposite conceptions. The "young" Marx is not an "abstract philosopher," nor is the "old" an "austere scientist": Marx's thought from beginning to end is a revolutionary humanism, and only when it is considered as a whole can it serve as an adequate theoretical basis of the revolutionary struggle for a democratic, humanistic socialism.

II

It is not difficult to formulate briefly the thesis about the continuity of Marx's thought, as I have done in the preceding essay. But to justify it completely one would have to analyze basic thoughts from his earliest published and unpublished manuscripts to his last writings. Nevertheless, although it is impossible in a short space to "prove" the thesis completely, it is possible to support it at least partially—by comparing the key ideas of *some* of his works that belong to different periods of his life and have a decisive importance for those periods.

What about considering, for example, the relationship between Marx's *Economic and Philosophical Manuscripts, Sketches for the Critique of Political Economy* and *Capital?* This choice may seem arbitrary, but it is by no means so. The three works belong to different periods of Marx's life: the first of them was written in the 1840s, i.e., in the first decade of Marx's theoretical work; the second, in the fifties, the second decade of his work; and the third mainly in the sixties and seventies, hence in the third and fourth decades of his work. Although the writing of the first two occupied Marx for only a small portion of the decades in which they were produced, and despite the fact that he did not himself either finish or publish any of the three,[1] these works are representative of the periods in

[1] *Economic and Philosophical Manuscripts* was written between February and August 1844, and published nearly half a century after Marx's death in 1932 in two editions with not quite identical texts: in K. Marx, F. Engels, *Historisch-kritische Gesamtausgabe,* Erste Abteilung, Band 3, Marx-Engels Verlag (Berlin, 1932); and also in K. Marx, *Der historische Materialis-*

which they were written. Marx's letters show that he was exceptionally anxious to write them and that he regarded them as more important than many other works that he finished and published. And comparing the contents of these works with other works from the same periods, we can establish that these are works where Marx discussed fundamental problems and came to decisive conclusions, conclusions that are basic for other works from these periods.

Taking the three works as a basis for analysis has one more special justification. Those who advocate the thesis about the two different Marxs very often put forward as their main argument the alleged unbridgeable gap between the *Economic and Philosophical Manuscripts* and *Capital*, maintaining that the first work shows the hand of Marx the abstract philosopher who solves concrete social questions by speculation, whereas in *Capital* we have before us Marx the scientist, the economist who bases his conclusions on scrupulous empirical investigation and the mathematical elaboration of a "mountain of factual mate-

_____

mus. Die Frühschriften, Erster Band, Herausgegeben von S. Landshut und J. P. Mayer, Alfred Kröner Verlag (Leipzig, 1932). The title under which they became familiar originates from their Soviet editors (Landshut and Mayer entitled them *Nationalökonomie und Philosophie*). The Sketches for the *Critique of Political Economy* were written between October 1857 and March 1858, edited and given a title by the Moscow Marx-Engels-Lenin Institute, and published by the Moscow Publishing House for Literature in Foreign Languages (Verlag für Fremdsprachige Literatur) in two volumes in 1939 and 1941. Owing to the war, most of this edition perished, so that the work became accessible only after it was republished in Berlin after the war (Karl Marx, *Grundrisse der Kritik der politischen Ökonomie,* Rohentwurf, 1857–58; Anhang, 1850–59, Marx-Engels-Lenin Institut, Moskau, Dietz Verlag [Berlin, 1953]). As is well known, the title of *Capital* (*Das Kapital: Kritik der politischen Ökonomie*), was given by Marx himself, and he succeeded in finishing and publishing the first volume of it in 1867. The second and the third volumes, however, were edited and published by Engels in 1887 and 1894.

rial." In disputing the thesis about the two Marxs, we
cannot bypass either the two works involved in this argument—or the third work, which is ignored because it
occupies the place reserved for the alleged "gap."

The fact that Marx did not finish and publish his
Economic and Philosophical Manuscripts does not mean
that it consists of purely private notes not intended for
publication. From Marx's Preface, where he informs us that
in preparing the manuscript for publication he gave up his
original intention of discussing in it law, morals, politics,
etc., which, he announces, he will elaborate critically in a
subsequent series of pamphlets, and in a separate work endeavor "to present the interconnected whole, to show the
relationships between the parts, and to provide a critique
of the speculative treatment of this material,"[2] it is obvious
that Marx wished to publish this work. That he did not
realize his intention is explained by the fact that after
meeting Engels at the end of August 1844 he devoted himself to the polemical work *The Holy Family,* which they
planned and wrote together (although much more of it
was written by Marx than by Engels). Marx did not believe that his unfinished manuscript thus lost its value and
interest, and he intended to finish and publish it later, as
can be seen from the fact that on February 1, 1845, he
signed a contract with C. W. Leske, a publisher from
Darmstadt, for a book entitled *A Critique of Politics and
National Economy.* Soon after finishing *The Holy Family,*
however, both he and Engels got involved in polemics
again and started writing the *German Ideology.*

Marx did not cease his work on the *Sketches for the
Critique of Political Economy* for any external reasons; he
did so because he was dissatisfied with what he had
written. He was dissatisfied, however, not with the content but with the form, which was, according to him,
affected by the liver disease that had suddenly attacked
him. This is vividly testified to in his letters of that time,
like the one to Lassalle of November 12, 1858, in which

2 Fromm, *Marx's Concept of Man,* p. 90.

he complained: "In all . . . that I wrote, I felt in the style the taste of the liver disease. And I have a double reason not to allow this writing to be spoiled by medical causes: 1) It is the result of a fifteen-year-long investigation, hence of the best years of my life. 2) It presents scientifically for the first time an important view of social relations. Consequently I owe it to the party not to distort the matter by the kind of dull, wooden writing that is proper to a sick liver."[3]

In Marx's letters we also find a partial explanation of his liver complaint. The illness was caused to a considerable extent by intensive night work, which was stimulated by the economic crisis of 1857, the fourth in the series of great economic crises of the nineteenth century and the first that really assumed a world character, embracing both Europe and America and all branches of economics. Optimistically expecting that the crisis would inflict a mortal blow on the capitalistic social order, Marx applied all his energy to work in order to round up his basic conceptions as soon as possible, at least in broad lines. "I work madly throughout whole nights, summarizing my economic studies," he writes to Engels in December 1857, "in order to have the foundations ready before the flood."[4]

III

The comparative study of the three works may at first give the impression that they agree both in the basic themes, which are economic, and in the literature on which they rely, which is also economic, but that they nevertheless differ, partly in subject matter—because the first work includes philosophical as well as economic topics—but even more in the method—because the first

[3] Marx and Lassalle am 12.XI, 1858, Lassalle-Nachlass, s. 136; quoted from K. Marx, Grundrisse der Kritik der politischen Ökonomie (Plans for the Criticism of Political Economy) (Berlin, 1953), s. XIII.

[4] Marx, Engels, Prepiska, vol. II, p. 279; cf. also, p. 285.

work is characterized by abstract philosophical reasoning and the second and third by concrete empirical analysis.

Such an assertion might seem convincing. In the *Economic and Philosophical Manuscripts*, in addition to sections devoted to such economic phenomena as wage, profit, rent, money, we also find special sections on distinctly philosophical themes such as alienated labor and Hegel's dialectics (the editor entitled those sections "Alienated Work" and "Criticism of Hegel's Dialectics and Philosophy in General"). In the *Sketches for the Critique of Political Economy* and in *Capital*, on the contrary, there is no chapter that is obviously devoted to a philosophical topic. The difference in method may also at first seem incontestable. *Capital* abounds in historical information, statistical facts and mathematical computations, whereas there are none of these in *Economic and Philosophical Manuscripts*.

Against the view that the *Economic and Philosophical Manuscripts* are abstract speculations without support in empirical investigations, there is, however, Marx's statement in the preface to that work: "It is hardly necessary to assure the reader who is familiar with political economy that my conclusions are the fruit of an entirely empirical analysis based upon a careful critical study of political economy."[5] This statement, of course, cannot be decisive when one asks to what extent Marx's results really were reached by an empirical analysis, but it must at least be taken into account when one discusses his conscious intentions and conscious methodological approach.

And if empirical analysis, or at least the intention of empirical analysis, was not alien to the "young" Marx, perhaps philosophizing was not extraneous to the "old." Indeed, is not the abundant use of philosophical terminology in the *Sketches* and in the *Capital* an indication of this?

The question leads us to the main thesis of this essay: despite the fact that the three chosen works are different,

[5] Fromm, *Marx's Concept of Man*, pp. 90–91.

they possess a basic unity, even an essential identity. First, all three represent a critique of the political economy and the economic reality of capitalism and of every class society from a viewpoint that is not purely economic but above all *philosophical*. And they all contain a theoretical foundation and a call for the realization of a truly human society in which man will no longer be alienated from himself, will no more be an economic animal, but will realize himself as a free creative being of praxis.

An external confirmation for the critical, "transeconomic" character of these works is provided by explicit statements of Marx. In the Preface to *Manuscripts* he stresses the critical nature of the work, characterizing it as one critique, which will be followed by others. And concerning the *Sketches*, Marx wrote to Lassalle: "The work that is first in question is the critique of economic categories, or, if you like, the system of bourgeois economy presented critically. This is at the same time the representation of the system and through the presentation its criticism."[6] The critical character of *Capital* was stressed by Marx in the subtitle —"Critique of Political Economy"—but also, for example, in the epilogue of the second edition (1873) where he says that he used the dialectical method in this work, and that it is "in its essence critical and revolutionary."[7]

Such single statements cannot be regarded as decisive confirmation of the identity of the basic position of the three works in question. The decisive confirmation is offered by the whole content of these works.

A fundamental idea of Marx's *Economic and Philosophical Manuscripts* is that man is a free creative being of praxis who in the contemporary world is alienated from his human essence, but that the radical form man's self-alienation assumes in the contemporary society creates real conditions for a struggle against self-alienation, for real-

[6] Marx, Lassalle, den 22.II, 1858, s. 116–17; quoted from Marx, *Grundrisse der Kritik der politischen Ökonomie*, s. IX.

[7] K. Marx and F. Engels, *Basic Writings on Politics and Philosophy*, edited by L. S. Feuer, Doubleday & Co. (New York, 1959), p. 146.

izing socialism as a de-alienated, free community of free men. And this is also the guiding idea of the *Sketches for the Critique of Political Economy* and of *Capital*.

IV

Every fragment of a great literary work expresses at least partly the meaning of the whole. Perhaps we will come closer to understanding Marx's *Sketches for the Critique of Political Economy* if we carefully consider the following passage:

"We never find in the ancients an investigation of which form of ownership of land, etc., is most productive, creates the largest wealth. Wealth does not appear as an end of production, although, of course, Cato may investigate which tillage of the ground is most remunerative, or Brutus may lend money at the best rate of interest. The investigation is always which form of ownership creates the best citizens. As an end in itself wealth appears only among a small number of commercial nations—monopolists of the carrying trade—which live in the pores of the old world like the Jews in medieval society. However, wealth is, on the one hand, a thing, it is realized in things, material products, which are confronted by man as a subject; on the other hand, as value it is a pure command over alien work, with the purpose not of domination but of private enjoyment, etc. In all forms it appears in a thing-form either as a thing, or as a relationship by means of a thing, which lies outside and accidentally beside the individual. In this way the old view, according to which man, although in a limited national, religious, political determination, appears as the end of production, seems very exalted compared with that of the modern world, where production appears as the end of man, and wealth as the end of production. But in fact, if one tears down the limited bourgeois form, what else is wealth if not universality of needs, capabilities, enjoyments, productive forces, etc., of individuals produced in a universal exchange? The full development of man's domination over natural forces, those of nature so-called as well as those of his own nature? The development of one's creative pre-dispositions—without any other presupposition but the previous historical development that makes this totality of development, i.e., the development of all human forces as such, not measured by some *previously given* standard—to an end in itself; where man does not reproduce himself in his definiteness but produces his totality? Where he does not endeavor to remain something become, but is in an absolute movement of becoming? In bourgeois economy—and in the epoch of production to which it corresponds—this full development of the internal in man appears as a complete emptying, this universal objectification as total alienation, and the demolition of all one-sided ends as the sacrificing of the end in itself to an entirely external end. Therefore, the childish old world on the one hand appears higher. On the other hand, it really is so in everything where a closed appearance, form, and definite limitation is required. It is satisfaction from a limited standpoint; whereas the modern world leaves man dissatisfied, or is, where it appears satisfied within itself, banal."[8]

What is the meaning of this passage? What topics are discussed here? What is the author's approach? What are his theses?

If we consider carefully the beginning of the passage, we immediately notice the terms: "ownership of land," "most productive," "wealth," "production," "tillage of the ground," "most remunerative," "lend," "money," "interest." How many economic terms in only the first two sentences! But the rest of the passage is equally rich in economic terminology: "commercial," "work," "exchange," "produc-tive forces," etc. Does this not show that economic themes are being discussed here? It is perhaps a too superficial way of reasoning to judge the subject matter of a text on the basis of the terms used. It is not, however, only the terms that are economic here. The main content of the passage seems to be a comparison of ancient and contem-

[8] Marx, *Grundrisse der Kritik der politischen Ökonomie,* ss. 387–88.

porary conceptions about the end of production. And is not production, at least in the sense in which it is used in the text, an economic category?

One may object that Marx is not speaking about production here, or even about the end of production, but about *views* concerning the end of production. And he does not engage in general theoretical considerations about any view, but compares *ancient* and *contemporary* views. He does not directly discuss an economic phenomenon, nor does he here consider any phenomenon theoretically and systematically. He gives an historical comparison of two different conceptions. This objection can, however, be answered convincingly: the view of the end of production is not a "material" economic phenomenon, but it is nevertheless an *economic* view. Thus the historical consideration of ancient and contemporary views about the end of production, although it is not a direct investigation of economic reality, is still an historical investigation of the development of *economic* views, and consequently belongs to the sphere of economic investigations in a broad sense. At least it is an investigation on the borderline between economics and history.

Let us look more carefully at the question with which Marx is here concerned: in what way and what sense is he concerned with the question about the ancient and the contemporary views about the end of production. Marx first establishes what is the immediate difference between the two views. According to the ancient view, the end of production is man; according to the contemporary, capitalist conception, the end of production is wealth, and the end of man is production. These statements can be regarded as a constituent part of a science that establishes the difference between the views of different periods by an objective investigation of historical documents.

Marx, however, does not stop at an objective registration of the difference between the ancient and the contemporary views about the end of production; he maintains that the ancient is "very exalted" compared with the modern. The main thesis of the whole passage is that the ancient conception, according to which the end of production is man, is the "more exalted" (better, higher, more human) view. It is difficult to call this fundamental thesis "economic," because it is first concerned not with economics, but with man.

Not only is this thesis not "economic," it is not really "scientific." It might be possible to establish by scientific methods whether one of the two views was actually widespread in the ancient, and the other in the modern world. But what scientific methods can establish whether one view is more "exalted" than the other? What kind of observation, experiment, measurement, in other words, what empirical method can establish "exaltedness"?

But the fact that Marx's thesis cannot be "scientifically proved" does not make it meaningless or unsupportable. Indeed, Marx tries to persuade us of its truth. This "persuasion" begins with the sentence: "But in fact, if one tears down the limited bourgeois form, what else is wealth if not universality of needs, capabilities, enjoyments, productive forces, etc., of individuals produced in a universal exchange?"

At first this sentence may be embarrassing. Marx here seems to jump to quite another question: what wealth really is. What is even more curious, in answering the question Marx denies what he said about it in the first half of the passage, where he said that wealth is, on the one hand, a collection of material products, things, and, on the other hand, command of the work of others for the purpose of private enjoyment. Now all at once we are informed that wealth is *in fact* something else, quite different, namely universality of needs, capabilities, enjoyments, productive forces, etc., of individuals. What do these differences and inconsistencies mean?

If we reflect a little more about Marx's text, we realize that his thought is really pretty clear and consistent: if wealth is conceived of as a collection of material things and command over the work of others, then the view that man is the end of production is "exalted" compared to the view that the end of production is wealth. But the view that the end of production is wealth need not be wrong or contrary to the view that the end of production is man, if "wealth" is interpreted in another way as:

1.) "universality of needs, capabilities, enjoyments, productive forces, etc., of individuals produced in a universal exchange";

2.) "the full development of man's domination over natural forces, those of nature so-called as well as those of his own nature";

3.) "the absolute development of one's creative predispositions—without any other presupposition but the previous historical development that makes this totality of development, i.e., development of all human forces as such, not measured by some *previously given* standard, an end in itself";

4.) such development of one's creative predispositions in which man "does not reproduce himself in his definiteness, but produces his totality";

5.) such development of one's creative predisposition in which man "does not endeavor to remain something become, but is in an absolute movement of becoming."

Thus, according to Marx, man is rich not when he possesses many things or when he successfully exploits other people, but when he universally develops his needs, capabilities, creative forces; when he does not reproduce himself in his definiteness, does not endeavor to remain what he already is, but is in the "absolute movement of becoming." Can such a view of man's wealth be regarded as an "economic" doctrine? Is it a scientific conception that can be empirically proved, or is it a philosophical thesis founded on philosophical argument?

Marx's thought in the part of the passage analyzed so far can be summarized as follows: the ancient view that the end of production is man is superior to the new, capitalist view that the end of man is production, and the end of production, wealth. If, however, wealth is conceived of not as the possession of things, but as the development of the creative human personality, the difference between the two views disappears.

The analysis of the passage is still not finished. The

thesis that man's wealth lies in the universal development of his capabilities and that the end of production is the development of man might seem to be an idealization of man and his production to those who regard philosophical theses as empirical descriptions of what in fact is. That Marx was not given to idealization of man in his factual existence can be seen from the part of the passage already quoted. But in the text that follows Marx also directly warns that he is not talking of what is but of what can and ought to be, because he regards the existing world as an alienated world in which man does not realize his human nature, but something contrary to it: "In bourgeois economy—and in the epoch of production to which it corresponds—this full development of the internal in man appears as a complete emptying, this universal objectification as total alienation, and the demolition of all definite one-sided ends, as the sacrificing of the end in itself to an entirely external end."

Thus Marx testifies that he is concerned with a philosophical question and with a critical, not apologetic or neutral, attitude toward the existing world. But although he takes care to protect his thought from misinterpretation as an apology for, or embellishment of, the existing reality, Marx also warns against conceiving of it as a criticism of the contemporary world from the viewpoint of the past. Repeating, at the end of the passage, that the old world is in certain respects higher than the modern ("in everything where a closed appearance, form and definite limitation is required"), he at the same time characterizes this old world as "childish," and remarks that it is "satisfaction from a limited standpoint." This, however, does not do away with the thesis that the old world is, in a qualified sense, higher than the contemporary. The old world satisfies man from a limited standpoint; the modern world leaves him dissatisfied or satisfies him in a banal way.

V

It is not necessary to be an expert on the *Economic and Philosophical Manuscripts* to know that the view that man's wealth is not the mere possession of things and domination over other men, but rather the full development of his creative potentialities, was already stated in the *Manuscripts*. Nevertheless let us quote one passage:

"It will be seen from this how, in place of the *wealth* and *poverty* of political economy, we have the *wealthy* man and the plenitude of *human* need. The wealthy man is at the same time one who *needs* a complex of human manifestations of life, and whose own self-realization exists as an inner necessity, a *need*. Not only the *wealth* but also the *poverty* of man *acquires*, in a socialist perspective, a *human* and thus a social meaning. Poverty is the passive bond that leads man to experience a need for the greatest wealth, the *other* person. The sway of the objective entity within me, the sensuous outbreak of my life-activity, is the passion that here becomes the *activity* of my being."[9]

The two passages (this one from the *Manuscripts* and the other from the *Sketches*) are, of course, not identical, but it is not difficult to see that the conception of man's wealth is essentially the same in both.

The ideas expressed in the *Manuscripts* were further developed by Marx in the *Sketches*, and he did not abandon them in *Capital*. Let us consider only this passage from *Capital*:

"However terrible and disgusting, under the capitalist system, the dissolution of the old family ties may appear, nevertheless, large-scale industry, by assigning as it does an important part in the process of production, outside the domestic sphere, to women, to young persons, and to children of both sexes, creates a new economic basis for a higher form of the family and of the relations between the sexes. It is, of course, just as absurd to regard

[9] Fromm: *Marx's Concept of Man*, pp. 137–38.

the Teutonic-Christian form of the family as absolute and final as it would be to apply that character to the ancient Roman, the ancient Greek, or the Eastern forms, which, moreover, taken together, form a series in historical development. Moreover, it is obvious that the fact of the collective working group being composed of individuals of both sexes and all ages must necessarily, under suitable conditions, become a source of humane development, although in its spontaneously developed, brutal capitalist form, where the laborer exists for the process of production, and not the process of production for the laborer, it is a pestilential source of corruption and slavery."[10]

This quotation from *Capital* seemingly has nothing to do with the fragment from the *Sketches for the Critique of Political Economy*. A more careful comparison, however, shows interesting analogies: just as the passage from the *Sketches* at first seemed purely economic or economico-historical, so this fragment from *Capital* at first seems sociological or sociologico-historical. Just as in the passage from the *Sketches* Marx seemed to idealize the ancient view about the end of production, so in the fragment from *Capital* it may seem that Marx is extolling the old form of the family. In the first instance, however, Marx is not upholding either the ancient or the contemporary, capitalist viewpoint, but regarding past and present from the viewpoint of the future; and in the second, he characterizes as folly the absolutization of either the Christian-Germanic, the Graeco-Roman or the Oriental form of the family and attempts to discover in an observed present the germs of a human future. The passage from *Capital* is not only analogous to the one from the *Sketches;* it actually repeats its fundamental thesis, criticizing the brutal capitalistic order where "the laborer exists for the process of production, and not the process of production for the laborer." Instead of "man" he here speaks of the "laborer," but

[10] *Capital*, I, pp. 514–16; quoted in K. Marx, *Selected Writings in Sociology and Social Philosophy*, edited by T. B. Bottomore and M. Rubel, Penguin Books (1963), p. 259.

the fundamental idea about the relationship between production and the producer is the same.

This does not mean that in *Capital* Marx only repeated the *Sketches*, and in the *Sketches*, the *Manuscripts*, so that there is nothing new in either the *Sketches* or *Capital*. To give only one example, when in the *Sketches* Marx says that man is really man when he "does not endeavor to remain something become, but is in the absolute movement of becoming," this is certainly one of the ways of expressing the essence of his philosophical position, which is also inherent in his other works, but which, so far as I know, is not expressed at any other place in exactly this way. The same holds for many other ideas expressed in the *Sketches* and in *Capital*.

The passage from the *Sketches* was not chosen entirely at random, but it is by no means the only one that is rich in interesting and important philosophical considerations. There are many like it. But the substance is not only in single passages. This whole unfinished manuscript is full of philosophical intentions, guided by philosophical ideas, and rich in philosophical insights. Thus it is a convincing testimony of the continuity of Marx's thought and makes it easier to grasp the essential continuity of the *Economic and Philosophical Manuscripts* and *Capital*.

Dialectical materialism and the philosophy of Karl Marx

Discussion of Marx as a philosopher has not yet been reduced to such questions as: "What are the main themes and theses of Marx's philosophy?" "What is the essential meaning of his philosophical thought?" "What is the historical value and importance of his philosophical work?" The question "Is Marx a philosopher at all?" is still controversial. There is nothing wrong with this question. But not every possible answer to it is equally valid.

The thesis that Marx is a philosopher has been disputed not only by many "experts" and "critics" of Marxism but also by many prominent Marxists. During the Second International it was disputed by orthodox revolutionary Marxists (e.g., F. Mehring), by centrist opportunists (e.g., K. Kautsky) and by open revisionists (e.g., E. Bernstein). It is disputed by many contemporary Marxists as well. But those who agree that Marx is not a philosopher do not all agree on what he is. The thesis that Marx is a philosopher is most often countered with one of the following: "Marx is a nonphilosopher"; "Marx is an antiphilosopher"; "Marx is a transphilosopher." Each of these theses has its particular attractions and its particular "arguments." These are, however, false attractions and shaky arguments.

One view, once widely held and still encountered, is that Marx was not an opponent of philosophy, but was never seriously concerned with it or at least did not make any major contribution to it. Those who share this view differ only on the question of why he did not achieve much in this "field." His critics are rather inclined to deny him any sense of or aptitude for philosophy; his followers and supporters frequently insist that he was continuously over-loaded with other, more urgent work and so could never find enough time for philosophy. Whatever one may think of these "explanations," their common presupposition seems at first acceptable. With the help of Marx's own statements it is possible, for instance, to show that he never realized some of his philosophical "wishes" and "plans." But what author has ever realized all his wishes and intentions? Whatever the amount of his unrealized philosophical plans, one thing is indisputable: Karl Marx, Doctor of Philosophy, left, beside his doctor's thesis, several expressly philosophical works (*A Contribution to the Critique of Hegel's Philosophy of Right; Economic and Philosophical Manuscripts; The Holy Family; German Ideology*, etc.).

In his youth, some people say, Marx was a philosopher, but in the *German Ideology* he broke with philosophical speculation to become a critic and opponent of philosophy as such, from the positions, and in the name, of empirical, positive science. This is borne out by his explicit state-ments: ("Phrases about the world cease and real knowl-edge has to take their place. When reality is depicted, philosophy as an independent branch of activity loses the medium of existence"). This is also attested to by the fact that after the *German Ideology* he stopped working on philosophy and devoted himself to economic, historical and political studies and practical revolutionary activity. Facts are facts, of course; but it is also a fact that Marx's "mature," "nonphilosophical" works do not contain "real knowledge" only, but also philosophical "phrases about the world" (*Capital* is written throughout in "philosophical phraseology"). It is also a fact that Marx's "nonphilosoph-ical" ("economic," "political," "historical") works are in their deepest sense *philosophical*, because they are di-rected at the essence of the modern world and man, and because they present a radical criticism of an alienated society and a "nonscientific" vision of a human commu-nity.

If Marx is not an a-philosopher or antiphilosopher, perhaps he is a transphilosopher? Perhaps Marx's most essential thought is that philosophy should not be simply rejected or ignored, but that, through being realized, it should be overcome, superseded, abolished. Is it not Marx's "ideal" that reality should become philosophical, and that philosophy as something specific should disappear? The idea is very attractive. But for this very reason it must be carefully examined. Convincing arguments do not preclude still more convincing counterarguments.

One argument says Marx taught that the proletariat cannot be abolished without the realization of philosophy. But how can philosophy realize itself without abolishing itself? To this one could reply: philosophy can be abolished only by being completely realized. And only a completed, closed philosophy, by which the completed man thinks of himself in his completed world, can be completely realized. An incomplete, open philosophy can be realized more and more, but never definitively. The complete realization of philosophy presupposes the end of history. History can be broken forever by a cosmic catastrophe or a thermonuclear war. But history cannot say to itself: whatever has been has been, and now I am going to sleep. Completed history is a *contradictio in adjecto*. There is no evidence that Marx was at any time ready to accept such a contradiction.

The second argument runs: Marx's "philosophy" is not set out according to traditional philosophical disciplines. There are no such things as Marx's ontology, epistemology, logic, ethics, aesthetics, etc. Furthermore, Marx's "philosophical" thought is so deeply merged with his "sociological," "economic," "political" and other thought that one cannot tell where one ends and another begins, and where philosophy is not separated from nonphilosophy and articulated into disciplines, there is no philosophy. Here the answer is clear: the essence of philosophy does not lie in its formal separation from science, art, religion, or in an academic grouping in disciplines. Plato and Nietzsche did not break their philosophies up into disciplines, nor did they separate them so strictly from the arts. Aristotle and Hegel may be said to have expounded their philosophies according to "disciplines," but it would be going too far to maintain that the essence and value of their philosophies lies in the distribution into disciplines.

The third argument may seem to be the most convincing: Marx reproached the philosophers for having only interpreted the world, whereas the point was to change it. Does not this reproach reveal the meaning and essence of Marx's "philosophical" thought? Is it not Marx's basic intention to give up trying to interpret the world philosophically and instead to embark upon its practical revolutionary change? To this one could reply with the counter-question: is the essence of philosophy as philosophy a mere "interpretation," which refrains from revolutionary change? Did not, say, the French thinkers of the Enlightenment consciously aim at a revolutionary change of the world on the basis of their philosophy? And did not even those philosophers who wanted to keep exclusively to interpretation, in fact, by their very "interpretations," encourage a revolutionary change of the world and take part in it?

Finally, somebody may remark: granted that Marx was a philosopher after all, does this not diminish the essential novelty of his message? Does this not make him just one in an endless series of philosophers? If Marx is one among many, however, it does not follow that he is no better than anyone else. And the novelty of his thought, and his thought in its wholeness, is certainly endangered by the demand that philosophy should be definitively "realized" and "abolished." A definite reconciliation of thought with reality is possible only as a definitive capitulation of revolutionary thought before reactionary reality. A definitive abolition of philosophy is imaginable only as a definitive victory of blind economic forces or political violence. Thus it is unimaginable.

II

The thesis that Marx is a philosopher does not solve the inevitable question of what constitutes the essence and importance of his philosophy. And this question does not require discovering the general or common characteristics of all the philosophical conceptions that have appeared under the name of "Marxist" or "Marx's" philosophy, since these terms have been used to describe conceptions that have almost nothing in common; their systematic exposition may be interesting, but it does not answer our question. Nor does our question mean: what are the philosophical conceptions that Marx always stood for? What philosophical conceptions did he express most frequently? What philosophical conceptions did he consider to be the most important? These and similar questions may be interesting; it is probably possible to give a precise answer to some of them but not to all.

The question of the essence of Marx's philosophy cannot be reduced to the question of what Marx's or Marxist philosophy has been so far; nor can it be answered by an empirical description or summing up of what Marx or some Marxist wrote about philosophy. The question of the essence of Marx's philosophy aims at discovering what makes Marxist philosophy what it is: the fundamental theoretical possibility of our times, the critical humanistic thought of modern man about himself and his world. Therefore the answer to this question cannot be a report on what has been or is still going on, but rather participation in the creation of something that can and should be. A correct answer cannot be obtained by a detailed comparison of quotations from Marx, but only by creative thinking in the spirit of Marx, by co-thinking with Marx and by thinking through Marx's guiding ideas.

Could it not be said that the essence of Marx's philosophy is that it is a "philosophy of action," "philosophy of deed" or "philosophy of praxis," that it is a "theory" that does not remain just theory but also demands the act of changing the world and at the same time participates

in this act? This could certainly be said, and it would not
be difficult to substantiate. There are many critical statements of Marx's against "theory" separated from "praxis,"
and his whole life offers evidence that cabinet thinking
for thinking's sake was not his ideal.

But it is not enough to say that Marx's philosophy is a
philosophy of action or a philosophy of praxis, because this
can be understood in various ways. It must therefore be
explained in greater detail to preclude wrong interpretations.

When we say that Marx's philosophy is a philosophy of
action (deed, praxis) this cannot mean that action is
added to the philosophy from outside by a coincidence,
or on the basis of a special decision of the philosopher.
If we characterize a philosophy as essentially a philosophy
of action (deed, praxis) this must mean that action (deed,
praxis) follows from the essence of its theoretical content,
that the transition from theory to praxis is its essential
"thesis." Thus if we characterize Marx's philosophy as a
philosophy of action, we must explain its essential theses,
according to which it cannot remain pure theory and must
turn into the action of revolutionary transformation of the
world.

The answer to the question is seemingly simple: Marx's
philosophy is a philosophy of revolutionary action because
its nucleus is the conception of "naturalism-humanism"
("naturalistic humanism" or "humanistic naturalism"), the
conception of man as a being of praxis who by his free
creative action molds and changes his world and himself.
There is no doubt that in his early works Marx developed
such a conception. And there is no ground for disputing
the view that Marx did not give up this conception in his
"mature" works, but continued developing and concretiz-
ing it. It would be more justified to dispute the names
quoted than the conception itself, but it must be pointed
out that these names can be arrived at on the basis of
some of Marx's writing. When, for instance, Marx says
that "communism as a fully developed naturalism is hu-

manism and as a fully developed humanism is naturalism"[1]
he obviously means that naturalism and humanism, which
in their incomplete "not fully developed" form may be
different and even contrary, become identical in their completed, "fully developed" form. The terms "naturalism-
humanism," "naturalistic humanism," "humanistic naturalism" suggest appropriate names for such a conception.
Since the two composite parts of these terms were understood in various ways, both up to Marx's time and afterward, the combined term may also be interpreted in different ways. It should therefore be kept in mind that in
the text below the term "naturalism-humanism" is used
to denote that philosophical conception by which Marx
tried to overcome the opposition between naturalism and
humanism.

Under the name of "Marx's philosophy," however, a
conception is often encountered that is more adequately
called "dialectical materialism," a conception that was developed by Engels, Plekhanov and Lenin, further elaborated by a number of Soviet philosophers between the two
world wars, and canonized in a simplified form by Stalin.
In the form given it by Stalin this conception is definitely
discredited, but many still think that it is "good" in the
form given it by Engels and Lenin. Even many who are
not quite satisfied with the form dialectical materialism
was actually given by Engels and Lenin consider that in
the classics of Marxism there is room for a "more creative,
better 'diamat' than we have today."

Under the name of "Marx's" or "Marxist" philosophy we
then encounter at least two philosophical conceptions, one
of which we have conditionally called "philosophy of
praxis" or "naturalism-humanism" (we could call it also
"Marx's humanism"), while the other is usually described
as "dialectical materialism." We must then consider the
question: what is the relationship between "naturalism-

[1] Fromm, *Marx's Concept of Man*, p. 127; cf., *ibid.*, p. 129,
the reference to the "realized naturalism of man and the realized
humanism of nature" and p. 181, reference to "consistent
naturalism or humanism."

humanism" and "dialectical materialism"? Are these two names for the same thing; two aspects of the same conception; two conceptions, one of which is part of the other; two different conceptions that complement each other; two different conceptions irrelevant to each other; or two conceptions that exclude each other? One could probably put forward some argument for each of these theses, but a detailed consideration of all theoretically possible hypotheses would take us too far. We will content ourselves with saying a little more about only the thesis that seems to be most correct, that "naturalistic humanism" and "dialectical materialism" are two different conceptions, which neither logically complement each other, nor are simply indifferent to each other, but at least in certain essential points are mutually exclusive.

III

In support of the thesis that Marx's "naturalism-humanism" is incompatible with "dialectical materialism" one could quote several statements by Marx, as, for instance, that "consistent naturalism or humanism is distinguished from both idealism and materialism, and at the same time constitutes their unifying truth."[2] But such statements are not decisive; it is more important to consider the main theses of dialectical materialism and see whether they can be reconciled with the basic ideas of Marx's humanism.

The basic ontological thesis of traditional dialectical materialism is the thesis of the primacy of nature in relation to the spirit, of matter in relation to mind, of the physical in relation to the psychic. This is not exclusively Stalin's thesis. It is well known that Engels regarded as the great basic question of all philosophy the relationship of thinking to being, of the spirit to nature; and, according to the way in which they replied to this "paramount question of the whole of philosophy," to the question "which is primary, spirit or nature?" he divided all philosophers into

[2] *Ibid.*, p. 181.

"two great camps": the idealists who insist that the spirit
is primary, and the materialists who regard nature as primary.[3]

Engels' thesis on the relationship of thinking and being
as the basic question of philosophy was also endorsed by
Plekhanov, who often formulated it in terms that were
more customary in the philosophy of his time—for instance,
"the question of the relationship of subject to object"[4]
or the "question of the relation of "I" toward "Non-I.""[5]
Although he did not classify all replies to this question
simply as materialist or idealist but took into consideration nonmonistic solutions such as dualism as well, Plekhanov, too, believed that the fundamental philosophical
trends were materialism and idealism, and the only correct
solution—materialism.

Engels' formulation of the basic question of philosophy
and his thesis of the primacy of matter, or nature in relation to consciousness or spirit, was endorsed by Lenin as
well, at least during the phase in which he wrote his
Materialism and Empirio-Criticism. As can be seen from
the titles of two sections of this work, Lenin considered
as essential components of the basic question of philosophy
two "more concrete" questions: "Did nature exist before
man?" and "Does man think by means of brains?" Both
these questions Lenin answered in the affirmative, and we
can agree with his replies; what is disputable is whether
Lenin's subquestions exhaust the meaning of Engels' "basic
question" and whether this question is really the "basic
question of philosophy."

I do not maintain that the basic philosophical question,
as understood by Engels, Plekhanov and Lenin, is meaningless. But everything that is meaningful is not "basic."
Besides, every question rests on certain assumptions, and
it will be well to ask whether Engels' "basic question"

[3] K. Marx and F. Engels, *Basic Writings on Politics and
Philosophy*, edited by L. S. Feuer, Doubleday & Co. (Garden
City, New York, 1959), pp. 206–7.

[4] G. V. Plekhanov: *Sočinenija* (*Works*), vol. XVII, p. 18.

[5] *Ibid.*, vol. XVIII, p. 296.

does not already contain certain assumptions. Does it not assume that the world is divided or split into two main "parts," "sides," "aspects" or "forces": matter and spirit? If the object of philosophy is the world in which we live, and if matter and spirit are the two fundamental realities of this world, it is indeed the fundamental task of critical thought about the world to determine the relationship between these two fundamental realities.

But is the world really divided in essence into "nature" and "spirit," "matter" and "consciousness," "being" and "thought"? No reply is really possible if we do not know what "nature," "spirit," "matter," etc., are. Let us assume for the present (what could be easily disputed) that "matter," "nature," "being" are the same and that we know what they are; but what about the other side of the relation, spirit or mind?

Spirit can be conceived in various ways, among other things as a nonhuman mind, independent of man, objective and absolute, popularly called "god." If we assume the existence of such a spirit, the question of the relationship of nature or matter toward absolute spirit will naturally emerge, and the various aspects of this question will call for an answer. There are, however, no convincing arguments in favor of this assumption, and those who have advocated dialectical materialism have, as a rule, rejected it outright. But if there is no such thing as absolute spirit, then there is little sense in asking about its relationship to matter or nature.

"The basic question of philosophy" can also be interpreted as concerning not the relationship of nature to absolute spirit, but the relationship of nature to man's spirit. Man is, however, not merely spirit; "spirit" is but one "part," "side" or "aspect" of man. It would be strange if the question of the relationship of one part of man to matter or nature were to form the basic question of philosophy. Is not the relationship of integral man toward the world in which he lives a more important question?

Faced with this objection one might try to save the "basic question of philosophy" approximately as follows:

the spiritual side of man's being can be one of the two sides of the basic relationship in which philosophy is interested, for the other side is not matter or nature in general, but man's matter or nature. The object of philosophy is man, and in man we can distinguish the "material" or "natural" and the "ideal" or "spiritual" side. The division into "matter" and "spirit" is the fundamental internal division of man, and thus the question of the relationship of matter and spirit in man is the basic question of philosophy.

Such rescue efforts, however, are of no great use. Man is a united being whose integrity does not exclude internal differentiation. His practical activity is differentiated in many forms, but it is very difficult to regard these forms as divided into two main kinds, material and spiritual. Hardly any activity of man is exclusively material or exclusively spiritual. Let us take, for instance, political activity: Is man, when acting politically, active as matter or as spirit? Or man's artistic activity: Is the activity of a painter or sculptor spiritual or material?

Consequently, division into matter and spirit is not the basic division of the world we live in, nor is this basic division within man. How, then, can the basic question of philosophy be the question of the relationship between matter and spirit? Is not the question possible only when given certain dualistic assumptions, which Marx's "naturalism-humanism" excludes?

It is very difficult to say if there is a basic question in philosophy and how it could be formulated most adequately. But are we not entitled to maintain that the question of man's relationship to the world is wider and more fundamental than the question of the relationship of spirit to matter (or subject to object) and that the latter is only a distorted form of the former?

IV

Dialectical materialism cannot be reduced to simply the thesis of the primacy of matter over spirit. A vital component of this conception is the theory of reflection, which has been discussed in the greatest detail in Todor Pavlov's well-known book *Theory of Reflection*. Stalin, too, was strongly in favor of this theory, but it does not belong exclusively to Stalin and Pavlov. In his book, Pavlov merely "elaborated" the thoughts contained in Lenin's *Materialism and Empirio-Criticism*, while Lenin only followed Engels, who, in discussing the basic question of philosophy, maintained that this question had yet another side: "Is our thinking capable of the cognition of the real world? Are we able in our ideas and notions of the real world to produce a correct reflection of reality?"[6] The formulation of the question clearly indicates Engels' reply.

The theory of reflection belongs to dialectical materialism not only because it was endorsed by Engels and Lenin, but also because it seems to be the most adequate complement to the materialist thesis of the primacy of matter over consciousness. But while it fits well with the theory of the primacy of matter over spirit, it does not fit with Marx's view of man as a being of praxis. If man is really a free and creative being, how could his cognitive activity be a mere reflection of reality? The theory of reflection obviously contradicts Marx's concept of man. What is more important, it cannot satisfactorily explain the phenomena of consciousness, knowledge and truth.[7]

While one can say with considerable certainty that the materialist "aspect" of dialectical materialism (including the theory of reflection) contradicts Marx's conception of man as a being of praxis, things are neither so clear nor so simple when the dialectical aspect is considered. Very different things have been understood by "dialectics" in the history of philosophy; and even among those who consider dialectics the essence, or an essential aspect, of Marx's philosophy, there are greatly different views of this matter.

[6] Marx, Engels, *Basic Writings on Politics and Philosophy*, p. 207.

[7] This is further developed in "Truth and reflection," pp. 190–98.

Regardless of all these different viewpoints, one thing is fairly certain: dialectics, as understood by the founders of dialectical materialism—Engels, Plekhanov, Lenin, is neither only a method nor only logic or theory of knowledge, but also ontology. Its essential aspect or element is the conception that there are certain most general, "dialectical" laws according to which everything that exists changes and develops. No matter how exactly we may formulate and systematize these laws, it seems legitimate to pose the question to what extent the idea of the inevitable, exceptionless general laws of every being can be reconciled with Marx's idea of man as a free creative being of praxis. If all that exists is subjected to dialectical "laws," how can man be exempted? And if man is not excepted, how can we speak of his freedom and creativity?

These thoughts and remarks by no means solve the question about the relationship between Marx's humanism and dialectical materialism, but they warn us that at least certain essential theses of dialectical materialism are full of difficulties and are irreconcilable with Marx's humanistic conception of man.

The criticism may be put forward that the difficulties have emerged because we have considered dialectical materialism "undialectically," first only in its materialistic aspect, and then only in its dialectical aspect. The materialistic thesis on the primacy of matter should be examined in dialectical form, i.e., not simply as a thesis on the primacy of matter, but as a thesis on the unity and interaction of what is material and what is spiritual, with matter having the primacy, but with the spirit possessing a relative independence and importance.

To this possible criticism we can reply that the dialectical-materialistic solution of the question on the relationship between "matter" and "spirit" is certainly "better," "more flexible," etc., than the vulgarly materialistic one; but this does not change the fact that both these variants of materialism start from the same question, which is based on dualistic presuppositions. In the same way, regardless of whether we interpret the most general laws of dialectics materialistically or idealistically, the fundamental difficulty will remain: how to reconcile the existence of exceptionless laws of being with the demand for free creative Being (Sein).

In pointing to these difficulties with the inherited conception of dialectical materialism and contrasting it with Marx's humanism, I do not mean that Marxist philosophy should or could be limited to anthropology. When we say that the essence of man is praxis, we are making use of the "metaphysical" concept of "essence," and when we say that man is a being that realizes its human (or nonhuman) potentialities, we use modal categories ("possibility," "reality," "necessity"). When speaking about the present, the past and the future we refer to time. Marx's entire work as a struggle for man who will be realized as a being of praxis presupposes the distinction between authentic and nonauthentic Being. And the meaning of Being, the question of what "to be" means is involved here.

Thus what is called Marx's conception of man is not narrowly anthropological, but a conception that rises from the question about man to fundamental questions about the meaning of Being. An essential feature of Marx's philosophy is that it has such continuity and constant "interplay," such a constant relationship between essential questions of ontology and anthropology (to use the traditional language). And it is for this very reason that Marx's philosophical conception is what it is: a radical humanistic criticism of an inhuman world. Is not the root of its criticism of inhumanity in its humanistic conception of man, and is not the source of its radicality in that it does not limit itself to man alone or try to isolate him, but rises to the question of the meaning of Being in general?

I have not spoken critically of the conception of dialectical materialism in order to diminish the importance of the persons who developed this conception, persons such as Engels, Plekhanov and Lenin, who made great contributions to the revolutionary movement and to Marxist theory (including Marx's humanistic philosophy). Nor is my criticism directed personally against those who in our times have tried, or are still trying, to combine Marx's humanism with dialectical materialism. Nor has it been my intention simply to belittle dialectical materialism: on the contrary, it is because I regard it as a possible philosophical conception that I think it should be seriously considered and criticized and neither declaratively accepted nor tacitly discarded.

PART II

Marx's concept of man

I. Introduction

1. What is the poet doing (for example, D. Vasiljev) when he passionately assures us: "Oh, I am a Man! a Man!" or when he grievously sighs: "Oh, when a man is not a Man"? Is he rambling disconnectedly, or is he saying something meaningful?

If the poet is talking nonsense, then all the rest of us are continually talking nonsense too. Nearly every day we praise somebody by saying that he really is a man, and we reproach somebody else by saying that he is not a man at all. In reading a newspaper we cry shame upon the inhuman act of a mother who has abandoned her child and express our indignation over inhuman behavior of some colonialists in Africa. We criticize contemporary society, which despite its civilized form dehumanizes man, and we contrast it with socialism as a society in which man comes into his own and relations between men become human. We argue whether contemporary man is a master or a servant of his technology, and we ask ourselves what cosmic flights and the discovery of californium will bring to man.

Are words like "man," "human" and "inhuman" only empty words that move us emotionally or do they have a meaning also? What does it mean, for example, to be a man?

If we cannot answer the question, our talks of man and the human may remain empty talks. But the purpose of raising the question of man is not solely to bring order and sense into our discourse, to learn how to use the word "man" meaningfully and consistently. Our time, more than any before it, imperils man's humanity as well as his bare existence; but it also offers him a chance to realize a truly human society and full humanness. The great practical struggle around the question "What is man?" is deeper and sharper today than it ever was before.

It is not philosophers who have fabricated the question "What is man?" but it is an important question of our existence, which philosophy, if it does not want to remain apart from life, cannot pass by in silence.

2. Meanings of words we use are registered, systematized and explained in dictionaries. Is the answer to the question "What is man?" to be found in a dictionary?

According to Webster's *New World Dictionary of the American Language* the word "man" has ten main meanings.[1] In its first and broadest meaning a man is "a human being; person, whether male or female." Every man is a man in this sense; and all men in this sense together form man in the second sense, which is "the human race; mankind." In meanings that follow (meanings three to seven) not every man is a man; man is called a man if he possesses certain special biological, social or psychological properties. And in the last two, dislocated meanings a man is not a human being at all but a piece in a game or a ship.

The multimeanings of the word "man" are not a peculiarity of the English language. The Serbocroatian word *čovjek* and the French word *homme* also have the same

---

[1] "1. a human being; person, whether male or female. 2. the human race; mankind: used without *the* or *a*. 3. *a*) an adult male human being. *b*) sometimes, a boy. 4. *a*) an adult male servant, follower, attendant, or subordinate. *b*) a male employee; workman: as, the employer talked to the *men*. *c*) *usually in pl.*, a soldier, sailor, etc.; especially, one of the rank and file: as, officers and *men*. *d*) [Archaic], a vassal. 5. *a*) a husband: as, they are *man* and wife. *b*) a lover. 6. a person with qualities conventionally regarded as manly, such as strength, courage, etc. 7. manly qualities; virility. 8. a player on a team. 9. one of the pieces used in chess, checkers, etc. 10. in *nautical usage,* a ship: used in compounds, as *man-of-war, merchantman. Man* is also used as a term of address." *Webster's New World Dictionary of the American Language,* College Edition (Cleveland and New York, 1960), p. 889.

basic meaning and very similar derived, specialized and dislocated meanings as the English "man."

It is not difficult to find the way to narrow the meaning of these words with the same basic meaning. In all cases in which not all men are regarded as men, only those men are regarded as men who are supposed to possess in a higher degree one or more of the basic human properties that make every man a man in the broader sense of that word.

In order to understand the plurality of meaning of the word "man," we must therefore understand its primary meaning, according to which man is "a human being; person, whether male or female."

What, then, is man as a "human being" or a "person, whether male or female"? It is useless to seek an answer in dictionaries that fix the everyday usage of the word "man."

Can etymology of the word "man" provide an answer?

3. The etymology of the word "man" is very interesting and can stimulate reflection. But if we expect it to answer our question, we may be disappointed. Far from being able to arbitrate in philosophical controversies about man, the etymology of the word shows that the question "What is man?" was controversial before philosophers started disputing about it.

The Latin *homo*, French *homme*, Italian *uomo* and Spanish *hombre* all originate from the Indo-European root *khem*, which means "earth, soil." The connection between man and soil is most easily seen in Latin. Soil in Latin is *humus*. *Homo* is *ex humo*. In the etymology of the word "man" in the Romance languages lies the idea of man as an earthly being. Man is thus radically contrasted with gods.

The German words *Mann* and *Mensch*, the English and Swedish *man* and Danish *mand* originate from the Indo-European root *men*, which means the movement of mind, thinking. From the same root are derived, among others, the English word "mind" and the German verb *meinen* (to think or opine). In the root of the word "man" in the Germanic languages we thus have the idea that man is one who thinks, a mind. Man is in this way radically opposed to animal.

For nations speaking Romance languages man is originally earth, soil; for Germanic nations man is mind; how is it with us Slavs? The Serbocroatian *čovjek*, Slovene *človek*, Czech *člověk*, Russian *čelovek* and Polish *czlowiek* are derived from old Slavonic *čelověk*. *Čelověk* is *čelo-věk*. With Slavs, then, man is not simple, he is compounded from *čel* and *věk*. What is even worse, the specialists in linguistics cannot agree either where *čel* comes from or what *věk* means. Both are controversial, and the dispute will probably never be settled.

Věk is very often considered in connection with the Lithuanian *vaikas*, which means "child, boy, youth." I find it more probable, however, that this *věk* is the same we have in the words *věk* (century, age, lifetime), *vekovati* (spend one's life, live) and *večnost* (eternity) and that it contains the idea of time. The man would be, then, according to his second part, one who his lifetime lives. The question remains: What does *čel* mean?

Daničić thinks that *čel*, which we find in the words *čelovek* (man) and *čeljad* (people, folks, inmates) is derived from the Indo-European root *skar* (today it is usually written *quel* or *kwel*), which means revolve, jump, swing, strike, cut, work, strew, cover, fill, sate, explode, shout, burn. According to this, man would be one who lives his lifetime working, revolving, burning.

Today the prevailing opinion is that *čel* comes from the sense of *quel* as a herd, drove, troop, genus, tribe, clan, group, community. According to this conception man is primarily not one who works but one who lives his lifetime in a herd, swarm, community.

Such an interpretation of man may conveniently be joined with that in which *věk* means child. If *čel* is genus or clan and *věk* child, then *čelověk* is a child, a member of a community.

These are only some of the hypotheses that have been produced so far, and they are the result of speculations not by philosophers but by philologists.

Is only one of them right? Or does the original Slav idea of man contain in itself the idea of time as well as the idea of activity and the idea of life in a community?

There is also one more idea in the Slavonic root of the word "man." The plural of *čovjek* is *ljudi,* which originates from the Indo-European root *leudh,* which means to raise oneself or to grow up. From this root are derived the Greek word *eleutheros* and Latin *liber,* both of which mean free. In the etymology of the Slavonic word for man we have the idea of freedom too.

Perhaps it is not uninteresting to mention that the idea of man as an earthly being, which is contained in the Romance root of the word "man" is most fully developed in the French materialist philosophy of the eighteenth century, whereas the idea of man as a spirit is most fully realized in German classical idealism. And by an irony of history, the ideas contained in the Slavonic root of the word "man" are most profoundly developed by a thinker who did not always regard Slavs very highly, but who nevertheless has had much success among them—Karl Marx.

4. If the etymology of the word "man," instead of settling the question "What is man?" makes it more complicated, could biology offer us a desired solution? As a science that studies all living creatures, biology cannot omit man.

There have been passionate disputes among biologists on the problem of man. Whereas Linné classified man together with monkeys and lemurs in the order of *Primates,* Cuvier thought that the difference between man and monkey is considerably bigger, so that they form two different orders: *Bimanes* (two-handed animals) and *Quadrumanes* (four-handed animals). Later anatomical and physiological investigations confirmed Linné's opinion that man, monkey and lemur belong to the same order, *Primates,* which, in turn, is only one of the orders in the subclass *Placentalia* in the class *Mammalia* of the subbranch *Amniota* of the branch *Craniota* of the subphylum *Vertebrata* of the phylum *Chordata* of the subdivision *Deuteros-*

tomia of the division *Coelemata* of the subkingdom *Metazoa* in the big kingdom *Animalia*.

According to the biological conception, man is only a small species in the huge animal kingdom. According to this view the difference between man and monkey is negligible in comparison to the difference between a monkey and a bear, or between a turtle and a frog.

But in everyday life and language we do not oppose man as a species of *Primate* to monkeys as another species; we oppose man to the whole animal and even, indeed, to the whole natural kingdom. The difference between man and animal seems to us deeper than any differences among animals. Whether such a view can be justified is a philosophical question. Can man really be opposed not only to one or another of animal species but to animals in general?

II. *Marx's View of Man's Essence*

5. People often doubt the legitimacy of the question "What is man?" in its general form. This question, they say, is sometimes posed by certain philosophies, but it is a false question, and it cannot be asked by Marxism. Different special sciences explore different aspects of man's activity; no aspect remains unexplored; and all "special" sciences together give a complete picture of man. On the other hand, man in general, man as such, does not exist; there is only a concrete man of a concrete society; slave owner or slave, landlord or serf, bourgeois or worker.

Man is not, however, the sum of his parts or aspects, but an integral being; and no special science does or can answer the question of what he is as an integral being, that is, what makes him man and each of his activities or aspects human. Although man is not always and everywhere the same, although he historically changes, there is something that allows us to call a proletarian as well as a capitalist, a landlord as well as a slaveowner, a man.

What makes a man—man? What, if anything, makes somebody more and somebody less a man?

If Marx had bypassed these questions, they would still

demand an answer. But nothing is more false than the assumption that Marx condemned discussions about man in general.

It is unnecessary to quote texts from *Economic and Philosophical Manuscripts* because it is well known that Marx speaks there about man as man. But it is sometimes held that Marx later came to the conclusion that all general speculations about man are inadmissible. In support of this assumption some passages from *German Ideology* can be quoted. But is *German Ideology* Marx's last word in philosophy? Did not he also write *Capital?*

According to *Capital*, the labor process is "human action with a view to the production of use-values, appropriation of natural substances to human requirements; it is the necessary condition for effecting exchange of matter between man and Nature; it is the everlasting nature-imposed condition of human existence, and therefore is independent of every social phase of that existence, or rather, is common to every such phase. It was, therefore, not necessary to represent our laborer in connection with other laborers; man and his labor on one side, Nature and its materials on the other, sufficed. As the taste of porridge does not tell you who grew the oats, no more does this simple process tell you of itself what are the social conditions under which it is taking place, whether under the slave-owner's brutal lash, or the anxious eye of the capitalist, whether Cincinnatus carries it on in tilling his modest farm or a savage in killing wild animals with stones."[2]

Marx in *Capital*, then, stresses that we can speak not only about laborer, capitalist and slave-owner, but also about man, labor and nature in general.

In another place in *Capital* Marx writes against the Utilitarian Bentham: "To know what is useful for a dog, one must study dog nature. This nature is not to be deduced from the principle of utility. Applying this to man, he who would criticize all human acts, movements, relations, etc., by the principle of utility, must first deal with

[2] Marx, *Capital*, vol. I, pp. 204–5.

human nature in general, and then with human nature as modified in each historical epoch. Bentham makes short work of it. With the driest naïveté he takes the modern shopkeeper, especially the English shopkeeper, as the normal man. Whatever is useful to this queer normal man, and to his world, is absolutely useful. This yardstick, then, he applies to past, present and future."[3]

Marx thinks that a dog has its dog nature and man his human nature, but that man differs from a dog by having a "human nature in general" as well as one "modified in each historical epoch." He reproaches Bentham for regarding the modern shopkeeper as a normal man, ignoring in this way general human nature and its historical development.

Marx not only "permits" discussion of human nature in general, in *Capital* he criticizes bourgeois society precisely because in it universal human nature cannot express itself, because in it "a general or a banker plays a great part, but mere man [man as man], on the other hand, a very shabby part."[4]

In accordance with this, Marx in the third volume of *Capital* opposes to capitalism a society in which the socialized man, the associated producers, will produce under conditions "most adequate to their human nature and most worthy of it."[5]

Marx thus without any hesitation speaks about human nature and about man as man. Without any fear that we will come into conflict with Marx, we may ask: What is man?

6. What does it mean to ask, What is man? Perhaps it means to start a search for that one human quality or property through which man differs from all other animals?

If this is the sense of our question, then it admits of many different answers. There are many distinctive traits peculiar to man. Traditionally, it was most frequently held

[3] Marx, *Capital*, vol. I, p. 668.
[4] *Ibid.*, p. 51.
[5] *Ibid.*, vol. III, p. 954.

that man differs from animal by reason. But we can distinguish him also by speech, economic production, moral activity, the creation of art. And, we can distinguish him by a quite special property or activity. Only man, for example, uses concepts. Only man can be a hypocrite. Man is also essentially different from animal in the way in which he prepares food. The difference between man's and animal's "intellectual" and "emotional" life is perhaps smaller than the difference between the animal devouring of food and contemporary culinary and gastronomical art. Men's methods of mutual killing and torturing, although we sometimes call them bestial, are also something of which the beasts are incapable.

To ask, What is man?, does not mean to ask about that one property that only man has. Nor does it mean to ask for an enumeration of man's specific properties, not only because the properties that are peculiar to him are many, so that it is difficult to enumerate them all, but also because man is not a chaos of qualities or properties but something structured and integral.

To ask, What is man?, means to ask what is it by virtue of which man is that integral being that differs essentially from everything else that exists.

That by virtue of which something is what it is, was traditionally called "essence." Is not the division of things into essence and existence one of the characteristics of scholastic philosophy? Certainly. But essence (*Wesen*), which, in its broadest sense, Hegel contrasts with Being (*Sein*) and in its narrower sense with existence (*Existenz*) and appearance (*Erscheinung*), is also one of the principal categories of his *Logic*. The distinction between essence and appearance plays an important part in the work of Marx and Lenin.

Hegel, Marx and Lenin relativize the opposition between essence and appearance, emphasizing that essence necessarily appears and that appearance is essential. But they think that without these categories theoretical thought is impossible. Marx, for example, holds that "every science would be unnecessary if the apparent form and the essence of things immediately coincided"[6] and Lenin writes: "Man's thought perpetually penetrates from the appearance to the essence, from essence of, so to speak, the first order, to essence of the second order, and so on, *without an end.*"[7]

Should not we nevertheless try to think without the categories of "essence" and "appearance"? Probably yes, if by "essence" we mean the hidden and unchangeable basis of the visible and changeable "appearance," if by the categories of "essence" and "appearance" we divide the world into two clearly separated and entirely different but nevertheless connected parts.

But is this the only possible interpretation of essence and appearance? And can we think without using anything similar to the traditional concept of essence? Some attempts in that direction seem to end by reintroducing the rejected concept of essence under another name.

In his work *Sein und Zeit* Martin Heidegger, for example, does not ask about man's essence, but about his fundamental constitution (*Grundverfassung*), Being (*Sein*), and sense of Being (*Sinn des Seins*). His answer is that man (*Dasein*) is being-in-the-world (*das In-der-Welt-sein*), man's Being (*das Sein des Daseins*) is anxiety (*Sorge*), and the sense of his Being (*der Sinn des Seins des Daseins*) is temporality (*die Zeitlichkeit*). The traditional question about essence is here replaced by three questions (about structure, Being and the sense of Being), but we would probably not be mistaken too much if we said that in these questions the talk is mainly about what Lenin would call man's essence of the first, second and the third order. Heidegger regards the sense of the Being of man (temporality) as that by virtue of which man is in the first place man, consequently as man's deepest essence.

7. Just as the sense of Marx's question about man has been misunderstood, so has his answer to this question.

[6] Marx, *Capital*, vol. III, p. 952.
[7] Lenin, *Philosophical Notebooks*, p. 237.

Expounding different conceptions of man, Max Scheler mentions as one of the five basic conceptions the positivistic, according to which man is an instinctive being, and as one of three subclasses of positivistic conception the "Marxist" or "economic" conception, according to which man is determined by his impulse for food. He obviously does not know that, according to Marx, animals "produce only under the compulsion of direct physical need, while man produces when he is free from physical need and only truly produces in freedom from such need."[8]

A view similar to Scheler's is also found in some "Marxists" who attribute to Marx Benjamin Franklin's definition of man as a tool-making animal. It is true that Marx quotes Franklin's definition with a certain sympathy in the first volume of *Capital*. But those who have noticed this often overlook the fact that in the same volume Marx characterizes this definition not as his, but as typically American. Of Aristotle's definition of man as a political animal he comments: "Strictly, Aristotle's definition is that man is by nature a town-citizen. This is quite as characteristic of ancient classical society as Franklin's definition of man as a tool-making animal is characteristic of Yankeedom."[9]

Marx believes that Aristotle's and Franklin's definitions of man are important—like Hegel, he thinks that no fundamental philosophical thought can be either simply false or worthless—but neither Aristotle's nor Franklin's definition is his.

When he rejects the traditional conception of man as a rational animal Marx does not do so simply because this gives reason the primary place, but first of all because he considers that neither reason nor political activity, neither production of tools nor any other special activity or property can be man's essence. Man is not a mechanical sum of his "spheres" (economical, political, moral, artistic, etc.), and even insofar as it is possible to distinguish such "spheres" they do not maintain for eternity the same re-

8 Fromm, *Marx's Concept of Man*, p. 102.
9 Marx, *Capital*, vol. I, p. 358.

lationships. Therefore, what makes a man man is not his "main sphere," but his whole way of Being, the general structure of his relationship toward the world and toward himself. This way of Being, which is peculiar to man, Marx designates by the word "praxis." Man for Marx, is, the being of "praxis."

8. When we define man as praxis all questions are not answered; many only begin. First of all, what is praxis? Praxis is human activity. But a certain kind of activity is also peculiar to all animals. What is it that distinguishes praxis as human activity from animal activity? In answering this question people often lose what they gained in defining man as a being of praxis. Difficulties in answering the question are seen in Marx also.

About the activity of man and animal we read in Marx's *Economic and Philosophical Manuscripts* of 1844: "The animal is one with its life activity. It does not distinguish the activity from itself. It is *its activity*. But man makes his life activity itself an object of his will and consciousness. He has a conscious life activity. It is not a determination with which he is completely identified. Conscious life activity distinguishes man from the life activity of animals."[10]

One can agree that man's life activity is conscious, whereas animals' is not. But can one agree that it is first of all consciousness (or perhaps even only consciousness) that distinguishes man's activity (praxis) from animal activity? If man differs from animal by praxis, and if praxis differs from animal activity by being conscious, then man differs from animal by his consciousness and we are back to the traditional definition of man as a rational animal.

Is this unavoidable, or is it possible to give an interpretation of praxis that would determine its general structure and also contain its determination as a conscious and free activity?

I think that such is the interpretation of praxis as a universal-creative self-creative activity, activity by which

[10] Fromm, *Marx's Concept of Man*, p. 101.

man transforms and creates his world and himself. Exactly such an interpretation prevails in Karl Marx.

In *Economic and Philosophical Manuscripts* he writes, for example: "Animals construct only in accordance with the standards and needs of the species to which they belong, while man knows how to produce in accordance with the standards of every species and knows how to apply the appropriate standard to the object. Thus man constructs also in accordance with the laws of beauty."

It is precisely in his work upon the objective world that man proves himself as a *species-being*. This production is his active species life. By means of it nature appears as *his* work and *his* reality. "The object of labor is, therefore, the *objectification of man's species life;* he no longer reproduces himself merely intellectually, as in consciousness, but actively and in a real sense, and he sees his own reflection in a world that he has constructed."[11]

9. The interpretation of praxis as a universal-creative self-creative activity contains its determination as a free, conscious activity. From this conception, the conception of man as a social history also follows. If man is a creative self-creative being that constantly creates and changes himself and his world, he is necessarily not always the same.

Animal species are also not always the same. But whereas an animal changes by adapting to and transforming its environment without any plan or purpose, man can by his creativity change purposefully his world and himself. "In short," says Engels, "the animal merely *uses* external nature and brings about changes in it simply by his presence; man by his changes makes it serve his ends, masters it."[12]

Therefore only man has a history. One can speak only figuratively of a "history" of the animal kingdom. But man's history is not only the history of the transformation

[11] *Ibid.,* p. 102.
[12] F. Engels, *Dialectics of Nature,* Foreign Publishing House (Moscow, 1954), p. 241.

of nature; it is also and in the first place the history of man's self-creation: "Since, however, for socialist man, *the whole of what is called world history* is nothing but the creation of man by human labor, and the emergence of nature for man, he therefore has the evident and irrefutable proof of his *self-creation*, of his own *origins*."[13]

Just because man is praxis and history, he is also the future. If man's essence is universal-creative and self-creative activity by which he historically creates his world and himself, then, if he does not want to cease being man, he can never interrupt the process of his self-creation. This means that man can never be completely finished, that he is not man when he lives only in the present and in the contemplation of past, but only insofar as he in the present realizes his future. Man is man if he realizes his historically created human possibilities.

At this point one can see clearly the difference between Marx and Hegel. For Hegel, man is also an active being, but he conceives man's activity primarily as an activity of self-consciousness, the final goal of which is the absolute knowledge of the absolute reality, a definitive completion of man and absolute. Absolute, which without man is only *an sich*, becomes through man *für sich*. Man's philosophical knowledge, which is at the same time the self-knowledge of the Absolute, means the end of human history. Man can be completed, and in Hegel's philosophy he is completed. For that reason he can also be fully described.

For Marx, man is an active being, but his activity is not the self-knowledge of the Absolute, but the transformation and creation of the world and of man himself. Therefore for Marx man can be never completed and never finally defined.

For that reason Marx's conception of man can never remain only a conception. Only to conceive man would mean only to conceive what man already was. But man is not only what he has been; he is in the first place what he can and ought to be. Marx's turn to praxis follows from

[13] Fromm, *Marx's Concept of Man*, p. 139.

this in the sense that his conception of man cannot remain a mere conception, but is also a criticism of alienated man who does not realize his human possibilities and a humanistic program of struggle for humanness. Marx's conception of man can thus not be separated from his humanistic theory of alienation and de-alienation.

10. The theory of alienation was outlined by Marx in those of his works that were published in *German-French Yearbooks*, and it was extensively developed in *Economic and Philosophical Manuscripts*; however, already in *German Ideology*, he and Engels speak very critically about alienation, self-alienation, man's essence, human nature, so that it appears as if they came to reject the theory. In *German Ideology* they maintain that philosophers, in conceiving human history as the process of man's self-alienation, transformed the whole of history into the process of the development of consciousness. This could mean that the theory of alienation is idealistic. But if we read carefully the "mature" works of Marx, we discover that the "rejected" theory of alienation is present in them, not only implicitly but also explicitly, not only by content but also terminologically. In the third volume of *Capital*, for example, Marx speaks about alienation and about the "human nature" that ought to be realized in the future, rationally organized society.

This shows that, in this case too, the exposition of the "true" Marx is possible only as interpretation, that it is illusory to think that we can give an absolutely objective exposition of Marx's thought as it is in itself. On the other hand, so far as an objective historical reconstruction of Marx's views is possible, it cannot settle the question of the value of these views. If it were shown, for example, that Marx only temporarily held the theory of alienation, this in itself would be no obstacle to accepting it. On the other hand, even if Marx permanently held it, we may find that there are defects in it.

11. Two basic questions arise in connection with the theory of alienation as expounded in *Economic and Philosophical Manuscripts* and in other works of Marx and

Engels: First, what do "alienation" and "self-alienation" mean; what is it to be a self-alienated or a nonself-alienated man; and, secondly, are man's self-alienation and nonself-alienation historical products; does self-alienation characterize only one stage in the historical development of mankind or is it a permanent (or nontemporal) structural moment of man's existence, one of those characteristics that constitute man as man? If we make up our minds that alienation is a characteristic of one stage in man's development, then we must add a third question: How is self-alienation grounded in the nature of history, how and why does it come to be?

In considering the first question, What do alienation and self-alienation mean?, one might first of all ask whether man alienates *something from himself* or alienates *himself from something*. Some Marxists are inclined to reduce the whole problem to the idea that man alienates something from himself, and the solution of the problem to the description of the concrete forms of this alienation. Thus they enumerate and describe in detail what it is that man alienates and how he does it: he alienates the products of his material activity in the form of commodity and money, he alienates the products of his spiritual activity in the form of religion, morals, etc. For consolation some add that one should distinguish between objectification and alienation, and that in the future rational society the first will remain while the second will disappear. Perhaps they think that this makes the problem easier. But it is merely a seeming alleviation; if we interpret alienation in this way, it is still possible to ask, for example: Is it an historical phenomenon and if it is, why and how does it emerge? On the other hand, Marx did not conceive the phenomenon of alienation so narrowly.

According to Marx, the essence of self-alienation is that man at the same time alienates something from himself and himself from something; that he alienates himself from himself.

We can see for ourselves that this is the essence of Marx's thought if we analyze his well-known manuscript

Alienated Labor, where he speaks about the four aspects or characteristics of alienation.[14]

He begins with the alienation of the results of man's labor, the alienation of objects produced by man. The realization of labor is its objectification, and this objectification is, for the laborer, at the same time the loss of the object, i.e., alienation. The worker is related to the product of his labor as to an alien object. Products of his hands constitute a separate world of objects, which is alien to him, which dominates him and which enslaves him.

The alienation of the results of man's productive activity is rooted in the alienation of production itself. Man alienates the products of his labor because he alienates his labor activity, because his own activity becomes for him an alien activity, an activity in which he does not affirm but denies himself, an activity that does not free but subjugates him. He is home when he is outside this activity, and he is out when he is in it.

From this characteristic of alienated labor Marx deduces a third: by alienating his own activity from himself, man in fact alienates his essence from himself and himself from his essence. Man is in essence a creative, practical being, and when he alienates his creative activity from himself, he alienates his human essence from himself. Transforming his generic essence into a means for the maintenance of his individual existence, man alienates himself from his humanity; he ceases to be man.

Finally, as an immediate consequence of the alienation of man from himself, there is the alienation of man from other men. Every relationship in which a man stands to himself finds expression in his relation to other men. Thus the alienation of man from himself manifests itself as the alienation of man from man. As the worker alienates the products of his labor, his own activity and his generic essence from himself, so he alienates another man as his master from himself. The producer himself produces the power of those who do not produce over production.

[14] See Fromm, *Marx's Concept of Man,* pp. 93–109.

Marx thus differentiated four "characteristics" in the phenomenon of alienation. The first and the fourth of them (the alienation of products and the alienation of man from man) he regarded as consequences and forms of expression of the second and the third (the alienation of production and the alienation of man's essence), where the essence of the phenomenon (the alienation of man from himself) is immediately seen. Instead of four characteristics Marx could have enumerated three or five; the number is not important. What is important is the thought that self-alienation means alienation of man from himself, and that alienation may assume different forms. Not only the alienation of productive activity and the alienation of man's generic essence, but also the alienation of the results of production and the alienation of man from man, are, in essence, the alienation of man from himself, the alienation of man from his humanity. Accordingly, the self-alienated man is a man who is really not a man; a non-alienated man would be a man who is really a man.

12. What does it mean to say that man is man or that man is not man, and generally to say that something is what it is, or that it is not what it is?

Marx's answer would be that man is really man when there is no split between his essence and his factual existence. Man is not man means: man in fact is not what he in essence is.

But what does it mean to say that something in fact is not what it in essence is? If man's essence is conceived as something common to all men, something that must be possessed by everybody who is a man, then somebody alienated from man's essence cannot be a man in fact either. Accordingly, if alienation of man from his essence is to be possible, this essence must not be conceived as something all men have in common, as a general part of their factuality. Neither should it be conceived as man's factual past or future (what he up to now has been or will one day be), nor simply as the future that is present in the present. Why should a past or a future factuality have any advantage over the present one? Neither would it be in accord with Marx's philosophical conception if the essence of man were conceived as an eternal or non-temporal idea toward which the real man ought to strive.

What then, after all, is man's essence? I think that in the spirit of Marx's whole philosophical conception it can be conceived only as his historically created human possibility, possibility here understood not as the impotent "mere possibility," which is deep under the level of reality, but real possibility, which is above it.

That man alienates himself from his nature would mean, then, that man alienates himself from the realization of his historically created human possibilities. "Man is not alienated from himself" would not mean that man has realized all his possibilities; on the contrary, man is at one with himself if he stands on the level of his possibilities, if, in realizing his possibilities, he permanently creates new and higher ones. This is not the final solution of the problem, but it may be the direction in which one ought to seek it.

On the way to the "definitive" solution there are still many problems. One is how and on what basis do we know that man *can* be something that he in fact *is not* (and perhaps will never be). It seems that we can infer this only on the basis of what he in fact is, that in his factuality we have to discover a certain internal structure, structural elements or tendencies of development that indicate what man can be and what he in essence is. The indication of essence must come from factuality; another question is how this indication comes about and how far it goes.

Still another question is: Which of man's real possibilities are his *human* possibilities? Man's essence is not whatever he can be, but only what makes his human essence. Man can be a war criminal, but we would not say that war criminality is man's essence—we would rather agree that this is man's inhuman possibility. On what basis do we divide man's real possibilities into human and inhuman? The question cannot be solved by a simple appeal to the future factuality and to its specific presence in the present.

13. The second important question is: Is alienation an essential structural element of man's existence or is it characteristic of only one historical stage in man's development?

Martin Heidegger in *Sein und Zeit* also speaks about alienation. For him, alienation is a structural moment of man's existence. Man is alienated from himself in the mode of everyday existence, in the sphere of the impersonal *one (das Man)* where rumor *(das Gerede)*, curiosity *(die Neugier)* and ambiguity *(die Zweideutigkeit)* reign. In this sphere man is addicted to the "world" *(an die "Welt" verfallen)*, which, among other things, means that he is alienated from himself; but his alienation and, more generally, addiction, according to Heidegger, is neither a consequence of a historical event, of a "fall" from a purer and higher original condition, nor a bad ontic property, which on a higher level of culture could be abolished.

For Heidegger, then, man's alienation is not a historical stage, which in the course of further development can be overcome. Man as man is necessarily alienated; besides his authentic existence, he also leads a nonauthentic one, and it is illusory to expect that he will in the future live only authentically. At least on a social plane, this problem cannot be solved.

Opposed to such a conception of alienation we find another according to which the originally non-alienated man later alienated himself from himself, but will in the future again return to himself. We find this conception in Engels and to some extent in Marx, although one cannot maintain that Marx advocated without qualification the idea of an original non-alienated condition. A careful analysis of his "early" and "later" works would show, I think, that he was more a critic than an adherent of this idea.

The theory of man's original non-alienated condition has come to seem familiar in Marxism, thanks to Engels, who develops it at length in *The Origin of the Family, Private Property and the State*. After having described the social constitution of the Iroquois, he comments: "And this gentile constitution is wonderful in all its childlike simplicity! Everything runs smoothly without soldiers, gendarmes or police; without nobles, kings, governors, prefects or judges; without prisons; without trials. All quarrels and disputes are settled by the whole body of those concerned —the gens or the tribe or the individual gentes among themselves. . . . Those concerned decide, and in most cases century-old custom has already regulated everything. There can be no poor and needy—the communistic household and the gens know their obligations toward the aged, the sick and those disabled in war. All are free and equal —including the women. There is as yet no room for slaves, nor, as a rule, for the subjugation of alien tribes. . . . And the kind of men and women that are produced by such a society is indicated by the admiration felt by all white men who came into contact with *uncorrupted* Indians, admiration of the personal dignity, straightforwardness, strength of character and bravery of those barbarians."[15]

A similar conception can be found in H. Lefebvre, who enthusiastically writes about the primitive man: "In his reality he lived and realized all his potentialities. With no deep discord in himself he could surrender—in this wonderful equilibrium of the village community—to his spontaneous vitality."[16]

Thus some Marxists think that man was originally nonself-alienated, "uncorrupted," that he successfully realized *all* his possibilities.

Marx himself thought that man had thus far always been self-alienated, but that he need not always remain so. Like Engels, he thought that man could and ought to come into his own. In this sense, Marx in his *Economic and Philosophic Manuscripts* speaks about communism as a society that means "the *positive* supersession of all alienation and the return of man from religion, the family, the state, etc., to his *human*, i.e., *social* existence."[17]

15 F. Engels, *The Origin of the Family, Private Property and the State*, Foreign Languages Publishing House (Moscow, 1952), pp. 160–61; italics by Petrović.

16 H. Lefebvre, *Critique de la Vie Quotidienne*, L'Arche Editeur (Paris, 1958), vol. I, Introduction, p. 221.

17 Fromm, *Marx's Concept of Man*, p. 128.

Such a conception of communism as a negation of alienation is the basis of Marx's later works. Although he always
emphasizes that slavery, feudalism and capitalism are not
irrational states, but states that were necessary at a certain
stage of man's development, he never reduces the difference between those states and communism simply to the
difference between an earlier and later necessity, and not
even to the difference in the degree of realized humanness.
He clearly contrasts the contemporary and the future
society as the alienated and the non-alienated one, as the
inhuman and the really humane one. All this means that
Marx regarded alienation as a historically transient characteristic of man, a phenomenon characteristic of all previous history, but not necessarily of the future.

14. Finally, we come to the question of how and why
alienation and de-alienation come about. Is it a historical
accident or a deeper necessity?

In *German Ideology*, Marx and Engels at one place
criticize Stirner, who thinks that thus far men have liber-
ated themselves only to the extent needed to realize their
preconceived idea of man. In fact, comment Marx and
Engels, men have freed themselves to the extent to which
existing productive forces prescribed and allowed them.
This means that the question of the conditions of man's
freedom is not a philosophical but merely an economic
one. In accord with this, one could also say that the question of the conditions of alienation is likewise an economic
one. But if alienation is more than an economic phenomenon, then the question of its conditions and causes cannot
be solely economic.

In his *Economic and Philosophical Manuscripts*, Marx
directly poses the philosophical question about the foundations of alienation. In his fragment, *Alienated Labor*, he
writes: "We have taken as a fact and analyzed the *alienation of labor*. How does it happen, we may ask, that *man
alienates his labor*? How is this alienation founded in the
nature of human development? We have already done
much to solve the problem in so far as we have *transformed* the question concerning the *origin of private*

property into a question about the relation between alienated labor and the process of development of mankind. For, in speaking of private property, one believes oneself to be dealing with something external to mankind. But in speaking of labor one deals directly with mankind itself. This new formulation of the problem already contains its solution."[18]

At the end of the manuscript of *Alienated Labor*, Marx raises two questions, of which this is the second. Having raised the questions, he answers the first, which was not quoted here. He did not come to the answer to the second. The manuscript is unfinished. The question was left open. He says only that the raising of the question already includes its solution. It is a task of Marxists to develop this solution explicitly.

[18] Fromm, *Marx's Concept of Man*, pp. 107–8.

Man as economic animal and man as praxis

I

According to a rather widely held view, Karl Marx investigated and determined the relationship between the different "spheres" of man. In the material production of means of subsistence he discovered the permanently determining factor of social development. More specifically, he is said to have come to the conclusion that the condition of material productive forces always determines the existing relations of production among men, and that the relations of production in turn directly determine state and legal forms, and, indirectly, all forms of social consciousness (political and legal theories, morality, art, philosophy and religion).

This does not mean that the condition of productive forces mechanically determines the political and spiritual condition of an epoch. There is also mutual influence between the different forms of politico-legal and ideological superstructure as well as a reverse action of superstructure upon infrastructure. But ultimately priority always has and will belong to the "basis." Economic production (production of the material means for the maintenance of life) has always been and will always be the ultimately determining sphere of social life. In other words, man is in essence an *economic animal*.

Taking into account that, in the material production the productive forces determine the relations of production, and that tools or instruments of production are the main element of the productive forces, it is still more precise to say that man is a *tool-making animal*.

At first sight it appears that this view of man as an economic animal is authentically Marxist. It is easy to show that it is found in Marx and in the majority of the most important Marxists.

In the famous Preface to *A Contribution to the Critique of Political Economy,* Marx maintains that "legal relations" and "forms of state" are rooted in the "material conditions of life," that is to say in the "civil society," the "anatomy" of which is to be sought in "political economy." He also says that "material forces of production" determine the "relations of production," that is the "economic structure of society," and that the latter represents "the real foundation" for the "legal and political superstructure" to which definite "forms of social consciousness" correspond. When the "material forces of production" come into conflict with the existing "relations of production" the "period of social revolution" begins. Together with the change of the "economic foundation" goes the transformation of the "entire immense superstructure," that is to say of "legal, political, religious, aesthetic or philosophic," in short, "ideological" forms.[1]

It seems, then, that for Marx it is unquestionable that the development of material forces of production ultimately determines the whole social development. In this classical text he failed even to mention the reverse influence of the superstructure upon the foundation.

The above concept of the relationship between foundation and superstructure was very highly esteemed by Engels. Just as Darwin discovered the law of evolution in organic nature, so Marx discovered, according to Engels, the law of evolution in human history. But not only did Engels put a high value on Marx's conception of history, he persistently explained, defended and spread it. In fighting against the distortion and simplification of Marx's materialist conception of history, Engels severely criticized those who wanted to twist it into the view that the economic element is the *only* determining one in history. Nevertheless, even in his letter to J. Bloch of September

[1] Marx, Engels, *Basic Writings on Politics and Philosophy,* pp. 43–44.

21–22, 1890, where the emphasis is on the "interaction" of all elements of the social whole, he maintains clearly that the production and reproduction of real life is "the *ultimately* determining element in history" and that in the interaction of all elements "the economic movement finally asserts itself as necessary."[2]

All the important disciples of Marx and Engels seem to agree with them in these fundamental conceptions.

Antonio Labriola, an excellent interpreter of Marx's conception of history, sharply criticizes attempts to conceive it as a doctrine about the all-determining role of the economic factor, but he nevertheless sometimes calls it "economic materialism." The explanation of this should be sought in the fact that he, like Engels, considers the "economic element" as one that, although it is not the *only* determining factor, ultimately determines the rest of social development. In his well-known essay on *Historical Materialism*, Labriola splendidly underlines the "very complicated, often subtle, tortuous and not always legible" character of the process of transition from substructure to "all the rest," but he also firmly believes that the "underlying economic structure" ultimately "determines all the rest."[3]

George Plekhanov often scorns the term "economic materialism" and the theory that the economic factor is ultimately predominant in history. But this does not prevent his calling man several times "a tool-making animal." This apparent contradiction can be explained by the fact that by "economic factor" he means only "economic order" or "economic relations" and not also the material productive forces, whose development ultimately determines, as he thinks, the evolution of socio-economic relations. The view that it is wrong to speak about the determining importance of the economic factor did not prevent him from representing Marx's and Engels' view on the relations be-

[2] Marx, Engels, *Basic Writings on Politics and Philosophy*, pp. 397–98.

[3] A. Labriola, *Essays on the Materialistic Conception of History,* translated by Charles H. Kerr (Chicago, 1904), p. 152.

tween the *"foundation"* and the *"superstructure"* by means
of a "formula," according to which we have:

1.) The state of the forces of production;

2.) Economic relations conditioned by these forces;

3.) The socio-political regime erected upon a given
economic foundation;

4.) The psychology of man in society, determined in
part directly by economic conditions and in part by the
whole socio-political regime erected upon the economic
foundation;

5.) Various ideologies reflecting this psychology. . . .[4]

Lenin was also in agreement with the thesis that the
whole development of human society is determined by the
development of material productive forces: "The relations
in which men stand to each other in the production of
things necessary for the satisfaction of their human needs
depend upon the development of the productive forces.
And it is in these relations that the explanation is to be
found of all the phenomena of social life, human aspira-
tions, ideas and laws."[5]

Stalin, too, seems to have agreed with Marx, Engels
and Lenin. He thought that the source of the "spiritual
life of society" and of "political institutions" should be
sought in the "conditions of the material life of society" and
that the "chief force" in the complex of conditions of
material life is the *method of procuring the means of life*
necessary for human existence, the *mode of production of
material values*. The mode of production is composed of
productive forces and relations of production, and one of
the essential properties of production is that "its changes
and development always begin with changes and development of the productive forces and in the first place with
changes and development of the instruments of production."[6]

[4] G. Plekhanov, *Fundamental Problems of Marxism,* edited
by D. Riazanov, International Publishers (New York), p. 72.

[5] V. I. Lenin, *Marx, Engels, Marxism,* International Publishers (New York, 1935), p. 36.

[6] *History of the C.P. of the S.U.* (*b.*), pp. 181, 188–93.

On the basis of all this we can apparently conclude:

1.) Karl Marx and his most important adherents or followers hold that there are different spheres of man's activity, and that these spheres stand in a very intricate but, despite the many-sided interaction, mainly constant relationship: the "economic sphere" determines directly the "political" and the "legal," and indirectly all spheres of "social consciousness."

2.) Marx's conception of history is not "economic" if by this one means the view that the economic factor is the only determining factor in history, but it is "economic" if this term is used to designate the view that acknowledges the ultimately determining role of the economic factor. According to this view man is not *only* an "economic animal" (or "tool-making animal"), but he is this first and above all.

These conclusions seem irrefutable. But the outward appearance is sometimes delusive. Quotations in particular can be very deceptive.

II

Let us ask ourselves, then, how the famous "formula" of historical materialism stands—the formula Marx expressed so pithily, Engels explained so brilliantly, Labriola phrased so beautifully, Plekhanov schematized so conspicuously, Lenin propagated so passionately and Stalin canonized so definitely.

Was this formula regarded and *could* it be regarded by Marx as a formula that holds for all possible, or at least for all so-far-known and all now-predictable, history? Or did he think that his "formula" held only for one stage restricted in time and transient in the historical development of mankind?

At first glance the question may seem improper. There is no apparent temporal restriction in any of the above quoted texts of Marx and his adherents, and in his famous text Marx says quite plainly: "The *general conclusion* at which I arrived . . . may be briefly, summed up as follows. . . ." The quoted view of the relation between the "forces of production," "economic structure," "legal and political superstructure" and the "forms of social consciousness" seems to be proposed as a view that holds for all the known past and for all the predictable future.

The assumption that all the mentioned "spheres" (or "regions," or "factors," or "elements" or "forms"—call them what you will) of social life always were and always will be in the same relation presupposes in its turn that these "spheres" always existed and that they will always exist, that they are permanent constitutive moments (elements, aspects) of man's social being.

But did Marx and his followers believe in the perpetuity of all the mentioned "spheres" of social life? Did they not regard at least some of these "spheres" or "forms" as historically transient? Was Engels not expressing an opinion common to Marxists when he wrote that the state "has not existed from all eternity," that there have been societies "that had no conception of the state and state power" and that along with the disappearance of classes "the state will inevitably fall."[7]

If the state is not a permanent but only an historically transient form of human life, then what Marx, Engels and other Marxists say about the relationship between economic structure and state forms and institutions (for example, that the "material forms of life" determine the "forms of government" or that the "degree of economic development" forms the foundation on which "state institutions" develop) cannot be interpreted as the description of a constant relationship characteristic of every human society.

In the quoted accounts of historical materialism there is mention not only of the state but also of jurisprudence and laws, politics and religion, social ranks and classes, class struggles and social revolutions. Are these all indispensable moments, constitutive of every human society and

[7] Engels, *The Origin of the Family, Private Property and the State*, pp. 283–84.

every historical development, or are they merely transient historical phenomena? Is every society, for example, necessarily divided into antagonistic classes, and can the historical movement be realized only through class struggle and social revolution?

If we assume (with Marx and the Marxists) that state, law, politics, religion, classes, class struggles and social revolutions are only transient historical phenomena characteristic of a certain stage of human history, then the theory that explains their mutual relationship cannot be a general theory of history or society. This means that the famous "formula" of the relationship between different "factors" or "elements" of social life cannot hold for all time, but only for one determined, transient stage of historical development. Which stage is that?

The passage quoted from Marx ends with the words that those who quote it nearly always omit: "In broad outlines we can designate *the Asiatic, the ancient, the feudal, and the modern bourgeois methods of production* as so many epochs in the progress of the economic formation of society. The bourgeois relations of production are the last antagonistic form of the social process of production—antagonistic not in the sense of individual antagonism, but of one arising from conditions surrounding the life of individuals in society; at the same time the productive forces developing in the womb of bourgeois society create the material conditions for the solution of that antagonism. This social formation constitutes, therefore, the closing chapter of the *prehistoric stage of human society.*"[8]

This indicates that the relationship between foundation and superstructure outlined in the Preface to *A Contribution to the Critique of Political Economy* is supposed to hold only for the prehistory of human society, or, more precisely, for that part of it that Marx studied, namely the Asiatic, the ancient, the feudal, and the modern bourgeois modes of production. In the last part of the passage there

[8] Marx, Engels, *Basic Writings on Politics and Philosophy,* p. 44; italics are Petrović's.

is no mention of either the beginning of prehistory (the primitive preclass society) or the genuinely human history (the future classless society). It is logical to assume that these two epochs, which Marx passed over in silence, were differentiated by him in an essential respect from the epoch of class history.

III

If we assume that man is a being that historically emerged and seceded from the animal kingdom, and that the primitive preclass society was the first form of society in which man emerged as a being essentially different from the animal, it is natural to assume that this society was in its characteristics relatively "closest" to the animal kingdom, that biological laws, which govern the animal world, expressed themselves there much more strongly and in a much more authentic way than in any later society.

Engels, who devoted considerable study to this question, arrived at conclusions that agree with such an assumption. In the Foreword to *Origin of the Family, Private Property and the State,* he writes: "According to the materialistic conception, the determining factor in history is, in the last resort, the production and reproduction of immediate life. But this itself is of a twofold character. On the one hand, the production of the means of subsistence, of food, clothing and shelter and the tools requisite therefore; on the other, the production of human beings themselves, the propagation of the species. The social institutions under which men of a definite historical epoch and of a definite country live are conditioned by both kinds of production; by the stage of development of labor, on the one hand, and of the family on the other."[9]

These words of Engels were severely criticized in the U.S.S.R. Thus the editors of his work remark: "Engels is here guilty of inexactitude by citing the propagation of the species alongside of the production of the means of

[9] *Ibid.,* fn. 7, pp. 8–9.

subsistence as causes determining the development of society and of social institutions. In the text proper of *The Origin of the Family, Private Property and the State,* Engels himself demonstrated by an analysis of concrete material that the mode of material production is the principal factor conditioning the development of society and of social institutions."[10]

According to this criticism, Engels, in the quoted Foreword, advocates the theory that there are two equally important determining factors in history: the propagation of the species (biological factor) and the production of the means of subsistence (economic factor); and he regards it as a theory that holds for all history. His guilt is diminished by the fact that his work as a whole concretely confirms the correct theory about economics as the only determining factor.

It is not difficult to see that even in the quoted passage Engels does not advocate a theory of "two factors," such as is attributed to him, and that the conception he really advocates does not contradict his own analysis in the work, but on the contrary is an adequate summary of the results of the whole investigation. To the above quoted text Engels thus adds: *"The less the development of labor,* and the more limited its volume of production and therefore the wealth of society, *the more preponderatingly does the social order appear to be dominated by ties of sex.* However, within this structure of society based on ties of sex, the productivity of labor develops more and more; with it private property and exchange, differences in wealth, the possibility of utilizing the labor power of others and thereby the basis of class antagonisms; new social elements which strive in the course of generations to adapt the old structure of society to the new conditions until, finally, the incompatibility of the two leads to a complete revolution. The old society based on sex groups bursts asunder in the collision of the newly developed social

[10] Marx, Engels, *Basic Writings on Politics and Philosophy,* fn. 7, pp. 8–9.

classes; in its place a *new society* appears, constituted in a state, the lower units of which are no longer sex groups, but territorial groups, a *society, in which the family system is entirely dominated by the property system,* and in which the class antagonisms and class struggles, which make up the content of all hitherto *written* history, now freely develop."[11]

Engels, then, does not maintain that the "biological" factor (the propagation of species) and the "economic" one (the production of the means of subsistence) always were and always will be equally important. In the primitive classless society the biological factor was for a time predominant. But from the beginning the material production of means of subsistence—"the economic factor"—existed in this society and exerted a certain influence. With the development of productive forces this other factor became more and more important, and, with the transition to class society, predominant.

Accordingly, what Engels writes in the Foreword to *The Origin of the Family, Private Property and the State* is in complete agreement with what other Marxists and he himself say in the texts we quoted at the beginning of this paper. These maintained that the economic factor was predominant in class society, and it is maintained here that the economic factor in the primitive preclass society is in the beginning subordinated to the "biological" one, but that the relationship between the "biological" and the "economic" factor permanently changes, because in the course of time the "economic" factor becomes more and more important. In the class society the "economic" factor becomes predominant, and "the family system is entirely dominated by the property system."

IV

It would be possible to concede that in the primitive preclass society the economic factor was not the only determin-

11 *Ibid.,* fn. 7, pp. 9–10; the word "written" italicized by Engels, other italics Petrović's.

ing one and still defend the thesis that in human history the economic factor always was and always will be determining.

Thus one could say that the so-called primitive preclass society, if it ever existed in the way described, was not *human society* in the strict sense, but only a transient form between the animal herd and human society. Did not Engels himself divide this primitive "society" into the epochs of "savageness" and "barbarism," reserving the title of "civilization" for class society? If "savages" and "barbarians" are only a transient stage from animal to man, it is natural that the influence of biological and economical factors in their "society" should interweave. But man as man is an economic animal, and we can speak of human society only when the economic factor has become determining. At the moment when this factor became determining and when the above-described relationship among factors was established, man was finally constituted, and as long as man exists, these factors and their relationship will remain the same.

This raises the question: Is the so-called savage or barbarian only somewhere in between man and animal, or is he a "savage" or "barbaric" *man?* Is not the difference that divides a "savage" and a "barbarian" from the "civilized" man of class society less than that which divides the most savage savage from the most advanced monkey?

There is also the question: Is man a being condemned to stagnation; must he, once constituted, remain always the same?

For an answer to the latter question let us turn first to Plekhanov. Together with his conception of the permanently decisive role of the productive forces is another, according to which neither man as man nor society as society can be characterized by a constant relationship of factors because this relationship historically changes. In his "On the 'Economic Factor'" he writes: "We know that according to the teaching of modern materialists economic relations of every given society are determined not by the properties of human nature, but by the condition of social forces of production. Together with the growth of those, socio-economic relations change too. With the change of these relations the nature of social man changes also. *And with the change of this nature the mutual relation among the different factors of social life changes.* This is a very important 'point' and one might say that he who managed to understand it conceived everything."[12]

In what way do the relations among different factors change? "Sometimes 'economics' influences the conduct of man through 'politics,' sometimes by the way of art, or some other ideology, and only occasionally *in the later stages of social development* does economics appear in its genuine 'economic' form. Most frequently it influences people through all these factors together, so that their mutual relation, as well as the power of any one of them in particular, depends on precisely what kind of social relations have grown up on the given economic basis, which in turn is determined by the nature of that foundation. At different stages of economic development every given ideology to an unequal degree suffers the influence of other ideologies. In the beginning law is subordinated to religion, afterward—as, for example, in the eighteenth century—it succumbs to the influence of philosophy. In order to remove the influence of religion upon law, philosophy had to face a big struggle. This struggle appears as a struggle of abstract concepts, and it seems to us that every single 'factor' attains or loses its importance owing to its own strength and to the immanent laws of development of this strength, whereas in fact its destiny is entirely determined by the course of development of social relations."[13]

From this it follows that the relative importance of factors changes, but one thing remains unchanged: productive forces determine economics, which is the basis of all other factors. There are quite a lot of these other factors:

[12] G. V. Plekhanov, *Izbrannye filosofskie proizvedenija* (*Selected Philosophical Works*) (Moscow, 1956), vol. II, p. 286.

[13] *Ibid.*, p. 292.

"First, every particular scientific 'discipline'—'branch' of science—has to do with a particular 'factor.' Second, in single branches one can also enumerate several factors. Is literature a factor? It is. And dramatic poetry? Also a factor. And tragedy? I do not see on what ground we could refuse to acknowledge it as a factor. And bourgeois drama? It is a factor too. In a word, there is no end to factors."[14]

Plekhanov, then, thinks that there is an immense number of factors of social development and that the relationship among factors constantly changes, but that the economic factor in a broader sense is, in the whole course of history, decisive. It would be possible, with the help of corresponding quotations, to show that Marx and Engels agree with this opinion. But this thesis will probably not be much disputed, so it is better to turn to a question that might be more controversial: whether a changeable relationship between the factors, restricted by the predominance of the economic factor, ought to be preserved in the future classless society.

V

Marx's theory of alienation was often conceived as preaching a return to something that man already was. Nothing is more incorrect than such an assumption: *"The social revolution of the nineteenth century cannot draw its poetry from the past, but only from the future."*[15]

In what does this poetry of the future consist? In his "Something about History" Plekhanov severely criticizes the "economic materialism" of the French historian P. Lacombe. Lacombe's opinion that the economic factor must always be decisive is an indication to Plekhanov that Lacombe believes capitalist society is civilized man's necessary form of Being, that he regards as general human

[14] Plekhanov, *Selected Philosophical Works*, vol. II, p. 293.
[15] Marx, Engels, *Basic Writings on Politics and Philosophy*, p. 323.

nature the nature of man in capitalist society. Lacombe's "economic materialism," according to Plekhanov, is a "libel against mankind."

In criticizing Lacombe, Plekhanov admits that so far men have been the "slaves of their own social economy." But he believes that they are not condemned to remain so forever, that *the triumph of human reason over the blind forces of economic necessity is possible.*[16]

Is it not precisely of this that the poetry the social revolution of the nineteenth and twentieth centuries draws from the future consists?

Affirming that human reason can triumph over the blind forces of economic necessity, Plekhanov emphasizes that this is an idea of Marx and Engels: "Marx and Engels had an ideal, and a very definite *ideal:* the subordination of *necessity* to *freedom,* of blind *economic forces*—to the *power of human reason.*"[17]

We can easily see for ourselves that Plekhanov here correctly interprets Marx and Engels. To the question whether the productive forces will always be the determining factor of history, Engels gives a very clear answer when he says: "As long as we obstinately refuse to understand the nature and the character of these social means of production—and this understanding goes against the grain of the capitalist mode of production and its defenders—so long as these forces are at work in spite of us, in opposition to us, so long do they master us, as we have shown above in detail. But when once their nature is understood, they can, in the hands of the producers working together, be transformed *from master demons into willing servants.*"[18]

Developing the same thought, Engels writes: "With the seizing of means of production by society, production of commodities is done away with, and, simultaneously, the mastery of the product over the producer. Anarchy in

[16] Plekhanov, *Selected Philosophical Works,* vol. II, p. 233.
[17] *Ibid.*
[18] Marx, Engels, *Basic Writings on Politics and Philosophy,* p. 105.

social production is replaced by systematic, definite organization. The struggle for individual existence disappears. Then for the first time man, in a certain sense, is finally marked off from the rest of the animal kingdom and emerges from mere animal conditions of existence into really human ones. *The whole sphere of the conditions of life* which environ man, and which have hitherto ruled man, *now comes under the dominion and control of man*, who for the first time becomes the real, conscious lord of nature because he has now become master of his own social organization. The laws of his own social action, hitherto standing face to face with man as laws of nature foreign to and dominating him, will now be used with full understanding, and so mastered by him. *Man's own social organization,* hitherto confronting him as a necessity imposed by nature and history, *now becomes the result of his own free action*. The extraneous objective forces that have hitherto governed history pass under control of man himself. Only from that time will *man himself, more and more consciously, make his own history*—only from that time will the social causes set in movement by him have, in the main and in a constantly growing measure, the results intended by him. It is the *ascent of man from the kingdom of necessity to the kingdom of freedom*."[19]

Engels thinks that the ascent from the kingdom of necessity to the kingdom of freedom is possible, and he sees the content of this ascent in the change of relations between men and their conditions of life, between men and their social organization. When the ascent to the kingdom of freedom is realized men will cease to be determined by the material conditions of life and these will come under their dominion and control.

If the social being of man becomes "the result of his own free action," if he starts "more and more consciously to make his own history," will we be entitled to assert even then that men enter into "definite relations that are indispensable and independent of their will" and that "these

[19] Marx, Engels, *Basic Writings on Politics and Philosophy,* pp. 108–9; italics, Petrović.

relations of production correspond to a definite stage of development of their material powers of production"? The answer is fairly clear.

Thus we come to the conclusion that in Marxists one can find elements of a conception of man and society that can by no means be described as "economic materialism," and according to which the "economic condition" is not the factor that determines all social development, but rather that, in the historic development, different factors have different importance. In the beginning of human history the "economic" factor emerges, gradually supplants the "biological" factor, which was predominant up to that time, and eventually becomes determining. Other factors joined the interaction of factors, "political," "legal" and many others. And today we can already anticipate a condition in which the "economic" factor will lose its predominance.

If the economic factor ceases to be the determining one, which factor is likely to take its place?

Before we try to answer this question, it might be useful to see whether it is well posed. Is the question about man to be solved only by a theory of factors?

VI

There are different versions of the theory of factors, but they all have in common the assumption that man is a sum, a set or a combination of different independent factors (parts, elements, aspects, spheres) and that these factors stand in a determinate mutual relationship. Variants of the theory differ only in their answer to the question: How are these factors related, and which among them is the most important?

The theory that the determining factor in history is material could be called the "materialistic" and the theory that the decisive factor is ideal, the "idealistic" conception of history. According to which material factor is taken as decisive we could distinguish between, say, "geographical," "biological" and "economic" materialism, and similarly between different subclasses of idealism. Taking into account the extent to which one might acknowledge other factors besides the determining one, one could distinguish a "narrower" and a "broader" variant in each of these theories (a "narrower" and a "broader" economic materialism, etc.). If we could assert that there are two or more equally important factors, we would have a "dualistic" or a "pluralistic" conception of history, and if we consider that the decisive factor is not always the same, we could call such a conception "dialectical."

But before we decide to choose a variant of the theory of factors, it is advisable to ask ourselves whether the basic assumption of *every* theory of factors is acceptable.

Is it not a kind of caricature of man (whether we mean by man an individual or human society) to regard him as a mechanical sum, set or combination of mutually independent factors, which maintain external relationships of "determination," "action," "influence," etc.? Is not man something united and integral, which strictly speaking cannot be divided into independent "factors" or "spheres"?

In polemicizing against those who attribute to Marx the doctrine of the predominant role of the economic factor, Plekhanov maintains that "the genuine and consistent materialists are averse to dragging in the economic factor everywhere" and that "*even to ask which factor predominates in social life* seems to them pointless."[20]

The question is unjustified because "strictly speaking, *there exists only one factor of historical development, namely—social man*"[21] and different branches of the social sciences—ethics, politics, jurisprudence, political economy, etc.—"investigate one and the same thing: *the activity of social man.*"[22]

If there is only one factor in history, the social man, how can a theory of factors arise at all? "An historico-

[20] G. Plekhanov, *The Materialist Conception of History,* International Publishers (New York, 1960), p. 13.

[21] Plekhanov, *Selected Philosophical Works,* vol. V, p. 363; italics, Petrović.

[22] *Ibid.,* fn. 20, p. 15; italics, Petrović.

social factor is an *abstraction*, and the idea of it originates as the result of a process of *abstraction*. Thanks to the process of abstraction, various *sides* of the social *complex* assume the form of separate *categories*, and the various manifestations and expressions of the activity of social man—morals, law, economic form, etc.—are converted in our minds into separate forces which appear to give rise to and determine this activity and to be its ultimate causes."[23]

This answer may account for the theoretical possibility of the theory of factors. But why does it happen that the various manifestations and expressions of the activity of social man are converted in our minds into separate forces? Where is the historical root of the theory of factors? Why does it arise, maintain itself and develop? Plekhanov thinks that one or another variant of the theory of factors "is bound to arise whenever people who are interested in social phenomena pass from simply contemplating and describing them to investigating the connections that exist between them," and that "the theory of factors, moreover, grows with the growing division of labor in social science."[24]

Many questions arise in connection with this explanation. For example: Must the theory of factors necessarily arise whenever men begin to investigate connections between social phenomena? And, still more important, is the deepest root of the theory really in the investigation of connections between social phenomena and in the growth of the division of labor in social science? Or has the theory also some deeper roots, which are at the same time the roots of the division of labor in social science?

In criticizing the bourgeois national economy, the young Marx writes: "Suppose I ask the economist: Am I acting in accordance with economic laws if I earn money by the sale of my body, by prostituting it to another person's lust (in France, the factory workers call the prostitution of

23 *Ibid.*, p. 16.
24 *Ibid.*, fn. 20, p. 15.

their wives and daughters the nth hour of work, which is literally true); or if I sell my friend to the Moroccans (and the direct sale of men occurs in all civilized countries in the form of trade in conscripts)? He will reply: You are not acting contrary to my laws, but must take into account what Cousin Morality and Cousin Religion have to say. My *economic* morality and religion have no objection to make, but . . . but whom then should we believe, the economist or the moralist? The morality of political economy is *gain*, work, thrift and sobriety—yet political economy promises to satisfy my needs. The political economy of morality is the riches of a good conscience, of virtue, etc., but how can I be virtuous if I am not alive and how can I have a good conscience if I am not aware of anything? The nature of alienation implies that each sphere applies a different and contradictory norm, that morality does not apply the same norm as political economy, etc., because each of them is a particular alienation of man; [XVII] each is concentrated upon a specific area of alienated activity and is itself alienated from the other. . . . Thus M. Michel Chevalier reproaches Ricardo with leaving morals out of account. But Ricardo lets political economy speak its own language; he is not to blame if this language is not that of morals."[25]

Accordingly, if bourgeois political economy is not moral, it is not the fault of the economist. At least his fault is not in a purely theoretical, epistemological error. When political economy and morality come into conflict, it is not merely the consequence of ignorance, stupidity or mistakes in the reasoning of economists and moralists. When in his investigations an economist leaves aside morals or comes to conclusions that conflict with morals, he adequately exemplifies the fact that the bourgeois man is a self-alienated man, a man who does not succeed in realizing himself as a united integral being, a man split into mutually independent and conflicting spheres. We cannot accuse him of simply ignoring facts. His fault, on the contrary, is that he is too faithful to the factuality of class

[25] Fromm, *Marx's Concept of Man*, p. 146.

society, that he does not see the possibility of a revolutionary change of the existing order and the overcoming of man's split into independent, mutually opposed spheres.

We could, then, in the spirit of Marx, answer the question about the theory of factors: The theory is not an accidental result of a logical mistake. It is natural for the social thought of class society to move inside the limits of the theory of factors, because it is a self-alienated society split into mutually independent and conflicting spheres. The theory of factors represents adequately the immediate factuality of that society; it only overlooks that the society whose outward appearance it correctly represents is the self-alienated, dehumanized society, that man really is not only what he is in fact, but also what he can and ought to be.

VII

After these general considerations about the theory of factors we can return to the question of the determining factor in the future classless society. We have already seen the opinion of Engels and Plekhanov, that in the future classless society the economic factor cannot be determining. But from their texts it is not at once clear which factor must replace it.

On the basis of the above texts it might seem that the required factor is "human reason" or the "rational organization of social production." But it is fairly clear now that the future classless society cannot be one in which another factor is the predominant one, but that it ought to mark a new epoch in which man will not be split into mutually opposed spheres.

One of the forms of man's self-alienation is the alienation of different human activities from each other and of all of them from their humanity. The abolition of self-alienation therefore also means the abolition of this form of it. Marx says about this: "Religion, the family, the state, law, morality, science, art, etc., are only *particular* forms of production and come under its general law. The positive supersession of *private property* as the appropriation of *human* life, is therefore the *positive* supersession of all alienation, and the return of man from religion, the family, the state, etc., to his *human, i.e., social* life."[26]

But what does the return of man from religion, the family, the state, etc., to his human, i.e., social, life mean?

Does it mean that all concrete forms in which man's activity has developed so far must disappear, and that man has to become an indivisible whole in which it is impossible to distinguish any forms, sides or aspects? Such a view is too absurd to be attributed to Marx. Certain forms of man's activity may disappear and others appear (and we have good reason to think that some of those that exist today, such as state or religion, will one day disappear), but it is not clear how man could be anything if he could not be something really differentiated.

The return of man from a dispersed existence in "spheres" to his human existence does not mean the dissolving of all the differences between man's sides or aspects; it means first of all the overcoming of the mutual alienation of these really different aspects of a whole, and the dissolution of the appearance that they are self-sufficient spheres that exist independently of man, into which he can, but need not, enter.

Neither can the return of man from independent and conflicting spheres into his human existence proper mean a perfect "harmony" between his different aspects or forms of activity; nor can it mean such a "many-sidedness" as would arise if every individual developed all possible forms of activity. This would be the most radical form of man's alienation from himself.

The individual man does not alienate himself from his human nature if, in those activities that correspond to his individual nature, propensities and abilities, he realizes the common human content, if he fulfills himself as a free creative being. And the de-alienation of human society means the realization of the association in which a "free develop-

[26] Fromm, *Marx's Concept of Man*, p. 128.

ment of every individual is the condition of the free development for all."

An unalienated man is, then, a man who realizes himself as an integral, free and creative practical being. He is a differentiated, "rich" being, but one in which the whole controls the parts, and not one or another part the whole.

For this reason the overcoming of the determining part of the economic factor in the de-alienated society does not mean the disappearance of labor, in the narrow sense of production of means for immediate maintenance of life.[27] In *Capital* Marx emphasizes that the division of labor is historically transient, but that "so far as labor is a creator of use-value, is useful labor, it is a necessary condition, independent of all forms of society, for the existence of the human race; it is an eternal nature-imposed necessity without which there can be no material exchanges between man and Nature, and therefore no life."[28]

The labor of the freed man of classless society will differ from the labor of the man-working animal of class society: "It goes without saying that the time of labor itself, because it will be restricted to a normal measure, and because one no longer works for somebody else but for oneself, together with the abolition of social antagonisms between masters and servants, etc., as really social labor and finally as the basis of free time, gets quite another, freer character and the labor time of one man, who is at the same time a man with free time, must have a much higher quality than the labor time of a working animal."[29]

[27] "Labor" and "production" in the wide sense could mean the same as "praxis."

[28] Marx, *Capital,* translated from the third German edition by S. Moore and E. Aveling; edited by F. Engels; revised and amplified according to the fourth German edition by E. Untermann (Chicago, 1912), vol. I, p. 50.

[29] Marx, *Theorien über den Mehrwert* (Theories on the Relation between Work Necessary for Workers' Needs and Work Producing Profit for the Employer), Von Ricardo zur Vulgärökonomie, Herausgegeben von K. Kautsky, Vierte, unveränderte Auflage (Stuttgart, 1921), bd. III, pp. 305–6.

But, again, although labor in the narrower sense, labor as the "creator of use-values," has in a non-alienated society a "quite different, freer character," this region will always remain a kingdom of necessity. "The freedom in this field cannot consist of anything else but of the fact that socialized man, the associated producers, regulate their interchange with nature rationally, bring it under their common control, instead of being ruled by it as by some blind power; that they accomplish their task with the least expenditure of energy and under conditions most adequate to their human nature and most worthy of it. But it always remains a realm of necessity. Beyond it begins that development of human power, which is its own end, the true realm of freedom, which, however, can flourish only upon that realm of necessity as its basis. The shortening of the working day is its fundamental premise.[30]

VIII

Finally, let us briefly summarize the answer to the question with which we started: whether man, according to Marx, is an economic and, more specifically, a tool-making animal.

At first glance it might seem that he is. But a more careful analysis of the basic sense of Marx's philosophy shows that his conception is different. Bourgeois political economy regards the proletarian "merely as a worker," "merely as an animal"; Marx's basic intention is to rise "above the level of political economy."

To rise above the level of political economy means to understand that man in the full sense of the word is not an economic animal, but a practical, hence free, universal, creative and self-creative social being. What distinguishes him from every other being is his special way of Being—praxis.

[30] Marx, *Capital*, translated from the first German edition by E. Untermann; edited by F. Engels (Chicago, 1909), vol. III, pp. 954–55.

Man as praxis does not cease to be a biological being, any more than the animal as biological being is exempted from physical and chemical laws. But although man has his particular biological nature, this nature is not that by which he essentially differs from everything else that exists.

In the course of historical development, man's practical activity differentiates into different, apparently self-sufficient and opposing, "forms," "kinds" or "spheres," and the lowest among the forms of his practical activity, material production for the satisfaction of immediate living needs, becomes predominant. During a whole epoch of his development, man is primarily an economic animal, and as such he is split into antagonistic social classes, into exploiter and exploited. But even in this epoch man is not only an economic animal. As an economic animal he is, by this very fact, already the self-alienated and only partly realized being of praxis. Even in this epoch other higher forms of practical activity also develop, and the possibility of overcoming their independence and mutual opposition gradually emerges.

This shows that the predominance of the economic and the exploitation of man by man are not necessary forms of man's existence. The condition in which man is primarily an economic animal can and ought to be replaced by a condition in which man will be able to fulfill himself as universal creative being. This does not mean that man should cease to produce economically. Material production will always be necessary, just as, so long as man exists, his organs will always perform definite biological functions and obey certain physical and chemical laws. But the material production of the means of subsistence will cease to be an obstacle for a "free activity which unlike labor is not determined by the compulsion of an outward purpose."[31]

In *Capital* Marx has given a brilliant criticism of the economic animal—the self-alienated man of capitalist

[31] *Ibid.*, fn. 29, p. 305.

society. Marx's criticism of alienation has not become obsolete so far, but in a time when the self-alienated society has already become the object of practical criticism by revolutionary social forces, the humanistic vision of the non-alienated free being of praxis, which is inherent in this criticism, becomes more and more important.

What is freedom?

In the history of philosophy various opinions have appeared as to who man is. Attempts to find the answer have most often started from the seemingly undoubted "fact" that man is a species of animal and have then sought those particular qualities that distinguish this particular animal species. Thus a multitude of various theories on man has come into being, all remaining within the limits of the same general conception. At first glance acceptable, all these theories meet with unsurmountable difficulties. Yielding to their free play we can become so entangled as to end up not knowing where we are.

Let us assume that man is a *rational animal,* as he has most often been considered in philosophy hitherto. That seems acceptable; man possesses the faculty of abstract thought, and no other animal species has this faculty.

How is this wonderful faculty of man to be explained? Is it not due to the fact that only man possesses the faculty of speech? Is man a rational animal because he is first of all a lingual animal? One might thus put forward the thesis that man is first and above all an animal endowed with the faculty of *speech.*

But one could ask further why only man is endowed with speech? Is it not because he lives in a social community? If he did not live in a social community he would have no one with whom to speak. The "best" thesis might then appear to be that man is a *social* animal.

One could go further still, and ask why man is a social animal, why he lives in society. Might one not assert that man is a social animal because he is an animal that works and produces? Man, as an animal who not only gleans the finished products of nature but also produces what is necessary to him, could not exist as a lone individual. Work is possible only in society. Man is thus a *working* animal.

But why does man alone work and produce? The most plausible explanation seems to be that man alone works and produces because he alone possesses reason. So we come back to our initial theory according to which man is a rational animal.

Attempts to discover the single property that makes man man can catch us up in an unpleasant vicious circle.

But that is not the only trouble with such attempts. In addition to those properties already mentioned (reason, speech, sociability and work), there is a multitude of others that are also peculiar to man. Man alone develops varied forms of spiritual creativity—literature, painting, sculpture, music; man alone cooks food and cultivates the culinary art. Only man is capable of being malicious, narrow-minded, corrupted, hypocritical, ironic. There are very many properties that belong to man only, and it is difficult to say which of them is the "most important."

Perhaps it is not necessary to single out the most important, but simply to enumerate *all* the properties unique to man. But such an endeavor also meets with difficulty. There are very many properties which are possessed by man only. And man is not a chaos of these many properties but something integral and structured.

Perhaps then, instead of seeking the properties possessed by man only, one should seek the general structure of man's being that manifests itself in every one of man's acts and deeds, in all his properties and activities.

The best answer so far to the question of who man is was given by Karl Marx: *Man is a being that exists in the form of praxis;* or, more briefly: *Man is a being of praxis.* To be sure, other answers to this question have also been ascribed to Marx: the answer that man is a tool-making animal, and the similar view that man is a being whose entire activity is determined by the economic sphere of his existence. But these and similar interpretations only indicate the extent to which Marx has been misunderstood.

II

If we say that man is a being of praxis, the question "What is praxis?" naturally arises. To the extent that we cannot answer this question, the entire definition of man as *praxis* remains in the dark. Different opinions exist, however, as to the way in which this question should be answered.

Some hold that praxis is a concept that cannot be defined; a concept with whose help all other concepts are defined, but that can itself be directly comprehended or explained only by examples or by the undefined but comprehensible words of ordinary speech.

According to another view, the concept of praxis can be explained by enumerating various kinds or forms of practical activity (economic production, political activity, artistic creativity, scientific research work, philosophizing, etc.) and at the same time determining their mutual relationship.

If we assume, however, that praxis is something complex and structured, a third solution is also possible: we can try to determine the structure of praxis, to discover the fundamental characteristics that make praxis praxis.

Those who think that in Marxist philosophy praxis can be defined only in one of the first two ways obviously draw no distinction between the most important concept in a philosophy and the most simple. Were praxis, to Marx, the most general and the simplest concept, as pure being is with Hegel, it could not be explained except in one of the first two ways. But "praxis" is not the simplest concept in Marx's philosophy. As the concept of the being of the most complex being (man), *the concept of praxis is the most complex.* Therefore we *can analyze and define* this concept, indicating its elements or moments—which does not mean that we will ever analyze and define it exhaustively and finally.

Praxis is in the first place a definite mode of Being (*Modus des Seins*), which is peculiar to a definite being (*einem bestimmten Seiendem*), which transcends all other modes of Being and differs from them in principle. This initial statement compels us to attempt to indicate characteristics of praxis as a peculiar mode of Being. Though the question is not simple, it is easy to mention at least some of the characteristics by which praxis is differentiated from every other form of Being. For example, praxis is *free* Being, praxis is *creative* Being, praxis is *historical* Being, praxis is Being through the *future*. All these characteristics need to be more closely explained, but it is fairly certain that freedom is one of the essential "elements" of praxis. *There is no praxis without freedom, and there is no free Being that is not praxis.* The question of freedom is a constituent part of the question of praxis, and hence a constituent part of the question of man.

III

As a being of praxis, man is a *being of freedom. There is no freedom without man, and there is no humanity without freedom.* This does not mean that all men have everywhere and always been free. On the contrary, one of the most widespread phenomena in contemporary society is the escape from freedom.[1] People feel their freedom and the responsibility associated with it as a heavy burden of which they wish to be relieved, transferring it to others.

The escape from freedom was one of the most fundamental factors in the spread of Fascism and Nazism as movements in which individuals were freed of the burden of freedom and all responsibility was assumed by a leader (*il Duce, der Führer*). Those who so freed themselves of freedom were willing to submit without contradiction to the leader, silencing any inner human voice. They were ready for the most wicked crimes, but also for physical hardships and sacrifice. Without deliberation they killed and looted, froze on snowy plains and choked in the sands of the desert.

[1] See E. Fromm, *Escape from Freedom* (New York, 1941).

The burden of freedom is also heavy for people in "democratic" (capitalistic) countries. To them as well, the escape from freedom is a mass phenomenon, only the forms are different. One of these forms is avoidance of the effort of thought; uncritical, passive acceptance of opinions that are suggested by the media of mass communication, as well as other ways.

The escape from freedom makes its appearance in socialism too. Here too we encounter people who seek to avoid or be rid of freedom, who reduce or attempt to reduce themselves to blind executors of the directives of higher social or political forums, who are prepared to be active to the limit even of physical exhaustion only in order not to have to carry the invisible but nevertheless difficult and unpleasant burden of freedom.

The escape from freedom is a spreading phenomenon in the contemporary world, but to the extent that he evades freedom man is not man. *The escape from freedom is a form of man's self-alienation.*

The young Marx wrote: "A life danger for every being consists in loss of oneself. Unfreedom is thus a real death danger for man."[2] This is well said, but one should go even farther: *Unfreedom is not merely the death danger for man, unfreedom is man's death.* Through becoming unfree, man ceases to be man.

IV

The question of what freedom is cannot be reduced to the question of various kinds or forms of freedom. Every day we speak of the most diverse kinds, forms and aspects of freedom—metaphysical, ethical, psychological, economic, political, national and religious. We speak of freedom of the spirit, of the will, of thought, conscience, movement, activity, freedom of the press, radio and television, of freedom of assembly, speech and association. We speak of freedom from exploitation, oppression, hun-

[2] Marx, Engels, *Werke,* bd. I, p. 60.

ger, war and fear. We speak of freedom from tradition, convention, vice, passion, weakness, prejudice, of freedom in art, science, education, instruction. Of free behavior, free love, free time and so on.

But the enumeration of varieties of freedom does not resolve the question of what freedom is. Moreover, before resolving this question, we cannot say which of the kinds or types of freedom mentioned actually represent freedom, and which are only pseudofreedoms. *The question of freedom is in the first instance the question of the essence of freedom.*

This question is not purely a theoretical one, nor can its answer be some purely factual judgment. Nor does the inquiry about freedom's essence mean asking what freedom has meant hitherto, or what it in fact is, or, still less, which meanings the word "freedom" has or may have. To ask about freedom's essence does not mean to ask what freedom ought to be according to someone's subjective whim or wish either. To inquire into the essence of freedom means to inquire into that by virtue of which freedom is a constituent of man, into what freedom as human freedom can and should be, what it in essence is.

The question of the essence of freedom, like the question of the essence of man, *is not only a question. It is at once participation in production of freedom.* It is an activity through which freedom frees itself.

V

In what lies the essence of freedom? What is freedom in its essence? One cannot speak of what freedom is without speaking of what it is not. Replying to the question of what freedom is and is not, we will achieve our object soonest by setting out from the conceptions or theories that have already been developed in the course of the history of philosophy.

Theories of freedom are practically numberless. Here we will mention, and subject to criticism, three groups: first, theories according to which freedom is the absence of external impediments to movement or activity—more generally, the sum of external circumstances under which something exists; second, theories that assert that freedom is the knowledge of necessity, or an adaptation to the world and a transformation of the world, based on the knowledge of necessity; and finally, theories that regard freedom as self-determination.

The first group can be found in many philosophers in the course of the centuries. We find it in the seventeenth century in Thomas Hobbes, and also in the twentieth, in a paper by the American Marxist (or Marxologist) John Somerville at the Twelfth International Philosophical Congress in Venice in 1958. According to these theories, a being or body is free as long as no external impediments to its movement or activity exist.

This view of freedom may seem acceptable. In everyday speech we most frequently speak of freedom in just this sense. We say, for example, that the convict is not free when he is in prison, and that he is free when he escapes or is set at liberty. Similarly, we say that a caged tiger or a caged canary is not free, but that a tiger at large or a bird outside a cage is.

This conception of freedom makes it possible to speak of the freedom of not only beasts, birds and fish, but of inanimate things as well. In this sense we can say that water is not free while it is in a pot, that it is semifree when a hole is made in the pot and completely free when the pot is overturned.

These and similar conclusions, which Hobbes indeed draws, show that such a conception of freedom is not acceptable. If freedom is understood in this way, it is obviously not something specifically human, and we are concerned with freedom as something peculiar to man alone.

This first conception of freedom also has other "inconvenient" consequences. If freedom consists in the absence of external obstacles, then it is differentiated in species according to the kind of external obstacles. External obstacles, however, can be of the most varied sort, so that the existence of some is good, of others bad, and of still others a matter of indifference. For example, in this way one might say that man is free to speak when he is not hindered from saying what he wishes to, and that he has the freedom to kill or torture when he can kill or torture whomever he wishes without external hindrance to do this. Thus we arrive at very unusual and strange kinds of freedom such as the freedom to kill, the freedom to rob, the freedom to persecute. And then the conclusion follows (which Somerville draws) that freedom in itself is neither good nor bad. There are freedoms that are "good"; there are likewise "bad" and "indifferent" ones.

It is precisely this conclusion, however, according to which phenomena that we generally consider the most conspicuous examples of the negation of freedom are counted among the forms of freedom, that indicates that something is wrong with this theory.

In contrast to the theory of freedom as the sum of external conditions under which something exists, we may assert that freedom is a certain way of Being. *Freedom is not something outside one who freely is, it is his specific mode or structure of Being.*

VI

The second group is comprised of theories according to which freedom is in him who is free and consists in the knowledge of necessity or in activity founded on the knowledge of necessity.

The idea of freedom as knowledge of necessity can be found among the ancient Greeks, who conceived of freedom as the realizing and acceptance of fate, and also in such later philosophers as Spinoza, Hegel and Engels, which is not to say that the theory of freedom in these philosophers can be reduced to this idea; Hegel's conception, for example, is much more complex.

In any case, the idea that the knowledge of necessity is the essence or essential presupposition of freedom extends throughout the history of philosophy and appears in three main variants: 1.) freedom is the *knowledge of necessity;* 2.) freedom is the *adjustment to the known necessity;* 3.) freedom is *power over nature and over oneself based on the knowledge of internal and external necessity.*

In all three variants this conception has at the very least two basic defects: it is contradictory and conservative.

If everything is necessary, then neither knowledge of (and adjustment to) necessity, nor power over nature (and over oneself) can be something outside that necessity. The idea that freedom is the knowledge of necessity is based tacitly on two mutually irreconcilable assumptions: 1.) that everything is necessary, and 2.) that man can (but does not have to) know that necessity. But if everything is necessary, then man's knowledge (or failure to know) necessity must also be necessary. Therefore, to consider the knowledge of necessity as freedom and lack of knowledge as unfreedom is senseless.

This contradiction is observable to a still greater extent in the conception of freedom as the adaptation to what exists on the basis of the knowledge of necessity. If everything is necessary, then we are of necessity such as we are, and we are of necessity "adjusted" in the way in which we are. In order to be able to adjust freely, we would have to be, at least to a certain extent, excepted from necessity.

The contradiction comes to its fullest expression in the notion of freedom as power over nature and oneself, which is based on the knowledge of necessity. For if everything is necessary, if necessity already rules over nature and over man, it is not clear how *we* can achieve power over both of them.

The idea that we ought first to know "necessity" and then to gain sway over it has "something" to it. That idea arose out of a somewhat rash generalizing from some experiences in daily life, from certain practical teachings that make up an important part of the sagacity of the weak. A servant or a slave can possess great power over his master if he is familiar with his weaknesses. Then cannot our knowledge of nature similarly make power over nature possible?

The presupposition for the slave's power over his master is that the latter possesses some weakness. Accordingly, if we wish to dominate nature, it must have its "weaknesses" as well. At least some "points" must exist in it where universal necessity is obviated.

The other basic defect in necessity theories of freedom is that they are in essence conservative. If everything occurs of necessity, it is then natural to accept what is and not attempt to change it. Precisely on this account necessity theories of freedom can be, and often have been, used as a weapon by conservative forces wishing to maintain the existing social order.

It might be observed that revolutionaries have often been inspired by the idea of freedom as the knowledge of necessity. Indeed, such an idea can be the basis of a peculiar revolutionary deed. The revolutionary can say that he considers his activity as a constituent part of necessary happening and that he does not wish to think about whether he could act otherwise. Revolutionary activity on such a basis can, however, easily become counter-revolutionary. The necessity theory of freedom cannot be the basis for creative revolutionary action. At the very best it can be the basis for revolutionary fanaticism, which does not critically examine its objectives and methods and which is intrinsically conservative, albeit at some stage of human history it can for a certain time and to some extent have a progressive effect.

The third variant of this theory, according to which power over nature and over oneself is based on the knowledge of internal and external necessity, has yet another important defect. This variant insists on freedom as a kind or form of power—domination. It assumes that nature and man are collections of completed powers and that nothing else is necessary except to conquer these powers in order to harness, subordinate and utilize them.

The view of freedom as a kind of domination and exploitation is typical of the nineteenth and twentieth centuries.

Contemporary man is interested in everything only as a possible object of subordination and utilization. But this is not to say that such a view is "good." Such a concept of freedom is an alienated concept characteristic of an alienated society.

In opposition to theories of freedom as knowledge of necessity, we may maintain: *If freedom is conceived of as knowledge and acceptance of fate, destiny, universal necessity, then "freedom" is only another name for voluntary slavery.* Freedom is neither submission nor accommodation to external or internal necessity. *Only that action can be free by which man changes his world and himself.* Knowledge of necessity is only the knowledge of limitations to freedom. *The positive condition of freedom is the knowledge of the limits of necessity, the awareness of human creative possibilities.* Freedom is also not the heedless exploitation of nature. *Freedom lies in man's ability to make nature human, and to participate in its blessings humanely.* Man and nature are not aggregates of finished powers, which have to be merely mastered, subjugated and utilized. *The essence of freedom is not in subjection of the given but in the creation of the new, in the development of man's creative abilities, in the widening and enriching of humanity.*

VII

Finally, we are left with the third basic theory of freedom, the theory that considers freedom as *self-determination.*

This idea has often appeared in the history of philosophy and has attained various forms (compare, e.g., Kant and Sartre). The idea is to a great extent justified in contrast to those it opposes. No one will call an act free that is determined from outside. If someone does something by order, under hypnosis, in fear or under threat we will not say that he is free. For someone to be free he must first of all, himself, guide his own actions. But that is still not sufficient.

Some think that not every self-determination is free

but only *immediate self-determination* (spontaneity), so that the idea of freedom as self-determination turns into the idea of freedom as spontaneity. According to such a view, that act would alone be free that we ourselves determine and through which at the same time this or that inclination, ability, aspiration or need of ours is directly expressed. We are free, they say, only when we do not calculate, speculate, premeditate.

But is man really free when in a fit of anger he commits some thoughtless act he will later regret, or is he at that instant a slave of his passions? It seems that freedom does not consist in sheer spontaneity. Man is a being who is always both immediate and mediated; he is not always free when spontaneously manifesting particular aspects or elements of his being, he is free only when acting as an integral and many-sided being. This does not mean that man is free only while doing something great and important. The whole man may be present in the most minute trifle.

Activity in which the entire man participates is not, however, by virtue of that necessarily free. The tyrant or criminal whose whole activity is directed by inhuman, destructive motives is far from being free. Man is free only when what is human in him moves him to creative action by which the limits of humanity are extended and enriched.

In favor of and against the theory of freedom as self-determination we may maintain: *Even the most intensive and the most successful activity is not free if it is determined from the outside.* Disciplined soldiers, obedient officials, well-paid policemen may be extraordinarily active and successful; nevertheless their activity is anything but free. *Only that activity is free in which a man himself determines his deed.* Nor is every action inwardly determined of itself free. *Only that self-determined activity is free in which a man acts as an integral, many-sided personality, in which he is not a slave of this or that special thought, emotion or tendency.* Furthest from free deeds are those whose activity is the "free" destruction of humanity. Dictators craving power, cruel conquerors, insatiable exploiters are only the slaves of their own inhuman obsessions and ambitions. *Man is free only when that which is creative in him determines his acts, when by his deeds he contributes to an extension of the limits of humanity.*

The above theses on the essence of freedom do not resolve the problem "to the end," but they do indicate a conception that may be a basis for discussion.

VIII

In the foregoing discussion no mention was made of "greater" or "lesser" freedom. We spoke simply of "freedom" and "unfreedom." One could consequently conclude that freedom does not allow degrees, that man is always *either* absolutely free, *or* absolutely unfree.

One might object that such a concept is both undialectical and unhistorical: *undialectical* because it overlooks the facts that various degrees of freedom and unfreedom are possible and that a definite degree of freedom is also a definite degree of unfreedom; *unhistorical* because it does not realize that man has never been absolutely unfree and will never be absolutely free, that all of human history is a contradictory but unrestrainable progression toward ever higher degrees of freedom, an advancement in which every degree achieved can be considered as a "greater freedom" (or "lesser unfreedom") in relation to those lower, superseded degrees, but as "greater unfreedom" (or "lesser freedom") in relation to all prospective greater ones.

We may agree with the foregoing and similar objections. Man is a being of freedom, but he is always free only to a greater or lesser extent. Freedom is "relative." If we wish, all the theses on freedom presented so far can be translated into a "relativized" form. Instead of saying: "Man is a being of freedom," we can say: "Man is man to the extent that he is free." Instead of: "Unfreedom is man's death," we can say: "To the extent that he is unfree, man is dead" (or, man is not man). Similarly, instead of saying: "Man is free only when that which is creative in him determines his actions," we can say: "Man is free only in so far as the creative in him determines his actions."

Freedom is indeed relative, but theories on the relativity of freedom often go too far. Relativity, some say, is not something appended to freedom from outside; it is a constituent element of freedom's essence. Regardless of how we continue the definition of freedom, we have to begin with the words: "Freedom is a relative . . ." or "Freedom is a definite degree. . . ."

If freedom is thus made relative, the historically relative degrees of freedom are thereby made absolute. The theory that freedom is "in essence" relative does not differ essentially from the theory that the essence of freedom is slavery. *Freedom is indeed "relative," but that does not mean that relativity is what makes it free. Relativity is what makes it relative.*

IX

In the preceding discussion of freedom and of "man" we did not specify whether man was to be understood as an association (society), as a group (class, stratum, nation, tribe, family, etc.) or as an individual (personality). But such specification is not essential. Regardless of whether we have in mind society, a social group or personality, the essence of freedom remains the same. Just as society is not free if it does not itself determine its own destiny, neither is personality free if somebody else decides its fate. Just as society is not free if it hinders the development of creative human powers, so the personality is not free if it does not contribute to the developing of man's creativity.

Does this mean that free society consists only of free individuals, and unfree society only of unfree individuals? In other words, is a free person possible only in a free, and an unfree person only in an unfree, society? An affirmative answer to these questions would be a sign that the essence of society has been miscomprehended. Society is a community of personalities, but such a community is not a mere sum of individuals.

Society can develop creative human powers only so as to make possible, and to stimulate, the development of free human personality. *There can be no free society without free personality.* But this does not mean that in a free society all are free. Even *in a free society the individual may be unfree.* By using a relativized terminology: The individual may be less free than the society in which he lives. Society may be organized so as to render possible and to stimulate the development of the free personality, but *freedom cannot be given as a gift to anyone.* "Given" or "imposed" freedom is a *contradictio* in *adjecto.* Freedom is by definition the activity of one who is free. *Only by his own free deed can the individual achieve his personal freedom.*

Just as in a free society not all are free, so neither are all in an unfree society unfree. *Even in an unfree society an individual may be free.* More precisely, it is possible for the individual to elevate himself above the degree of freedom obtainable in society. External obstacles erected by an unfree society can make more difficult or limit a free human act, but they cannot completely prevent it. An unwavering revolutionary in chains is freer than the jailer who guards him or the torturer who vainly tries to break him down. If we were to deny the possibility of a free personality in an unfree society, we would be denying the possibility of transforming an unfree society by conscious revolutionary action.

If unfree personalities are possible in a free society, and if free personalities are possible in an unfree society, this does not mean that the freedom of a society is irrelevant to the freedom of the personality. The unfree society endeavors to destroy the free personality, while a free society makes possible and stimulates its flowering. Therefore the *struggle for a free society is a component part of the struggle for the freeing of personality.* When this part attempts to become everything, it ceases to be that which it ought to be. *The struggle for a free society is not a struggle for a free society unless through it an ever greater degree of personal freedom is created.*

Personal and social freedom are inseparably associated, but the relationship between them is asymmetrical; *there is no free society without free personality* (which does not mean that all individuals in a free society are free) *but a free personality is possible outside a free society* (which does not mean that the freedom of society is irrelevant for the freedom of personality or that a free personality is possible outside every social community!).

X

Man as individual is not only a member of a broader social community, he is also included in particular groups. Membership in antagonistic social groups, "classes," has been of decisive importance in history up to the present time.

The class struggle in all its variety of forms is a fundamental form of the development of class society. The struggle to achieve a higher degree of freedom has, in class society, a class character. By concrete historical analysis it can be established which class or stratum is the bearer of a higher degree of freedom in a particular situation, and which class or stratum the defender of unfreedom.

But every class society is alienated, inhuman, in essence unfree. Only classless society can develop into a realm of freedom. A progressive class that fights for a new, freer form of class society is striving for only a new "freer" form of unfreedom. *The radical champion of freedom can only be the class that fights for the abolishment of every class society, and of itself as a class.*

One free personality, or several, cannot transform an unfree society into a free one. The free personality succeeds in its transforming endeavors only to the extent that it manages to convince, inspire and stir to action those potentially revolutionary social groups.

This essential knowledge is often distorted and abused.

The personality is asked to "merge" completely with his class, to subordinate all his personal thoughts, wishes, hopes, apprehensions and passions to the requirements of the class struggle. Those who in this manner demand the subordination of the personality to "class" do not realize that *there is no revolutionary class struggle without free personalities* capable of raising themselves above the factual level of their class and of realizing its revolutionary, universally human potentialities.

The need of "class" for "personality" is often interpreted as the need for a "great" personality that "sees" and "leads." Great personalities are indeed necessary to class, nation and mankind, but no less necessary are those seemingly "lesser" personalities that, regardless of their own modest working and intellectual "capabilities," evince high qualities of humanity.

It might seem to some that I overemphasize the importance of personality, but, regardless of what anyone thinks, *socialism is the cult of personality*—although not, of course, in the politico-journalistic sense that is nowadays widespread (the term "cult of personality" is often used for the cult of impersonality).

XI

In discussing the meaning of the question of freedom, we have emphasized that the question of freedom cannot be reduced to the question of types or forms of freedom. The essence of the question of freedom is in the question of freedom's essence.

This does not mean that one cannot speak of various forms, types or aspects of freedom. We have just made several observations on certain important aspects of freedom (social, individual, class), and in an earlier section we enumerated many of freedom's various kinds, forms and types.

The analysis of forms and aspects of freedom has a great significance, which many contest. The denial of varieties of forms of freedom is most often motivated by the wish to render specific characteristics of one type of freedom as the norm for all remaining types. In contrast to such endeavors we may assert: In addition to the universal essence of freedom, every kind of freedom has its own specific essence by virtue of which it is precisely that kind of freedom. *"As in the solar system each individual planet revolves around the sun only while turning around itself, so in the system of freedom each of its worlds circles around the central sun of freedom by circling around itself."*[3]

The possibility of various types or forms of freedom should not induce us to assume that the various forms of freedom are completely peculiar and mutually dissociated. All the forms of freedom are mutually conditioned, and each of them is one form of freedom.

Trampling upon this or that form of freedom is often excused by the demand for maintaining or establishing some other, more important form. To such arguments we may answer: "Each form of freedom is the condition for the rest of them, as one member of the body is for the others. *Whenever a specific freedom is brought into question, then freedom itself is brought into question. Whenever one form of freedom is rejected, it is freedom that is rejected, and it can continue to carry on only a fictitious life because henceforward it is pure chance at which point unfreedom will manifest itself as the predominating force."*[4]

XII

Finally, it is necessary to say at least something about the relationship between the problem of freedom as a lasting human problem and the varied forms in which that problem appears historically.

In the foregoing analysis certain important aspects of

[3] Marx, Engels, *Werke*, bd. I, pp. 69–70; italics, Petrović.
[4] *Ibid.*, pp. 76–77; italics, Petrović.

the problem of freedom were brought out, but we did not systematically discuss the various forms assumed by the problem of freedom in various social formations ("primitive," slave, feudal, capitalistic, socialistic) and in various developmental phases of individual formations. This does not mean that the problem of freedom is always the same. It is "eternal" (in the sense in which we use that attribute to characterize all lasting problems of man), but in every epoch it assumes a different form.

The consideration of various historical forms in which the problem of freedom appears does not fall within the limits of this essay. Nevertheless, it may be mentioned: In our time it has become clear that a free society is not created only by expropriation of the expropriators, nor alone by raising the standard of living, nor yet by the combination of these two. In a society from which exploiters have been eliminated, man's freedom is threatened by the means by which he communicates with nature and with other men (technology) and by the social forms through which he effects that communication (social organizations and institutions). *The question of freedom appears today primarily as the question of freedom and socialism and as the question of freedom with technology.*

Those who stress the question of freedom and socialism are sometimes disdained because they neglect the more important question of freedom and capitalism. This objection seems only justified. Capitalism is still a great force, but socialism is not a lesser one. The problem of freedom in capitalism is still theoretically interesting; but the problem of freedom in socialism is nevertheless newer and more interesting. And, regardless of what is more interesting, the problem of freedom in socialism is certainly incomparably more important, not only from the standpoint of the internal development of socialism but also from that of the contemporary world as a whole. *The development of socialism as a free community of free personalities is the most effective criticism of capitalism.*

Those who emphasize the problem of freedom with technology are accused of uncritically transfering a grave question of capitalism to socialism. "Technology," it is claimed, is a mere instrument, which can be dangerous under capitalism, but which becomes "obedient" under socialism. There is something to this. *But the atomic bomb will not start producing edible mushrooms the moment we affix a socialist label to it.*

Alienation and de-alienation

The term "alienation" ("estrangement") has many different meanings in everyday life, science and philosophy; most of them can be regarded as modifications of the broadest meaning, which is suggested by the etymology and the morphology of the word, the meaning in which "alienation" (or "estrangement") is the act, or result of the act, through which something, or somebody, becomes (or has become) alien (strange) to something, or somebody, else.

In everyday life "alienation" often means turning or keeping away from former friends or associates. In law it usually refers to the transfer of property from one person to another (selling-buying or giving as a gift). In medicine and psychiatry "alienation" usually means deviation from normality, i.e., "insanity." In contemporary psychology and sociology it is often used to name the individual feeling of alienness toward society, nature, other people or oneself. For many sociologists and philosophers alienation is the same as "reification," i.e., the act (or result of the act) of transforming human properties, relations and actions into properties and actions of things independent of man and governing his life. For others, "alienation" means the same as "self-alienation" ("self-estrangement"), namely the process, or result of the process, through which a "self" (God or man) becomes alien (or strange) to himself (i.e., to his own nature) through himself (i.e., through his own acts).

The concept of "alienation" has been philosophically elaborated by Hegel. Some have maintained that the Christian doctrine of "original sin" and "redemption" can be regarded as a first version of Hegel's doctrine of "alienation" and "de-alienation." According to others, the concept of alienation found its first expression in Western thought in the Old Testament concept of idolatry. And some have maintained that the source for Hegel's view of nature as a self-alienated form of the Absolute Mind can be found in Plato's view of the natural world as an imperfect picture of the noble world of Ideas. As the investigation proceeds, many more forerunners of Hegel will probably be found. But one thing is likely to remain unshaken: G. W. F. Hegel, Ludwig Feuerbach and Karl Marx first gave an explicit elaboration of "alienation," and their interpretation is the starting point for all discussions on alienation in present-day philosophy, sociology and psychology.

It is a basic idea of Hegel's philosophy that whatever is, is in the last analysis the Absolute Idea (Absolute Mind, Absolute Spirit, or, in popular language, God), and that the Absolute Idea is neither a set of fixed things, nor a sum of static properties, but a dynamic Self, engaged in a circular process of alienation and de-alienation. Nature is but a self-alienated (self-estranged) form of the Absolute Mind, and man is the Absolute in the process of de-alienation. The whole of human history is the constant growth of man's knowledge of the Absolute, and at the same time the development of self-knowledge of the Absolute, which through the finite Mind becomes self-aware, "returns" to himself from his self-alienation in nature. As the alienation of the Absolute Mind in nature is not an event in time but a "time-less" fact, it means that the starting point of world history is the already alienated mind, and that all of history is reduced to the process of de-alienation.

Not only the Absolute Mind alienates himself from himself in Hegel's philosophy. It is an essential characteristic of the finite mind (man) to produce things, to express himself in objects, to "objectify" himself in physical things, social institutions and cultural products; and every objectification is of necessity alienation: the produced objects become alien to the producer. Alienation in this sense can be overcome only in the sense of being adequately known. There is also another sense in which man can be regarded

as alienated in Hegel's system. It is the vocation of man as
man to serve as the organon of the self-knowledge of the
Absolute, and to the extent to which he does not perform
this function, he does not fulfill his human essence; to that
extent he is merely a self-alienated man.

Ludwig Feuerbach accepted Hegel's view that man can
be alienated from himself, but he rejected both the view
that nature is a self-alienated form of the Absolute Mind
and the view that man is the Absolute Mind in the
process of de-alienation. Man is not a self-alienated God.
On the contrary, God is a self-alienated man; he is merely
man's essence absolutized and estranged from man. And
man is not alienated from himself when he refuses to recog-
nize nature as a self-alienated form of God; man is
alienated from himself when he creates and puts above
himself an imagined alien higher being and bows before
him as a slave. The de-alienation of man consists in the
abolition of the estranged picture of man that is God.

Karl Marx praised Hegel for having grasped the self-
creation of man as a process of alienation and de-alienation. But he criticized Hegel for, among other things,
having identified objectification with alienation, and the
suppression of alienation with the abolition of objectivity;
for having regarded man as self-consciousness, and the
alienation of man as the alienation of his self-consciousness;
and for having assumed that the suppression of objectification and alienation is possible only in the medium of pure
thought.

Marx agreed with Feuerbach's criticism of religious
alienation, but he stressed that the religious alienation of
man is only one among many forms of man's self-alienation.
Man not only alienates a part of himself in the form of
God, he also alienates other products of his spiritual activity in the form of philosophy, common sense, art, morals,
etc.; he alienates products of his economic activity in the
form of commodity, money, capital, etc.; he alienates
products of his social activity in the form of state, law,
social institutions. So there are many forms in which man
alienates the products of his own activity from himself and

makes of them a separate, independent and powerful world of objects toward which he is related as a slave, powerless and dependent. He not only alienates his own products from himself, however, he also alienates himself from the very activity through which these products are produced, from the nature in which he lives and from other men. But all these kinds or forms of alienation are in the last analysis one: they are only different forms or aspects of man's self-alienation, different forms of the alienation of man from his human "essence" or "nature," from his humanity. The self-alienated man is a man who really is not a man, a man who does not realize his historically created human possibilities. A non-alienated man, on the contrary, would be a man who really is a man, a man who fulfills himself as a free, creative being of praxis.

The concepts of alienation and de-alienation were elaborated by Marx in his early writings, especially in his *Economic and Philosophical Manuscripts*, written in 1844 and published in 1932. Both concepts are also basic in his later works, but they are there used implicitly rather than explicitly. This is the main reason why their importance was overlooked. In no exposition or interpretation of Marx's views written in the nineteenth or in the first three decades of the twentieth century do the concepts of alienation and de-alienation play an important role. Some important aspects of alienation are discussed in G. Lukacs's *Geschichte und Klassenbewusstsein* (1932) under the name of "reification" (*Verdinglichung*), but there is no general and explicit discussion of alienation in the book.

The concepts of alienation and de-alienation became the object of ardent discussions after the publication of Marx's *Economic and Philosophical Manuscripts* in 1932, and especially after World War II. Those who have taken part in these discussions include not only Marxists, but also non-Marxists, especially existentialists and personalists, and not only philosophers, but also psychologists (especially psychoanalysts), sociologists, literary critics, writers, etc.

The revival of interest in the problem of alienation met

with violent opposition from a number of dogmatic Marxists who maintained that the concept of alienation was a Hegelian "stopgap" in young Marx, which the "mature" Marx abandoned. But more and more Marxists in France, Italy, England, the United States, Poland, Czechoslovakia, Yugoslavia and in other countries now think that the "young" and the "old" Marx are basically one, and that the concepts of "alienation" and "de-alienation" are indispensable for an adequate expression of the most essential theses of Marx.

Among those who regard the concepts of alienation and de-alienation as important tools of theoretical analysis, there are, however, differences in the way in which those concepts are used and interpreted. It is impossible to consider here all the different opinions on alienation. We shall mention only some of the controversial questions that are discussed by philosophers, psychologists and sociologists.

II

Some authors think that the concept of alienation can be applied both to man and to nonhuman entities ("God," "world," "nature," etc.); but there are many more who hold that it is applicable only to man. Some of those who apply it only to man insist that it can refer only to individuals, to single persons, and not to society as a whole. According to a number of such authors, the nonadjustment of the individual to the society in which he lives is a sign of his alienation. Others maintain that a society can be also "sick" or "alienated," so that an individual who is not adapted to the existing society is not of necessity "alienated."

Many of those who regard alienation as applicable merely to individuals make it even narrower by conceiving of it as a purely psychological concept referring to a "feeling" or "state of mind." Others insist that alienation is not a "feeling" only, but also an "objective fact," a way of Being.

Some of those who characterize "alienation" as a state of

mind regard it as a fact or concept of psychopathology; others insist that, although alienation is not "good" or "desirable," it is not strictly pathological. They often add that one should distinguish alienation from two related but not identical concepts: anomie and personal disorganization. "Alienation refers to a psychological state of an individual characterized by feelings of estrangement, while anomie refers to a relative normlessness of a social system. Personal disorganization refers to disordered behavior arising from internal conflict within the individual."[1]

Those who oppose the characterization of alienation as a psychological concept usually say that it is "also" (or "primarily") an economic, or political, or sociological, or ethical concept. And some insist that it is basically and first of all a concept of general philosophy, or a concept of "ontology" and "anthropology."

Owing to these differences in approach, those who nowadays use the term "alienation" differ greatly in their definitions of the term. According to Gwynn Nettler, alienation is a certain psychological state of a normal person, and an alienated person is "one who has been estranged from, made unfriendly toward, his society and the culture it carries."[2] For Murray Levin, "the essential characteristic of the alienated man is his belief that he is not able to fulfill what he believes is his rightful role in society."[3] According to Eric and Mary Josephson, alienation is "an individual feeling or state of dissociation from self, from others, and from the world at large."[4] For Stanley Moore, the terms "alienation" and "estrangement" "refer to the characteristics of individual consciousness and social structure typical in societies whose members are controlled by, instead of controlling, the consequences of

[1] Murray Levin in E. and M. Josephson, eds., *Man Alone* (New York, 1962), p. 228.

[2] *American Sociological Review*, vol. 22, no. 6, December, 1957, p. 672.

[3] E. and M. Josephson, *Man Alone*, p. 227.

[4] *Ibid.*, p. 13.

their collective activity."[5] According to Jean-Yves Calvez, alienation is "a general type of the situations of the absolutized subject which has given a world to oneself, a formal world, refusing in this way the true concrete and its requirements."[6] And according to Erich Fromm, "alienation (or "estrangement") means, for Marx, that man does *not* experience himself as the acting agent in his grasp of the world, but that the world (nature, others and he himself) remain alien to him. They stand above and against him as objects, even though they may be objects of his own creation. Alienation is essentially experiencing the world and oneself passively, receptively, as the subject separated from the object."[7]

When one is confronted with such a variety of definitions it is difficult to say which is the "best" one. Two basic approaches seem possible, however. One is to reserve the term for a specific phenomenon in which one is interested, and, consequently, to define it in such a narrow way as to make the majority of existing uses of "alienation" entirely inadmissible. The other is to define it in such a broad way as to make as many as possible of the existing uses at least partly admissible in order to account for the variety of phenomena and to prevent possible confusions. The latter course might seem more promising, and it really is—provided one does not remain at such a broad definition but proceeds immediately to distinguish between different forms of alienation and to the maximally unambiguous and clear determination of that decisive form that Hegel and Marx called "self-alienation."

III

All authors who have used the concept of alienation have distinguished between the different forms of alienation.

[5] S. Moore, *The Critique of Capitalist Democracy* (New York, 1957), p. 125.

[6] J.-Y. Calvez, *La Pensée de Karl Marx* (Paris, 1956), p. 51.

[7] Fromm, *Marx's Concept of Man*, p. 44.

But not all of them have dealt with the question explicitly.

There is no attempt at an explicit classification of the forms of alienation in Hegel; but as the essence of all development for him is a process of alienation and de-alienation, different stages in the development of the Absolute could be regarded as so many forms of alienation. It would be much more difficult to develop a similar classification for Feuerbach, the essence of whose philosophy was negation of systematic philosophy. A well-known fragment in Marx's *Economic and Philosophic Manuscripts* ("Alienated Labor") seems to suggest that we should distinguish between four different forms of man's alienation: the alienation of man from the products of his own activity, the alienation of man from his productive activity itself, the alienation of man from his human essence, and the alienation of man from other men. But such a classification seems too far from being a fair summary of the whole of Marx's views on the forms of alienation. In other places we find Marx talking about other forms and subforms of alienation. And the enumeration also seems to be defective because it puts on the same level "forms" of alienation that cannot be at the same level.

The twentieth-century writers differ widely in listing the basic forms of alienation. To mention just a few, Frederick A. Weiss has distinguished three basic forms of self-alienation (self-anesthesia, self-elimination and self-idealization); Ernest Schachtel, four (the alienation of men from nature, from their fellow men, from the works of their hands and minds, from themselves); Melvin Seeman, five (powerlessness, meaninglessness, social isolation, normlessness and self-estrangement); Lewis Feuer, six (the alienation of class society, of competitive society, of industrial society, of mass society, of race, of generations).

In listing five different forms of alienation Melvin Seeman tried to define them strictly. According to him, powerlessness is "the expectancy or probability held by the individual that his own behavior cannot determine the occurrence of the outcomes, or reinforcements, he seeks"; meaninglessness is "when the individual is unclear as to what he ought to believe—when the individual's minimal standards for clarity in decision-making are not met"; normlessness is the characteristics of a situation "in which there is a high expectancy that socially unapproved behaviors are required to achieve given goals"; isolation is characteristic of those who "assign low reward value to goals or beliefs that are typically highly valued in the given society"; and self-estrangement is "the degree of dependence of the given behavior upon anticipated future rewards, that is upon rewards that lie outside the activity itself."[8]

Other authors have avoided indicating either a full list of the forms of alienation or a precise definition of those forms. Eric and Mary Josephson indicate indirectly and roughly what they regard as basic forms of alienation when they say that "man in modern industrial societies is rapidly becoming detached from nature, from his old gods, from the technology that has transformed his environment and now threatens to destroy it; from his work and its products, and from his leisure; from the complex social institutions that presumably serve but are more likely to manipulate him; from the community in which he lives; and above all from himself—from his body and his sex, from his feelings of love and tenderness, and from his art—his creative and productive potential."[9]

Instead of trying to enumerate all classifications of the forms of alienation that have been made so far, we shall mention only a few of the basic criteria according to which such classifications could be and actually have been made.

According to the nature of that which is alienated we may distinguish between alienation of things and alienation of selves. And according to the basic types of things or selves we may add further subdivisions. For those for whom the only self is man, alienation of the self is only another name for the alienation of man. But depending

[8] *American Sociological Review*, vol. 24, no. 6, December, 1959, pp. 786, 788, 789, 790.

[9] E. and M. Josephson, *Man Alone*, pp. 10–11.

upon whether we consider man as an individual or man as a social group or community, we may distinguish between individual alienation and *social alienation*. As different kinds of social alienation we may distinguish the alienation of society as a whole (alienation of feudalism, alienation of capitalism, etc.), alienation of social groups (alienation of capitalist, alienation of worker, of intellectual, of bureaucrat, of producer, of consumer, etc.), alienation of social institutions (alienation of state, of church, of cultural institutions, etc.).

According to the question of what that which is alienated is alienated from, we can distinguish between the alienation from something or somebody else and the alienation from oneself. The distinction is not applicable to the alienation of things; a thing cannot be alienated from itself. But a self can be alienated either from something or somebody else or from itself. According to the different kinds of "others" and the different aspects or sides of the self, further subdivisions can be added (for example, alienation from nature, alienation from one's fellow men, from one's body, from one's feelings, needs, creative possibilities, etc.).

According to the question whether that which is alienated is alienated through its own activity or through the activity of another, we could distinguish between alienation through others and alienation through oneself. The alienation of a thing can obviously be only an alienation through others, while the alienation of a self can be both an alienation through others and an alienation through oneself.

The above criteria for differentiating alienation can be combined; the concept of self-alienation, as it is found in Hegel and Marx and as it is of the utmost interest for philosophy, is a result of a combined application of the above three basic criteria. What is called self-alienation by Hegel and Marx is the alienation *of* a self from itself through itself. The difference is that Marx knows only one self-alienated self (man), and Hegel, two (man and God, or Absolute). Some think that one could also speak about the self-alienation of "nature" or the "world." In religious myths we find self-alienated angels (e.g., Lucifer), and in children's stories and fables there are self-alienated animals (the cowardly lion, the naïve fox) and even plants (a humpy fir tree, a stinking rose). But outside of children's stories (which in speaking of animals aim at men) man is the only being that can be self-alienated in the proper sense of the word.

Someone might object that, by limiting the concept of self-alienation to man, we have made it too narrow. But if man is not only *one* being but *the* being (*dasjenige Seiende*), which is in the most authentic form of Being (*Form des Seins*) and expresses the meaning of Being as Being (*den Sinn des Seins als Seins*), this narrowing is not so drastic. If the highest possibilities of the whole of Being, of "totality," "world" or "nature" remain unrealized without man, then the alienation of man from himself can be regarded as a form of the self-alienation of the "world" or "nature" as a whole.

Our concept of self-alienation would be really too narrow, however, if we were to regard man's self-alienation merely as one among the many forms of man's alienation, because self-alienation is the decisive "form" of alienation, whose understanding opens up perspectives for understanding all the rest. Besides, much of what might seem only an alienation of man from something else is also a form of his self-alienation. Man's alienation from nature, for example, is also a form of man's self-alienation (because man is a natural being and a part of nature).

IV

It is not difficult to define self-alienation as the alienation of a self from itself through itself. But it is not so easy to say how and in which sense it is possible for a self (be it an individual man or a society) to be alienated from itself.

It seems plausible to say that to be self-alienated means to be internally divided, split into at least two parts, which have become alien to each other. But why should we talk of "self-alienation" instead of "internal division" or "split" in such a case? The term "self-alienation" seems to suggest some or all of the following points: 1.) the division into two conflicting parts was not carried out from the outside, it is the result of an action of the self itself; 2.) the division into conflicting parts does not annihilate the unity of the self, despite the split the self-alienated self is nevertheless a self; and 3.) it is not simply the split into two parts, which are equally related to the self as a whole; the implication is that one part of the self has more right to represent the self as a whole, so that by becoming alien to it the other part also becomes alien to the self as a whole.

One way to specify and clarify the inequality of the two parts into which a self-alienated self is split is to describe self-alienation as a split between man's real "nature," or "essence," and his factual "properties," or "existence." The self-alienated man in such a case is a man who in fact is not what he in essence is, a man whose actual existence does not correspond to his human essence. And a self-alienated human society would be a society whose factual existence does not correspond to the real essence of human society.

But how is it possible for the actual existence of man to deviate from his real essence or nature? If one conceives of man's essence as something shared by all men, then somebody alienated from man's essence could not be a man in fact either. Accordingly, if alienation of man from his essence is to be possible, his essence must not be conceived as something that all men have in common. But how should it be conceived then?

One possible interpretation would be to conceive it as an eternal or intemporal idea of man toward which the real man ought to strive. This interpretation is full of difficulties and leads to unanswerable questions. For example: Where and in which way does such an idea of man exist? What is the way or method to achieve an adequate knowledge of it? Why should a real man strive toward it? Etc., etc.

Another interpretation would conceive man's "essence"

as something actually belonging to men, but only to a part of them; for example, to the majority of all so-far existing men, or to the majority of future men, etc. But whichever interpretation one chooses, new difficulties arise. Why should a majority be more representative of the nature of man than the minority? If we already allow the split into "essence" and "existence," why should not we allow for the possibility that the split be present in the majority? And why should a future factuality have any advantage over the past and the present one?

A third, and perhaps the most promising, way seems to be to say that man's essence is neither an eternal idea nor a part of factuality, but the sum of historically created human possibilities. To say that a man alienates himself from his human essence would then mean that a man alienates himself from the realization of his historically created human possibilities. To say that a man is not alienated from himself would mean that a man stands on the level of his possibilities, that in realizing his possibilities, he permanently creates new and higher ones. The third interpretation seems more plausible than the first two, but it leads to difficult questions, too. In which way do the possibilities exist, and in which way do we discover them? And on what basis do we divide man's real possibilities into human and inhuman?

v

Another question has also been much discussed: Is self-alienation an essential, imperishable property of man as man, or is it characteristic only of one historical stage in man's development. Some philosophers (especially existentialists) have maintained that alienation is a permanent structural moment of man's existence. Man as man is necessarily self-alienated; besides his authentic existence, he also leads a nonauthentic one, and it is illusory to expect that he will one day live only authentically.

Opposed to such a view there is another, according to which the originally nonself-alienated man in the course of development alienated himself from himself, but will in the future return to himself. We find this view in Engels and in many contemporary Marxists; Marx himself seems to have been inclined to think that man had been always self-alienated thus far, but that he nonetheless could and should come into his own. In this sense, Marx in *Economic and Philosophical Manuscripts* speaks about communism as the *positive* supersession of all alienation and the return of man from religion, the family, the state, etc. to his *human,* i.e., *social,* existence. Such a conception of communism as a de-alienation of human community also forms the basis of all Marx's other works.

If we assume that all of history up to now was a history of man's self-alienation, the question may emerge: Was it characterized by the gradual elimination of alienation, or, on the contrary, by its permanent deepening? Those who believe in constant progress have maintained that the alienation has been steadily diminishing. But a great number of contemporary philosophers and sociologists have found that alienation has constantly increased, so that it is much deeper and more pervasive in contemporary capitalism and bureaucratic socialism than it ever was before. A third group of authors have maintained that the development of alienation is not easy to assess; it diminishes in one respect and increases in another. And some have insisted that the question cannot be answered simply by means of "more" or "less," that we should investigate different types of self-alienated characters typical of different periods in human history.

An interesting attempt in this direction has been made by Erich Fromm, who distinguished four basic types of "nonproductive" (self-alienated) character orientations (the receptive orientation, the hoarding orientation, the exploitative orientation and the marketing orientation) and took them as typical of four successive stages of historical development. According to Fromm, all four are found in the contemporary self-alienated society, but not all of them are equally typical of it. The receptive orientation is characteristic of "societies in which the right of one group to exploit another is firmly established"; the exploitative orientation "goes back to piratical and feudal ancestors and goes forward from there to the robber barons of the nineteenth century"; the hoarding orientation "existed side by side with the exploitative orientation in the eighteenth and nineteenth centuries"; and the marketing orientation is "definitely a modern product" and is typical of twentieth-century capitalism.[10]

Nearly every one of the outlined views can be supported. It is difficult to dispute the thesis that de-alienation is progressing. We live in a time when nations on all continents are showing an unprecedented activity and energy in the endeavor to become masters of their destiny, and the working man throughout the world (despite large variations in different countries) is gradually achieving not only more and more bearable conditions of life, but also more and more noticeable influence upon the determination of those conditions, and a greater and greater chance for a radical transformation of the society as a whole. But it is also difficult to dispute the thesis that alienation is growing and becoming stronger. We live in a time when the relations between people and individuals are more and more based on principles of a heartless egoism, and man regards himself as a commodity that ought to be sold well in the market.

If by such and similar arguments both opposite theses can be successfully defended, this means that it is also possible to defend the third, "middle" one, that alienation in one respect declines and in another increases. In connection with this, however, which in this form repels by its eclectic character, the question naturally imposes itself: Can we establish, or at least approximately assess, whether alienation as a whole is increasing or not?

It might seem at first that the answer is affirmative. But take only one aspect of alienation: Is man less man when he as a cannibal cooks another man in a pot, when he as an inquisitor from the Middle Ages tortures a heretic, or

10 Fromm, *Man for Himself* (New York, 1941), pp. 79–81.

when he as a contemporary Nazi scientifically kills women
and children in a concentration camp? Insisting on either
progress or regression here seems only an inhuman ped-
antry. But if it is impossible to compare numerically quali-
tatively different forms of the same aspects of alienation,
then it is certainly even less possible to find some general
numerical standard for the increase or the decrease of self-
alienation, which would hold for the society as a whole.

If the development of the process of alienation and de-
alienation cannot be expressed by means of numerical in-
dexes, does this mean that the only thing left is to say that
different forms of alienation have emerged in the course
of history and have been overcome in order to be replaced
by new forms? Such an answer seems too simple.

Should not the key for a better understanding of the
previous history of the relationship between the processes
of alienation and de-alienation be sought in their present
relationship? Does not the specificity of the present moment of world history lie in the fact that the swollen contradiction between alienation and de-alienation cannot be
solved any longer from the position of some new, more
refined form of alienation, but only from the position of a
radical de-alienation?

VI

For those who regard alienation as a historical phenomenon, the question about a possible "end of alienation" ("de-
alienation" or "dis-alienation") naturally arises.

According to one widespread answer, absolute de-
alienation is possible; all alienation, social and individual,
can be once and for all abolished. The most radical among
the representatives of such an optimistic viewpoint have
even maintained that all self-alienation has already been in
principle eliminated in socialist countries, that it exists
there only as a case of individual insanity or as an insignifi-
cant "remnant of capitalism." The more realistic among
the representatives of this view have not denied facts
showing that in countries considering themselves socialist

many "old" forms and even some "new" forms of alienation exist. But they insist that in the more mature stages
of socialism all these forms of alienation are foredoomed
to disappear.

It is not difficult to see the untenability of these views.
Absolute de-alienation would be possible only if mankind
were something given once and for all and unchangeable.
Against the advocates of absolute de-alienation, we may
therefore maintain that only a relative de-alienation is possible. It is not possible to wipe out alienation because human "essence" or "nature" is not something given and unchangeable that could be fulfilled once and for all. But it
is possible to create a basically non-alienated society that
would stimulate the development of non-alienated, really
human individuals.

Depending on the view of the essence of self-alienation,
the means recommended for overcoming it also differ.
Those who regard self-alienation as a "psychological" fact,
as "a fact of the life of the individual human self," dispute
the importance or even relevance of any "external" changes
in "circumstances" and suggest the individual's own moral
effort, "a revolution within the self" as the only cure.[11]
And those who regard self-alienation as "a result of the
neurotic process" are quite consistent in offering a psycho-
analytical medical treatment, regarding "the new creative
experience of acceptance and 'meeting' in a warm, truly
mutual, trusting doctor-patient relationship" as "the main
therapeutic factor."[12]

At the other pole stand those philosophers and sociologists who, basing their ideas on a degenerate variant of
Marxism called "economic determinism," regard individuals
as passive products of the social organization, the whole of
social organization, as the consequence of a certain organization of economic life, which is the inevitable result of the
dominating form of property (which, according to such a

[11] R. Tucker, *Philosophy and Myth in K. Marx* (Cambridge,
1961), pp. 240–41.
[12] F. A. Weiss in E. and M. Josephson, *Man Alone*, p. 479.

conception, can be either private or collective-state property). For such "Marxists" the problem of de-alienation reduces to the problem of social transformation, and the problem of social transformation to the abolition of private property.

In criticizing "the materialist doctrine that men are products of circumstances and upbringing," Marx stressed that "it is men that change circumstances" so that "the coincidence of the changing of circumstances and of human activity can be conceived and rationally understood only as *revolutionizing practice* [*praxis*]."[13]

Starting from this thought it is possible to elaborate a different conception about the roads of de-alienation, a conception according to which de-alienation of the society and of individuals is closely connected, and neither can be carried out without the other, nor can one be reduced to the other. It is possible to create a social system that would enable and even stimulate the development of de-alienated individuals, but it is not possible to organize a society that would automatically produce such individuals. A non-alienated individual is an individual who fulfills himself as a free and creative being of praxis, and free creativity is not something that can be given as a gift or forced upon anyone from outside. An individual can become free only through his own activity.

But not only can de-alienation not be reduced to de-alienation of society, the de-alienation of society in its turn cannot be conceived of as a change in the organization of the economy that will be followed automatically by a change in all other aspects or fields of social life. Far from being an eternal fact of social life, the split of society into mutually independent and conflicting spheres (economy, politics, law, arts, morals, religion, etc.) and the predominance of the economic sphere are, according to Marx, characteristics of a self-alienated society. The de-alienation of society is therefore impossible without the abolition of the

[13] Marx, Engels, *Basic Writings on Politics and Philosophy*, p. 244.

alienation of the different human activities from each other.

Equally, the problem of de-alienation of economic life cannot be solved by the mere abolition of private property. The transformation of private property into state property (be it a "capitalist" or a "socialist" state property) does not introduce an essential change in the situation of the working man, the producer. The de-alienation of economic life requires also the abolition of state property, its transformation into real social property; and this cannot be achieved without organizing the whole of social life on the basis of the self-management of the immediate producers.

But if the self-management of producers is a necessary condition of the de-alienation of the economic "sphere" of man's life, it is not of itself a sufficient condition. The self-management of producers does not solve automatically the problem of de-alienation of distribution and consumption; it is not by itself sufficient for even the de-alienation of production. Some forms of alienation in production have their root in the nature of the contemporary means of production and in the organization of the process of production, so that they cannot be eliminated by a mere change in the form of managing production. Some ways of working toward de-alienation have already been found and verified; others have to be invented and tested.

Philosophy and politics in socialism

We live in a time when even children all over the world know something about socialism, and theoreticians have written mountains of books and articles on the "topic." Nevertheless, it would be wrong to think that the question of what socialism means and what its prospects are has been "solved" and is therefore out of date. Indeed, at a time when among socialists (or those who declare themselves to be socialists) there are dozens, and even hundreds, of different interpretations of socialism, and many of these interpretations are backed not only by single lonely thinkers or groups of thinkers, but also by strong social groups, organizations, and institutions, sometimes even by dominant national forces, or whole states (this is why people sometimes talk of a "Chinese," "Yugoslav," "Italian," "Cuban," "Algerian," "Indian," "Burmese," etc., conception of socialism), it would be ridiculous to assume that the question of the meaning of socialism has been solved. Similarly, at a time when the prospects of mankind as a whole are neither clear nor certain (because the very existence of the human race has become endangered), it would be naïve to assume that the prospects of socialism are quite clear and certain.

What holds for the general question of the meaning and prospects of socialism largely holds also for the subject, "Philosophy and Politics in Socialism." This subject is by no means new; it can be found as far back as Plato. But it is still not out of date, although, it seems, there is more "agreement" here than there is in the general question about the meaning of socialism. In a great number of socialist countries the relationship between politics and philosophy is very similar: philosophy performs the function of a servant of politics. Even in those socialist countries where this relationship does not exist, there are influential groups and individuals who long to create such a relationship and from time to time try to establish it. Karl Marx never depicted the relationship between philosophy and politics in socialism in such a way, and this leads us to ask: Is there something wrong with Marx; or is something wrong with the relationship between philosophy and politics in socialism, and with that socialism where such a relationship exists? This question can be approached in different ways. Why not approach it by asking first what socialism is?

The term "socialism" has been used so far for three different areas. It has been used as a name: 1.) for a certain social order that should arise, or is already arising, as a negation of capitalism; 2.) for the political movement fighting for the realization of socialism in the first sense; and 3.) for the theory that establishes the possibility and shows ways and means for furthering socialism in the second sense and for achieving socialism in the first sense. In this essay we will discuss socialism in the first of these three meanings. We believe, however, that much of what holds good for socialism as a social order also holds good for socialism as a political movement and for socialism as a theory. The relation between philosophy and politics in socialism as a social order is certainly not independent of the relationship between the two that exists or existed in socialism as a theory and in socialism as a social movement. It is also clear that by determining the field of application of the concept, the question about its content is not yet solved. Different interpretations are still possible.

In the conception of socialism that was canonized by Stalin and that is still widespread in some socialist countries, the term "socialism" denotes the "lower phase of communism," which comes after the "period of the dictatorship of the proletariat" and before the "upper phase of communism." According to this conceptual and terminological scheme, we have the following sequence of social orders: capitalism, dictatorship of the proletariat, the lower phase of communism (socialism), the upper phase of communism (true communism). According to the proponents of the scheme, the period of the dictatorship of the proletariat lasted in the Soviet Union up to the proclamation of the Stalin Constitution; after the Stalin Constitution the period of socialism or the lower phase of communism began; and today, after the building of socialism has been completed, there is already a transition from socialism to communism.

I think that this scheme is defective for a number of reasons. Before criticizing it, however, I would like to make clear that this favorite Stalinistic scheme is not an arbitrary Stalinistic invention; it has its root in Marx. In his *Critique of the Gotha Program* Marx speaks of the two phases of communism, although he does not terminologically fix them as "socialism" and "communism." In the same work he also refers to "the period of the revolutionary transformation of the one into the other" (of the capitalist society into communist), as something that differs from both capitalism and communism, some third thing to which "there corresponds . . . also a political transition period in which the state can be nothing but *the revolutionary dictatorship of the proletariat.*"[1]

In connection with the conception of the transition period as a period of the dictatorship of the proletariat, which differs essentially from both capitalism and socialism, it is necessary to remark, first, that this is a very dangerous theory, which can be used, and actually has been used, for antisocialist purposes. If the transition period is neither capitalism nor socialism, if it has some properties of its own that distinguish it essentially from both capitalism and socialism, then it is possible to maintain that, although the developed capitalist society is characterized by political democracy, and although the developed socialist order will be democratic, the transition period from capitalism to socialism—that is, from bourgeois democracy to socialist democracy—need not be democratic. Moreover, it may even be maintained that inhumanity, unfreedom and violence make the best, or the only possible, "dialectical" road to socialism; that they are those dialectical means that

[1] Marx, Engels, *Basic Writings on Politics and Philosophy*, p. 127.

lead to their opposite—to the true democracy, freedom and humaneness of the socialist society. Of course, when we say that it is possible to maintain this in the framework of the theory regarding the dictatorship of the proletariat as a special transitory period, it does not mean that this *must* be maintained, that such an interpretation necessarily follows from the essence of the theory. But one must not overlook the fact that this is not only one among many possible interpretations, but is *the* interpretation that was promoted by Stalinism, in deeds as well as words. If Marx could have foreseen such an interpretation of his theory about the dictatorship of the proletariat as a special transitory period, he would perhaps never have formulated it, not even in the passing way in which he did in the *Critique of the Gotha Program*. He would probably have more firmly adhered to another version of his theory about the transitory period, which excludes the above-mentioned Stalinistic interpretation. This is the version according to which the transitory period is characterized not only by the dictatorship of the proletariat but also by communism and socialism. In order to make this theory clearer, we must for the moment leave aside the question of the transitory period and consider more carefully the theory of the two phases of communism.

On the basis of what Marx says in the *Critique of the Gotha Program*, one might get the impression that he distinguished the two phases of communism according to the ruling principle of distribution, ascribing the principle of distribution according to work to the first phase, and the principle of distribution according to needs to the second phase. In the lower phase of communism, according to Marx, "the individual producer receives back from society —after the deductions have been made—exactly what he gives to it,"[2] whereas in the upper phase of communism the society will be able to inscribe on its banners: "From each according to his ability, to each according to his needs!"[3] Marx stressed that society will be able to pro-

---

[2] *Ibid.*, pp. 117–18.
[3] *Ibid.*, p. 119.

claim the principle of distribution according to needs only
when certain conditions have been fulfilled, namely, "after
the enslaving subordination of the individual to the division
of labor, and therewith also the antithesis between mental
and physical labor, has vanished; after labor has become
not only a means of life but life's prime want; after the
productive forces have also increased with the all-around
development of the individual, and all the springs of co-
operative wealth flow more abundantly."[4] But this enumeration of the conditions for distribution according to
labor does not exclude the view that this principle is the
essential characteristic of the higher phase of communism. As if he himself felt that he might be misunderstood,
Marx expressly warned: "Quite apart from the analysis so
far given, it was in general a mistake to make a fuss about
so-called *distribution* and put the principal stress on it.
Any distribution whatever of the means of consumption
is only a consequence of the distribution of the conditions
of production themselves. The latter distribution, however, is a feature of the mode of production itself. . . .
Vulgar socialism (and from it in turn a section of democracy) has taken over from the bourgeois economists the
consideration and treatment of distribution as independent
of the mode of production and hence the presentation of
socialism as turning principally on distribution."[5] Thus,
after having seemingly attributed the decisive part in distinguishing the two phases of communism to differences in
distribution, Marx criticized those who believe that socialism turns on distribution and asserted that this view had
been inherited from the bourgeois economists. Such a
criticism is in accordance with Marx's basic view that production is more important than distribution and that forms
of distribution are dependent on forms of production.

One could ask whether one should not distinguish the
"lower" and the "higher" phase of communism according
to the forms of economic production. A positive answer

[4] Marx, Engels, *Basic Writings on Politics and Philosophy*,
p. 119.
[5] *Ibid.*, p. 120.

to this question would not be in the spirit of Marx, however. According to Marx, in an epoch of human history, the epoch of alienated class society, man really was an economic animal; his whole life was, in the last analysis, determined by the sphere of economic production. When we speak of that epoch, it is justifiable to distinguish different stages of development primarily according to the ruling mode of production. But the society that has to arise as a negation of capitalism has to be, according to Marx, not merely a negation of the capitalistic economic order; it must also negate the relationship between the "spheres," which was characteristic of class society; it must abolish not only the primacy of the economic sphere, but also the split of man into mutually estranged spheres. Accordingly, the criterion for distinguishing phases in that society cannot be the difference in the mode of economic production, it must be much more complex.

If we look at the familiar distinction between the lower and the higher phase of communism from the point of view of content, we see that not only the Stalinists, but even Marx himself, did not succeed in clarifying it. The lack of clarity is not only in content, it is also in terminology. Marx did not call the two phases "socialism" and "communism." These names were fixed later. Despite that, many Marxists still accept not only this distinction, which really is derived from Marx (although it does not agree with some of his fundamental views), but also the terminology, which is not his. This terminology as such is not "false," but it is not adequate for distinguishing the main phases of the communist society. Although the Stalinistic conception of socialism and communism has already been criticized, the terminology it used has remained untouched. The view that socialism is a finished social system essentially different from communism has been criticized, as has the view that inhumanity is allowed in socialism as a means for achieving humaneness in communism. But none of the critics, as far as I know, have called into question either the division of the development of communist society into two phases or the terminological fixation of the two phases as "socialism" (the "lower" phase) and "communism" (the "higher" phase).

The texts of Marx speak in favor of regarding socialism as a higher phase compared with communism. The etymology of the words also supports such a terminology. "Communism" (compared with *communis*—common) suggests a society in which means of production are common, and "socialism" (corresponding to *socius*—comrade) points to a society in which a man is comrade to another man. And the second is certainly higher and more difficult to achieve than the first.

That Marx really considered socialism "higher" than communism can be shown by help of a text that is well known and often quoted, but inadequately interpreted, because Marx is still much read through Stalinistic glasses. Marx writes: "*Atheism,* as a denial of this unreality, is no longer meaningful, for atheism is a *negation of God* and seeks to assert by this negation the *existence of man.* Socialism no longer requires such a mediation; it begins from the *theoretical* and *practical sense consciousness* of man and nature as essential beings; it is positive human *self-consciousness,* no longer a self-consciousness mediated through the negation of religion; just as the *real life* of man is the positive reality of man no longer mediated through the negation of private property, through communism."[6] As we see, communism for Marx is that mediation ("roundabout method") through which private property is abolished, and real life is the positive reality of man no longer mediated through that abolishment. In other words, communism is the "lower" phase, and real life is the "higher" phase. The relationship between "atheism" and "socialism" is analogous to this relationship between "communism" and "real life." Atheism is the affirmation of the existence of man through the negation of God. Socialism on the contrary needs no mediator. It is positive human self-consciousness, which is not mediated by the abolishment of religion. Consequently, whereas commu-

[6] Cf. Fromm, *Marx's Concept of Man,* p. 140.

nism is the humane society mediated through the abolition of private property, socialism is an aspect of that higher form of society, which is immediately humane. Socialism is not that society as a whole, it is merely an aspect of "real life," its self-consciousness. Of course, if Marx regarded communism as the "lower" phase and socialism as one aspect of the "higher" phase (its self-consciousness), this does not mean that we must accept his terminology and his view (because this is not merely a terminology). But is it not of vital importance for mankind today to distinguish between the social condition in which private property is abolished (communism), and the humane community of men in which a man is a *socius* to another man (socialism, or, more adequately, humanism)?

In discussions of socialism and communism, the question is often asked whether socialism or communism represents the final goal, the end of human history; and Marxists and Marxologists answer unanimously that, of course, it does not. When uninformed people ask what then has to follow after communism, the experts explain patronizingly that it is a scholastic question that goes too far into the future. It is clear that communism will not last forever, and that something will happen after it, but what is going to happen we do not and cannot know. So if a "scholastic" calls attention to the fact that Marx sometimes spoke of communism as a "solved puzzle of history" and sometimes stated that "communism as such is not an aim of human development" but only a "necessary form and an *energetic* principle of the nearest future," he will get the explanation that this is "dialectics." If we study Marx more attentively, however, we will see that "dialectics" in the sense of simultaneous assertion of contradictory theses was not allied to him. We will also discover that Marx clearly answered the "scholastic" question: What is going to happen after communism? He wrote: "In the same way, atheism as the annulment of God is the emergence of theoretical humanism, and communism as the annulment of private property is the vindication of real human life as man's property. The latter is also the emergence of practical humanism, for atheism is humanism mediated to itself by the annulment of religion, while communism is humanism mediated to itself by the annulment of private property. It is only by the supersession of this mediation (which is, however, a necessary pre-condition) that self-originating *positive* humanism can appear."[7]

Consequently, according to Marx, communism is in essence the emergence of humanism; but in contradistinction to atheism, which is the emergence of theoretical humanism, it is the emergence of practical humanism. As the emergence of humanism, it cannot be essentially different or contrary to humanism; it already is humanism, but a humanism mediated through the abolishment of private property. Only through and after this mediation can the positive humanism emerge, a humanism that begins positively from itself. This positive humanism has no reason to call itself "communism," because this name suggests that we have to do with a community that emerged as a negation of the society based on private property.

When he insists that communism is a mediated humanism, Marx does not want to say that communism is not humanism at all. On the contrary, he remarks: "But atheism and communism are not flight or abstraction from, or loss of, the objective world which men have created by the objectification of their faculties. They are not an impoverished return to unnatural, primitive simplicity. They are rather the first real emergence, the genuine actualization, of man's nature as something real."[8]

In this way Marx does not advocate the replacement of capitalistic society through another form of class society, or through another form of the self-alienated society in which the economic sphere would still dominate; he advocates an essentially different, *humanistic* society. And communist society is humanistic society in the process of emergence. *Communism*, in fact, is the *"transitory period"* *from capitalism (and class society in general) to human-*

[7] Fromm, *Marx's Concept of Man*, pp. 188–89.
[8] *Ibid.*, p. 189.

ism, but this does not mean that it is somewhere in the middle between capitalism and humanism. Communism is communism to the extent to which it is humanism. And socialism is one of the aspects of the humanistic society, because in the society in which man really *is* man, man is a comrade to other men too.

What is the more precise meaning of communism conceived as the emerging of humanism? In his "Private Property and Communism" (a well-known fragment in the *Economic and Philosophical Manuscripts*)[9] Marx writes in a detailed way about communism and its three main phases. It seems to me that the division into three phases is not essential. What is much more important is what Marx has to say generally on communism. And he speaks on communism in general, even when he is concerned with the description of a single phase. Thus, in connection with the first two phases, he writes: "In both forms communism is already aware of being the reintegration of man, his return to himself, the supersession of man's self-alienation. But since it has not yet grasped the positive nature of private property, or the *human* nature of needs, it is still captured and contaminated by private property. It has well understood the concept, but not the essence."[10]

In this way Marx clearly states the humanistic essence of communism: the abolition of man's self-alienation, the reintegration, or return of man to himself. Discussing the "third phase," he specifies this explanation when he maintains that religion, family, the state, morals, science, art, etc., are merely special modes of production, and that "the positive supersession of *private property,* as the appropriation of *human* life, is therefore the *positive* supersession of all alienation, and the return of man from religion, the family, the state, etc., to his *human,* i.e., *social,* life."[11]

If one wished to summarize Marx's answer to the question of what communism and humanism are, one could say

[9] *Ibid.,* pp. 123–40.
[10] *Ibid.,* p. 127.
[11] *Ibid.,* p. 128.

that they are the appropriation of man's life through the abolishment of man's self-alienation, especially through the abolishment of man's split into separate spheres that stand in relationships of external determination. Communism is, accordingly, not simply a new socioeconomic formation, it is the abolishment of the primacy of the economic sphere and of the predominance of economic criteria in distinguishing human communities.

This conception of communism, socialism and humanism requires a determined relationship between philosophy and politics in a society that is communist, socialist or humanist (the three are not identical, but they are not essentially different, because, as has already been said, communism is the merging of humanism and socialism, one aspect of communism and humanism).

I shall not try to give here a precise definition of either philosophy or politics. It is well known that the different definitions of philosophy are legion, and controversy about which is best will probably never end. I have explained my own viewpoint on the essence of philosophy elsewhere in this volume, and it is not necessary to repeat it here. I will merely mention again I do not regard philosophy as a branch of either science or art, I consider it a separate form of spiritual activity through which a man not only discovers his own essence and his place in the world, his capabilities for changing the world and for enriching his own nature, but also stimulates the deed of transforming the world, and participates in it in a creative way.

It is also well known that there are a lot of different definitions of politics, from narrow ones, which treat politics as an activity of ruling the state, to wider ones, which regard politics as a way of administrating society as a whole, to those that identify politics with every directed human activity, or with the way of life of a people. I cannot enter into the controversy about the best definition of politics here. I will mention only that in this context I do not mean by politics either every directed human activity or merely the activity of ruling the state. Under politics I mean here every activity of administrating social life, whether this is done through the state or through a stateless form.

Despite the fact that philosophy and politics have always been and still are different, they have always had certain common characteristics. Both philosophy and politics have been so far special activities, parallel to many other activities (economic, artistic, scientific, religious, legal, etc.), clearly separated from the rest and from one another, but connected through the external relationships of mutual influencing and conditioning. Both activities have also been bound up with special social groups—politicians and philosophers. Although other people have taken part in both politics and philosophy (there is almost no one who has no interest at all in politics, or who is without at least an "amateurish" philosophy), and although the participation of "masses," especially in politics, may attain a very high degree of intensity (for example, in revolutions), these activities have always been performed and furthered mainly by a narrow circle of people, politicians and philosophers. Although many philosophers and politicians throughout history have been at the same time slave owners, landlords, capitalists, merchants, lawyers, etc., with the development of class society, especially of capitalism, the tendency to professionalize both activities, to turn both philosophers and politicians into special social strata, which by performing these activities make their living, secure their means for life, has increased. A bureaucratic, or, in Marx's words, "rough and thoughtless communism," does not oppose this tendency, it sometimes even brings it to the absurd by transforming politicians into politicants and philosophers into schoolmen. The originality of such a communism is that it "dialectically" abolishes the opposition between the two strata by transforming one ("philosophers") into the servant of the other ("politicians").

But if this happens in fact, must it necessarily happen? Does such a relationship follow from the essence of communism, philosophy and politics? Or does from the essence of these phenomena follow quite another relationship, which is, in turn, not merely an ideal project or a powerless wish, but a real possibility and the already existing tendency of historical development, albeit a possibility that cannot be realized without our active engagement?

What, accordingly, could and should happen to philosophy and politics under communism and humanism? In accordance with the sketched conception of communism, philosophy in communism and humanism should disappear as a special activity separated from all others. But it should remain and develop as the critical thought of man about himself, as a self-reflection that penetrates the whole of his life, as a co-ordinating force of his whole activity, as a form through which he achieves the wholeness of his personality. Philosophy should also cease to be a professional duty or privilege of a special social stratum. This does not mean that all people can or must become great philosophers, but it does mean that philosophy must break its narrow limits, that it must turn to the essential human questions of its time and develop through broad, free and equal discussion among all those who think about these questions.

In communism and humanism, politics should develop in a similar direction. It should disappear as a special activity exercised by a privileged stratum and determined primarily through the economic interests of social classes (and of that stratum). It should be transformed into an activity that is not a privilege of professional politicians, but through which the social community as a whole, on the basis of critical reflection about its problems, solves the important questions of its life.

Consequently, if questioned about the relationship of philosophy and politics in communism (socialism, humanism), my answer would be that philosophy as man's critical self-reflection should direct the whole of his activity, including his political activity. But I do not think that political acts could or should be prescribed by any philosophy or by a philosophical forum. These should come about by a democratic, free decision of all those interested.

If one depicts in this way, on the one hand, what the relationship between philosophy and politics has been up to now, and, on the other hand, what their relationship should be in socialism, one might ask what roads, if any, lead to the realization of such a relationship. In answer it should be remarked, first, that such a relationship cannot be established if we first start going in the opposite direction, i.e., if we "temporarily" employ philosophy as the handmaid of politics and instead of developing democratic forms of government strengthen bureaucratic ones. Without awaiting the "right time" for the development of the humanistic essence of communism (for those who wait for it the right time never seems to have come) we must today, and now, try to realize the maximum of what according to our beliefs it could and should be.

Without passively waiting for the "future," philosophy must make the real world, including politics, the object of its criticism. In answering the question whether one should discuss politics in a philosophical way in newspapers, the young Marx replied that newspapers have not only the right but also the obligation to write about political questions, and that philosophy, as the "wisdom of the world," must care for the state as the "kingdom" of this world. "The question is here not whether one should philosophize about the state, the question is whether one should philosophize about the state well or badly, philosophically or unphilosophically, in a prejudiced way or without prejudices, with consciousness or without consciousness, consequentially or unconsequentially, quite rationally or semirationally."[12]

Philosophy must make the real world, including its politics, the subject of criticism. But this is not enough. Philosophy must also break the limits of discussion within a narrow circle of professional philosophers; it must turn itself to nonphilosophers, not only to scientists, artists, politicians, but to all those who think about the living problems of our time.

In order to establish the described relationship between philosophy and politics, politics must also develop in a

[12] Marx, Engels, *Werke*, bd. I, s. 100–1.

given direction. It must more and more become the concern and work of the whole community. It must also become more and more the function of critical thought and discussion, not of accidental or arbitrary decision. Developing in this direction, philosophy and politics can free themselves from being separated "sectors" or "spheres" of a split social life, and fulfill themselves and develop as essential "aspects" or "moments" of the whole man.

On such a road various obstacles may arise. This may occur partly because the bearers of the process of superseding philosophy and politics can be only philosophers and politicians, and that only insofar as they are able to raise themselves above the egoistic interests of their own social strata can they look from the standpoint of the whole of mankind and of that social class that can today be the bearer of the social transformation, i.e., the working class.

Although both professional philosophers and professional politicians are interested in retaining the social privileges of their strata, and this (not insurmountably) can obstruct them in taking a revolutionary standpoint, there is a considerable difference between philosophers and politicians as social strata. The difference is not only in the kind or quantity of social privileges, although this difference can be fairly large and easily observable. There is an even greater importance in the following fundamental asymmetry: in order to make the activity of ruling society common, the stratum of politicians that has ruled so far must restrict its activity. In order that all may be able to rule, those who have ruled so far must rule less. In order that all can think critically about fundamental problems of contemporary man and world, however, no philosopher ought to renounce his right and duty to think critically. The "space" for that is wide enough for all. On the contrary, the greater the number of those who think and discuss philosophical questions is, the more stimulating the atmosphere for philosophical thought will be, and the greater the possibility for every individual to develop his own philosophical thinking to the maximum.

The asymmetry in the social being of politicians and philosophers may result in certain misunderstandings between the members of the two strata in the beginning of the construction of communism and humanism. It may happen, for example, that some politicians who are not able to raise themselves to the universal social standpoint, and who strive to keep their privileged position as social rulers together with the corresponding material privileges, may regard philosophy directed against all privileges as a danger to themselves. Such politicians will have an entirely negative attitude toward philosophy and philosophers, but they will avoid an open discussion of controversial questions, and they will try to represent the defense of their material interests and privileges as a defense of socialism against "nonsocialist" strivings.

Such conflicts and tensions can be avoided or solved in different ways. One way would be to liquidate philosophy or to transform it into a subservient handmaid of politics. In some socialist countries this has largely succeeded. In others (primarily in Yugoslavia) such a danger does not exist. But where there are no real conditions for transforming philosophy into the servant of politics, there may be the danger that politicians will try, by surrendering a part (more accurately, a small particle) of their power to "corrupt" philosophers, to divide their power over all society with philosophers and scientists (although, of course, not equally). This is the most dangerous trap philosophers in socialism have to avoid. It is the duty of philosopher-Marxists to develop a critical consciousness toward themselves as a special social stratum, toward politicians and toward anybody else who may try or wish to maintain or to achieve a privileged position in society. In these efforts philosopher-Marxists can find their best allies among those politician-Marxists who do not confine themselves to the standpoint of their own social stratum, but take the standpoint of society as a whole.

PART III

Praxis and Being

I

What makes a man man is neither this or that quality or activity that is his alone, nor any set of such qualities and activities, but the general structure of his Being (*Sein*), which Marx called "praxis." Man is, according to Marx, a being (*Seiendes*) that is in the mode of praxis.

By characterizing man as a being of praxis not all problems of man have been solved; the most difficult questions have just begun. If we cannot explain what praxis is, we do not gain very much by our definition. To be sure, it might seem unnecessary to explain what praxis is. The word is Greek, but we Yugoslavs (Englishmen, Russians, Frenchmen, Germans, etc.) understand it well and use it easily! We use the words "praxis" and "practice" so often and so easily, however, that we do not notice that we use them in many different and even incompatible meanings. At one time we mean by practice an established *custom* or *habit* (for example, when we say "the practice is to do so and so"), another time *new events* that show the untenability of some established views (for example, when we say "practice has disproved this generally accepted view"); a third time practice means the same as *experience* (e.g., somebody has "a lot of practice" in the work he does); a fourth time we mean by practice *exercise* ("More practice!" the music teacher advises his pupil); a fifth time, a lawyer's or doctor's professional *business* (a doctor with "private practice"), etc. Hence the word "practice" has more than one meaning in everyday language. It has more than one meaning in philosophy also. "Praxis" does not mean the same for Plato, Aristotle, Kant, Hegel, James. The thesis that man is praxis (or a being of praxis) requires us to consider the question, what praxis is.

As a form of Being of the most complex being, praxis is

something very complex. Therefore, the concept of praxis is also most complex, and we can analyze and define it, but we can never analyze it and define it to the end. It is difficult to give a perfect and complete definition of praxis, but one might say that praxis is, among other things, universal, free, creative and self-creative Being. One could also say that praxis is historical Being, or Being through future. Of course, such definitions of praxis commit us to many further questions. For example, What is creativity? What is freedom? What is history? But such characterizations lead also to a "nearer" question: What is Being and what is its relationship to praxis? Is praxis only one among the many modes of Being or is it in an exceptional relationship to Being?

II

What is Being? This question also is too difficult and complex to allow a brief and simple answer. But this is not a sufficient reason for not raising it.

When one speaks of Being, one cannot disregard what has been said about it by great thinkers. But anyone who tried to report everything that others had said about Being would never manage to say anything about it himself. Therefore, without entering into the history of the concept "Being," we will recall only some "details" that may be "important" for us here.

In discussing the ontological proof for the existence of God, Kant, in passing, explains nicely what Being is not: "*Being* is obviously not a real predicate, i.e., the concept of anything that can be added to the concept of a thing." But he is much less specific when he wants to say what Being is: "It is only the positing of a thing, or of certain determinations in themselves."[1]

No more illuminating are the examples of which Kant

[1] I. Kant, *Kritik der reinen Vernunft* (Critique of Pure Reason), Herausgegeben von Dr. K. Kehrbach, Reclams Universal Bibliothek (Leipzig), s. 472.

makes use. What do I not do when I maintain, for example, that God is? In this way "I do not add any new predicate to the concept of God." This is beautifully said. But what do I do in this way? In this way "I merely posit the subject in itself with all of its predicates, i.e., the *object* in relation to my concept."[2]

Kant believes that the real (e.g., hundred real Talers) does not contain anything more than the merely possible (e.g., hundred possible Talers), but this does not mean that between the real and the possible there is no difference. I am most certainly better off when I have one hundred real Talers than when I merely have a concept of them! Thus Kant feels that Being is not a "quality" of an object or of a thing like all the rest, but is something exceptional and essentially different from everything else, and nevertheless not less important, but perhaps even more important. But he does not know how to say what this so unusual and important entity is.

The concept of Being is not even terminologically fixed in Kant. He uses interchangeably *das Sein* ("Being"), *das Dasein* ("existing") and *die Existenz* ("existence"). He is in one respect very specific, however: Being cannot be a "characteristic" of any concept, so that we cannot attribute Being to any object on the basis of its concept alone. Only by the help of perception can we establish whether an object of our senses exists; when objects of pure thinking are in question, there are no means whatsoever to establish whether they exist.

All this reasoning has an exactly determined aim in Kant: to show the impossibility of an ontological proof for the existence of God. In his attempt to refute Kant's criticism of the ontological proof, Hegel insists that one should make a distinction between a hundred Talers and God. In everything, final Being is different from concept. But the infinite is in principle different from the finite. The unity of Being and concept makes the very concept of God! In trying to substantiate the assertion that the concept of God

[2] *Ibid.*

includes Being, Hegel writes: "It would be strange, one really may say, if this innermost inner of the mind, concept, or if I, or the entirely concrete Totality which is God, were not rich enough to contain in itself such a pure determination as *Being*, which is among all the poorest, the most abstract. Nothing can exist more trifling in content than *Being*. Only what is sometimes first imagined as Being, i.e., *external sensory* existence, such as the existence of the paper I have here before me can be even smaller; but nobody will in any case want to speak of the sensory existence of a limited, passing thing."[3]

For Hegel, Being is consequently the "poorest, most abstract" among all determinations. In respect to content there is "nothing more trifling" than Being! These expressions have not slipped incidentally into Hegel's writing during the ardor of polemics. Hegel's determination of Being in the beginning of his *Logic* is in harmony with them. "Being is the indeterminate immediate (*das unbestimmte Unmittelbare*); it is free from determination in relation to the essence, and also from every determination that it can get within itself."[4]

The first among Hegel's determinations of Being is not at the same time the last, however. That pure Being, which is the "indeterminate immediate," cannot in its purity and indeterminateness either be or be thought of. "Being, the indeterminate immediate, is really *nothing*, and neither more nor less than nothing."[5] But "nothing" is also not the last word in Hegel's analysis of Being. The immediate truth of "Being" and "nothing" is their unity, "becoming" (*das Werden*). Nevertheless, becoming is still far from being the definitive truth about Being. Being is not

[3] G. W. F. Hegel, *Encyclopädie der philosophischen Wissenschaften im Grundrisse* (Encyclopedia of Philosophical Knowledge), Neu herausgegeben vom G. Lasson, Dritte Auflage (Leipzig, 1923), s. 80.

[4] G. W. F. Hegel, *Wissenschaft der Logik* (The Science of Logic), Herausgegeben von G. Lasson, Zweite Auflage (Leipzig, 1932), Teil I, s. 67.

[5] *Ibid.*

only "pure Being," "nothing" and "becoming," Being is also "existence" (*das Dasein*) and "Being-for-Self" (*das Für-sichsein*); quality, quantity and measure; essence, appearance and reflection; identity, difference and contradiction, etc. In the full sense of the word "only the Absolute Idea is *Being*."[6] The sense of the requirement to show Being is to realize the notion. The "fulfilled" Being is the "concept which conceives itself," "Being as a concrete, and equally absolute *intensive* totality."[7]

In this way Hegel rises from the view of Being as the "indeterminate immediate" to the view of Being as the concrete totality, as the most determinate mediate. Thus "Being" appears in Hegel at least in two senses: as the simplest category, which does not presuppose any other, and the most complex category, which includes all the rest of them. Being in the first sense is a "pure indeterminateness and vacuity," the content of Being in the second sense can be uncovered only by systematic deduction of all forms of Being from one another. Both views of Being provoke a certain uneasiness. The first is too "vacuous," the second too "full"; in neither of the two cases do we know how we will approach it.

III

Ludwig Feuerbach opposes Hegel's critique of Kant. He holds that Kant's insistence on the difference between the hundred imagined and hundred real Talers is fully justified. "Because I have these Talers in my *head* only, and those in my *hand*, these are *here* only *for me,* and those also *for others*—they can be felt, seen. And only that exists which is at the same time for me and for others, in which I and others agree, which is not only mine—which is common."[8]

[6] *Ibid.,* Teil II, s. 484.

[7] *Ibid.,* s. 504.

[8] L. Feuerbach, *Sämtliche Werke* (Collected Works) (Leipzig, 1846), bd. II, s. 308.

On the basis of this, somebody might think that *to be* means for Feuerbach to be a common object. His thought is different: "Being is something where not only I take part, but also others, first of all the *object* itself. To be means to be a *subject*, means to be *for oneself*."[9]

Hence, to be means to be not only a common object, but also subject. Through what kind of activity, however, do we discover what really is, what is not only an object, but also a subject? "In thinking I am the absolute subject, I leave everything to hold only as an object or predicate of me, one who thinks; I am intolerant. In sensory activity I am on the contrary liberal, I allow the object to be what I myself am—subject, real, *self-active* being. Only senses, only perception give me something *as subject*."[10]

If only senses and perception give us something as subject (consequently as being), then it is obvious that an abstract, thinking being possesses no idea of Being. Being is the limit of thinking. And Being as conceived by speculative philosophy is a pure ghost that contradicts both real Being and what man means by Being. "Under *Being* man as a matter of fact understands *existence, Being for oneself, reality, existence, actuality, objectivity,* in conformity with matter and reason. All these determinations or names express one and the same thing only from different viewpoints."[11]

Abstracting from every content of Being and trying to think of Being separated from this content, Hegel substitutes unfounded abstraction for what the human mind correctly and intelligently means by Being. "*Being is not a general concept separable from things. It is one with what it is.* It can be thought of only mediately by the help of predicates which make a thing's essence. Being is the positing of essence. *My Being is what my essence is.*"[12]

[9] *Ibid.,* s. 309.
[10] *Ibid.*
[11] *Ibid.,* s. 310.
[12] *Ibid.,* s. 311.

Feuerbach, especially, points out that the merely thought Being is not real, and that the question about Being is not only theoretical. "The question about Being is a practical question, a question in which our Being takes part, a question of life and death."[13]

A being without perception, sensation and love would be unable to conceive the difference between Being and non-Being. "Abstract thought without sensation and passion abolishes *the difference between Being* and *non-Being*, and this difference, what disappears for thought, is reality for love. To love means nothing else but to be aware of this difference. For those who do not love anything—whatever the object may be—it is entirely irrelevant whether something is or is not. As only through love, however, generally through sensation, Being is given to me as distinct from non-Being, so, owing to it, object is given to me as distinct from me. Pain is a loud protest against identification of subjective and objective. . . . Thus love is a true *ontological* proof of the existence of an object outside our head—and there is no other proof of Being except love and sensation in general. Only that *is* which gives *joy* by its *Being*, and *pain* by its *non-Being*."[14]

In laying down this principle the new philosophy is fundamentally different from the old. "If the *old* philosophy said: what *is not thought of*, that *is not*; the *new* philosophy, on the contrary, says: what is not loved, *what cannot be loved*, that does not exist. . . . If the *old philosophy* had for its starting point the proposition: *I am an abstract, merely thinking being, body does not belong to my essence*, the *new* philosophy, on the contrary, begins with the proposition: *I am a real, sensory being: body belongs to my essence, what is more, body in its totality is myself, my essence which is only mine*."[15]

If only what can be sensed and loved is (exists), and if one can love only what is bodily, then it is not far to the

[13] *Ibid.*, s. 313.
[14] *Ibid.*, s. 322–23.
[15] *Ibid.*, s. 324–25.

conclusion: *"Space and time are not mere forms of appearance—they are essential preconditions, rational forms, laws both of Being and thinking."*[16]

In his polemics against Dühring, Engels starts from Hegel's initial conception of Being as indeterminate immediacy. Against Dühring's reasonings, he writes: "When we speak of *Being*, and *solely* of Being, unity can consist only in that all the objects to which we are referring—*are*, exist. They are included in the unity of this Being, and no other unity, and the general statement that they all *are* not only cannot give them any additional qualities, whether common to them all or not, but provisionally excludes all such qualities from consideration."[17]

After thus in his own words expressing the view of Being as the indeterminate immediate, and after giving some more explanations of this determination, Engels criticizes Dühring's view that the unity of the world consists in its Being: "The unity of the world does not consist in its Being, although its Being is a precondition of its unity, as it must certainly first *be* before it can be *one*. Being indeed is always an open question beyond the point where our sphere of observation ends. The real unity of the world consists in its materiality, and this is proved not by a few juggling phrases, but by a long and protracted development of philosophy and natural science."[18]

While he here distinguishes so strictly between materiality and Being, reducing Being to that pure indeterminateness we get when we abstract from all qualitative determinations of Being, Engels then follows Feuerbach and, radicalizing his viewpoint, writes that "the basic forms of all Being are space and time, and Being of time is just as gross an absurdity as is Being out of space."[19]

Feuerbach and Engels were followed by Lenin. In *Ma-*

[16] *Ibid.*, s. 332.

[17] F. Engels, *Anti-Dühring*, Lawrence & Wishart (London, 1934), p. 52.

[18] *Ibid.*, pp. 52–53.

[19] *Ibid.*, p. 62.

terialism and Empirio-Criticism he quotes with approval the above ideas of Feuerbach and Engels and, maintaining that space and time are "objective-real forms of Being," goes on: "There is nothing else in the world except matter which moves, and matter which moves cannot move otherwise than in space and in time."[20]

Lenin, consequently, identifies being and matter, i.e., Being and materiality. In accordance with this view, the authors of a philosophical dictionary wrote in 1952 that Being is a "philosophical concept which designates nature, matter, external world, objective reality as distinct from consciousness, thinking, sensation."[21]

The view of Being that identifies Being with material, spatiotemporal Being is certainly not only theoretically possible but also very widespread. It is the everyday, natural, commonsensical, vulgarly materialistic view to which we all tend spontaneously, a conception according to which only material objects have Being.

I do not deny that such a conception of Being has meaning and value. In so far as it opposes religious, mythical, idealistic and solipsistic views on Being (for example, the view that to be means to be perceived), it can be important, positive and progressive. But it cannot by any means be a satisfactory solution for us. If we seriously accept it and think it through consistently to the end, we will be confronted with unbridgeable difficulties. If "Being out of time is just as gross an absurdity as Being outside space," what about our human pains, sufferings, hopes, joys and anxieties? Are they merely non-being nonsense, or is everything located somewhere in man's body or outside of it? Is it not too much to say that man's love is in his heart, hatred in his knife, greed in his stomach, generosity in his hands and stinginess in his pocket?

[20] V. I. Lenin, *Materializm i empiriokriticizm,* Ogir 1945, p. 151.

[21] *Kratkij filosofskij slovarj,* Pod redakciej M. Rozentalja i P. Judina (Izdanie tretje, 1952), p. 48.

IV

In supporting his thesis about the inseparability of Being and essence ("*My Being is what my essence is*") Feuerbach also wrote: "Fish *is* in water, but you cannot separate its essence from this Being. Language already identifies Being and essence. Only in man's life, and even then only in abnormal, unlucky cases, is Being separated from essence—it happens that where somebody has his Being he does not have his essence, but just because of this separation he is not in truth, with his soul, where he really is with his body. Only where your heart is, *are you*. But all beings—if one excepts contranatural cases—are glad to be where they are, and enjoy to be what they are."[22]

After quoting the above ideas of Feuerbach, Marx comments: "A splendid apologia for the existing. Except in contranatural cases, in a small number of abnormal cases, you may contentedly at the age of seven be a porter in a coal mine, fourteen hours alone in darkness, and as this is your Being, it is also your essence. The same applies to a *piecer* on a *self-actor*.[23] It is your 'essence' to be subsumed under one branch of work."[24]

Feuerbach's argumentation for the identity of Being and essence was also discussed by Marx in the *German Ideology*: "As an example of the recognition and at the same time miscognition of the existing, still common to Feuerbach and our opponents, we recall the place in the *Philosophy of the Future* where he explains that the Being of the one thing or man is at the same time his essence, the definite existential relationships, ways of life and activities of animal or human individuals are those in which their 'essence' feels satisfied. Any exception is here ex-

---

[22] Feuerbach, *Sämtliche Werke,* bd. II, s. 311.

[23] The *self-actor* is part of a spinning machine which works automatically, and a *piecer* is a young girl who supervises the machine and binds any broken threads.

[24] Marx, Engels, *Werke,* bd. III, s. 543.

pressly conceived as an unlucky accident, as an abnormality which cannot be changed. Hence if millions of proletarians do not feel satisfied in their conditions of life, if
their 'Being' . . . to their . . . in reality also for the *practical* materialist, i.e., *communist,* the task is to revolutionize
the existing world, to effect practically and change what
they find."[25]

Despite the deletions in the text, Marx's thought is sufficiently clear. Obviously the two texts quoted complement
each other. Both unambiguously show that Marx did not
regard "metaphysical" discussions such as that about the
relationship between "Being" and "essence" as mere speculative absurdities but as important controversial questions,
which deserve attention. The texts also show that Marx
has a definite view concerning this "metaphysical" question: he rejects the identification of Being and essence.
But Marx's texts also show something even more important: the angle from which he approaches the problem,
his basic philosophical position and the intention with
which he philosophizes.

In trying to determine the general relationship between
Being and essence, Feuerbach starts from the relationship
between Being and essence in fish, and looks from this fish
perspective at the relationship between Being and essence
in general and the relationship between Being and essence
in man. Therefore there is nothing strange in the fact that
what really is an abnormality in man, but a "normal" abnormality (because both the possibility of this abnormality,
of man's alienation from himself, and the possibility of a
revolutionary abolition of this abnormality, the possibility
of de-alienation, are founded in "human nature") is regarded by him as a pure abnormality, an irremediable,
unlucky accident to which we must reconcile ourselves.
In this way he not only misses the Being and essence of
man, but also accepts a conservative, or, to put it mildly,
nonrevolutionary philosophical position.

Marx, on the contrary, thinks that the general solution

[25] *Ibid.,* s. 42.

of the question about the relationship between Being and essence can be achieved only if we approach it from the perspective of man's Being and essence. The relationship between Being and essence in man is, for Marx, an essential signpost for solving the question concerning the relationship between Being and essence in general. And as a decisive "test" for the validity of the solution, Marx takes contemporary man and his Being, "millions of proletarians," seven-year-old porters in coal mines, young girls on self-actors. These examples, however, which illustrate Marx's "concrete" approach to "abstract" philosophical problems, can be misleading. One might think that Marx's philosophy has been "deduced" or "inferred" from such "concrete" examples. In fact, the basis of Marx's approach is a general philosophical viewpoint that cannot be "inferred" from examples, or from anything existing, the viewpoint that "the task is to revolutionize the existing world, to effect practically and change what is found."

The same basic principle is demonstrated by Marx when he criticizes Edgar Bauer for disregarding the difference between Being and thinking. "They (the workers) feel very painfully the *difference* between *Being* and *thinking*, between *consciousness* and *life*. They know that property, capital, money, wage, work, etc., are by no means ideal dreamings but very practical, very objective products of their self-alienation, which, consequently, must be abolished in a practical, objective way, in order that man may become man not only in *thinking*, in *consciousness*, but in the massive *Being*, in life."[26]

It would be possible to find a number of similar examples. This is not necessary, however. All examples would show the same thing: Marx never considered the question about Being from all sides and in detail. But there are in Marx interesting and important suggestions for approaching it. The most important may be the one just mentioned: the road to the understanding of Being does not start from fish but from man, not from those most simple,

[26] Marx, Engels, *Werke*, bd. II, ss. 55–56.

most empty "modes" of Being, but from the most complex
and fullest—from man's praxis.

V

According to Martin Heidegger, the question about the
meaning of Being is the main question of contemporary
thought and the contemporary world in general. Philosophy has not only not succeeded in answering this question,
but does not even ask it any more. Not only do we not
really know what to be means, but we are not in the least
embarrassed because we don't. In the race for a complete
and exhaustive knowledge of being, the question about
Being has fallen into oblivion. The awakening of understanding on this question is regarded by Heidegger as his
historical mission.

It is impossible to summarize here everything that
Heidegger wrote about Being. We will content ourselves,
therefore, with only some brief remarks.

While he wishes to attain an understanding of the
meaning of Being in general, Heidegger, like Marx, holds
that the question about the meaning of Being in general
cannot be separated from the question about the meaning
of man's Being (*Dasein*). In his chief work, *Sein und Zeit*,
this idea appears in radical form: the analysis and the
solution of the question about man's Being should *precede*
the analysis of the question about Being in general. The
fundamental endeavor of *Sein und Zeit* is to force one's
way through the analysis of the meaning of man's Being to
the meaning of Being in general.

Heidegger did not proceed to the end of the road that
he took in *Sein und Zeit*. He stopped when he had finished
with the question about the meaning of man's Being, and
just as he got to the question about the meaning of
Being in general. After he had analyzed the meaning of
man's Being and concluded that the fundamental constitution of *Dasein* is "Being-in-the-World," its Being, care and
the meaning of its Being, temporality, Heidegger at the
end of the first half of his main work gave hints of how he

would in the sequence solve the question about Being in general. "The existential-ontological constitution of the *Dasein* whole is rooted in temporality. Consequently an original mode of the temporalization of the extactic temporality must make possible the extactic project of Being in general. How one ought to interpret this mode of the temporalization of temporality? Does road from original *time* lead to the meaning of *Being*? Does *time* reveal itself as the horizon of *Being*?"[27]

An answer is certainly foreshadowed here. But it is not more than foreshadowed. The part in which this answer should have been developed, which was to bear the title "Time and Being," was never written.

The answer was not systematically developed in Heidegger's subsequent works, although it appears in some places in a fairly "explicit" or "clear" form. Thus, in his 1949 "Introduction" to his 1929 work, *Was ist Metaphysik*, Heidegger writes: " 'Being' in *Sein und Zeit* is not something other than 'time,' in so far as 'time' is given as a name for the truth of Being, which truth is the essencing (*das Wesende*) of Being and in this way Being itself."[28]

In his *Introduction to Metaphysics* (*Einführung in die Metaphysik*, a lecture from 1934, published in 1953), Heidegger addresses himself directly to the question about Being in general, while he only touches in passing the question about the meaning of man's Being. But even here the introductory explanations take sway over those that should be concluding. After he has in an interesting way discussed the grammar and the etymology of the word *sein* ("to be") Heidegger himself reduces the value of these considerations to the right measure by remarking that the "question about Being is not a matter of grammar and etymology."[29]

[27] M. Heidegger, *Sein und Zeit*, Siebente unveränderte Auflage (Tübingen, 1953), s. 437.

[28] M. Heidegger, *Was ist Metaphysik*, Siebte Auflage (Frankfurt) a.m. s. 17.

[29] M. Heidegger, *Einführung in die Metaphysik* (Tübingen, 1953), s. 66.

From ancient times to our day attempts have been made to explain Being by way of delimitation, by determining its relationship toward what is different from it, but as something different nevertheless belongs to it. Very often Being has been determined through its relationship to "nothing" or "non-Being"; not much more rarely, through its relationship to essence. The determination of Being through the oppositions mentioned is also found in some of Heidegger's writings. In his *Introduction to Metaphysics*, however, he maintains that there are four decisive, mutually connected contrapositions, which have their own necessity, which have developed in the course of the history of philosophy and which permeate our whole knowledge, action and talking outside philosophy also. These decisive oppositions are: 1.) Being and becoming (*Sein und Werden*); 2.) Being and appearance (*Sein und Schein*); 3.) Being and thinking (*Sein und Denken*); 4.) Being and ought (*Sein und Sollen*). The consideration of these oppositions brings Heidegger to the following conclusions:

"Being as opposed to becoming is remaining (*das Bleiben*).

Being as opposed to appearance is the lasting model, always the same (*das Immergleiche*).

Being as opposed to thinking is what lies in the foundation, the given 'before the hands' (*das Vorhandene*).

Being as opposed to ought is the always 'before-lying' (*das je Vorliegende*) as a not-yet or already realized ought.

Remaining, always-the-sameness, before-handness, before-lying—they are basically the same: the enduring presence (*ständige Anwesenheit*): *on* as *ousia*."[30]

What in these oppositions is opposed to Being (becoming, appearance, thinking, ought) is not, however, something merely imagined, a pure nothing; it is also a kind of Being. But becoming, appearance, thinking, ought cannot possess Being in that sense of Being in which they are opposed to Being. This means that the traditional inher-

[30] *Ibid.*, s. 154.

ited concept of Being is not sufficient for thinking about all that is. Thus, also in this work Heidegger concludes that the opposition that leads to a decisive clarification of Being is none of the four enumerated but what is expressed by the words *Being* and *time*. Unfortunately, even here Heidegger does not say much more about this decisive contraposition than he does in his main work.

VI

Both Marx and Heidegger regard the question about the meaning of Being in general as inseparable from the question about the meaning of man's Being. But their answer to the question about the meaning of man's Being is not the same, and neither is their answer to the question about the meaning of Being in general. The meaning of man's Being according to Heidegger is *temporality;* according to Marx, free creative activity, *praxis*. What Heidegger means under "temporality" has some points in common with what Marx calls *praxis*. The two concepts are nevertheless fundamentally different.

Determining the Being of *Dasein* as care (*die Sorge*), Heidegger points out that he uses this word "purely ontologically-existentially," and not in the sense of some ontic tendency of Being such as concern or lack of concern. Equally, in defining the meaning of care as temporality, Heidegger expostulates against the traditional conception of time according to which time times itself from the present. To the conception according to which time is only an infinite, passing and irreversible series of "now"-points Heidegger opposes his view according to which "extactic-horizontal temporality temporalizes itself *primarily* from the future."[31]

Without disputing Heidegger's merits for seeing the essential connection between Being and time, without denying the importance of his critique of the vulgar conception of time, one must nevertheless observe that seeing the fun-

[31] Heidegger, *Sein und Zeit,* s. 426.

damental significance of time is not a "discovery" of Heidegger. Understanding of the essential significance of time is found even in the everyday nonphilosophical conscience. A popular riddle whose answer is Time says: "He is the father of all things. He awaits and survives everything."

Heidegger is not even the first to develop the idea of the fundamental importance of time for Being philosophically. Kant believed, for example, that time is a subjective form of our inner sense, but, because of that, also the formal condition a priori of all appearance in general. While space as a pure form of external perception is the condition a priori only for external appearances, time is a condition a priori of all appearances in general, an immediate precondition of the "internal," and a mediate precondition of the "external." In other words, all "appearances" in general, all objects of the senses are, according to Kant, in time, and they are necessarily in time relations.

Heidegger's conception of time and of its relationship to Being is not identical with Kant's, or with anyone else before him. But even time conceived in a new way is not sufficient for determining the essence of man, and Heidegger's determination of man primarily through time has "unpleasant" consequences. Perhaps most "unpleasant" for Heidegger himself is that, despite his main antinihilistic direction, he himself retains the position of a kind of nihilism, which, by reducing man's Being to Being toward death, sees as the highest human vocation to endure in such a Being to be without trying to evade his most proper and most necessary possibility, to be without illusions in self-aware and anxious freedom to death.

This nihilism, clearly expressed in *Sein und Zeit* and brought to its logical consequence in *Was ist Metaphysik* —where the *Dasein* is determined as "stretchedness into nothing," and man as "placeholder" (*Platzhalter*) of nothing—is more verbally than actually overcome in Heidegger's later writings, where he declares that nothing is at the same time the "neighbor" and "shepherd of Being."

The other "unpleasant" consequence of reducing the

meaning of Being to temporality is that Heidegger in his praiseworthy endeavor to rise above the traditional abstract opposition between optimism and pessimism goes no further than a quietistic optimism. He maintains that the oblivion of Being, which in contemporary technology assumes forms unseen so far, is neither final nor inescapable, but he cannot say anything about where this possible way out is. In remarking helplessly that "nobody can know whether, when, where and how" thinking will make the decisive true step, he merely advises us to wait patiently for the coming of Being.

In the spirit of Marx we can counter this view: Man is certainly Being toward death, and his transitoriness is not merely an unimportant and accidental determination. But man is not that alone, and truly human Being is not a passive expectation of "nothingness" or "coming of Being." Man is man not when he passively and patiently awaits the inescapable burden that time brings us, but when he acts and fights to realize his real human individual and social Being. And truly human Being is not the proud expectation of nothingness, but free creative activity through which man creates his world and himself.

Should not we perhaps distinguish between creative human activity as authentic human Being (*bivstvovanje*) and through-Being (*bitisanje*) as alienated, purely transient Being? And is not even through-Being (*bitisanje*) something unattainable by an animal or plant, which in its it-Being (*bivovanje*) does not attain awareness of Being, although it is above the mere there-Being (*bićenje*) of dead beings?

The diversity of the forms and levels of Being should not conceal the unity of Being. And if the meaning of man's Being is not only temporality but free creative activity, is not the meaning of Being of nonhuman beings overlooked if it is reduced to time? Is not that conception of material things closer to truth that, among qualities proper to matter, gives first place to motion, "however not only *mechanical* and *mathematical* motion, but primarily as *drive, life, spirit, elasticity,* as *torment*—to use the expression Jakob Böhme uses—of matter."[32]

The question we raised in the beginning: "Is praxis only one among the many modes of Being, or is it in an exceptional relationship to Being?" can consequently be answered by another question: Is not praxis that most authentic "mode" of Being that reveals the true meaning of Being, and therefore is not a special mode but the developed essence of Being? Is not *praxis* the starting point that makes it possible for us to see both the essence of the nonauthentic "lower" forms of Being and the meaning of Being "in general"?

[32] Marx, Engels, *Werke,* bd. II, s. 135.

Truth and reflection

We sometimes talk a lot and say little. Often to say something is beyond our power, but the amount we talk depends on our will; therefore I will state briefly what I think about truth and reflection. I will sum it up in seven theses, adding to these only a few words of explanation.

1. Is truth a kind of reflection? The answer obviously depends on what one means by "truth" and "reflection."

2. We may answer someone who asks "What is truth?" by asking him: "If you don't know what 'truth' means *what* are you asking about? And if you know, *why* are you asking?" The ambiguous question "What is truth?" becomes definite if we specify the conditions to be satisfied by the answer, if we indicate the fore-concept whose conceptual fixation is required.

3. Truth-adequacy, truth-evidence, truth-coherence, truth-usefulness, truth-universal validity, truth-praxis, truth-man, truth-reality, truth-Being, etc.—each of these concepts could be the real concept of truth. In reality none of them is, in an absolute sense, either "real" or "false." They are all different concepts.

4. Many meanings of the word "truth" and variations of the concept "truth" are not mere historical accidents. Different meanings of truth cannot be reduced to one "real"; but there is something that mutually connects them. Therefore, philosophy cannot be satisfied simply by "defining precisely" some arbitrarily chosen meaning of truth (like the "semantic definition of truth"); it should show the inner sense of this multimeaningness. It is the task of philosophy, for example, to show how "ontological" truth makes possible "anthropological," "ethical," "aesthetical," "logical" and "epistemological."

5. The "theory of reflection" cannot be "refuted" by a simple indication that truth "really" is not a property of

the proposition, but the essence of man or Being. Because a theory of reflection, such as was advocated, for example, by Lenin, is not a theory of truth or knowledge at all, but a theory of thinking, consciousness or mind. Its essence is in the thesis that mind is a "function of brain, reflection of the external world." Even Lenin's theory of truth (theory of adequacy or correspondence), however, cannot be "refuted" by an appeal to "ontological" or "anthropological" theory of truth. One theory cannot be refuted by another theory about another question.

6. Taken literally, the theory of reflection is incompatible with Marx's conception of man as a creative being of praxis. The "corrected" variant of this theory, which could be made by starting with Lenin's *Philosophical Notebooks*, would be a "theory of reflection" in name only. Attempts at saving the theory of reflection do not have much chance of success.

7. Abandoning the theory of reflection need not mean accepting idealism and subjectivism. As one of the forms of man's practical, creative activity, thinking is nevertheless in a double sense thinking of being in its Being: in the sense that it belongs to a certain being as one of its modes of Being and in the sense that it clarifies, changes and enriches being in its Being, even when it is at first sight concerned only with nonbeing.

The above theses certainly do not say all that needs to be said about the question. Perhaps they do not quite adequately express even what I wanted to say. They are, however, an attempt to say something about the question from a certain standpoint. The question is whether consciousness, thinking, knowledge and truth are subjective reflections of objective reality, i.e., whether the theory of reflection held by many Marxists is tenable.

The starting position, expressed in the first theses, and especially in the fourth, is that the question about thinking is not entirely autonomous, that it necessarily presupposes the question about that being which thinks, man, and that the question about man as a being that has a specific way of Being is not independent of the question about Being in general. In other words, the starting point of this exposition is that the "epistemological" question cannot be solved without the "anthropological" or the latter without the "ontological."

The starting point of the theses is also that the "epistemological" question cannot be reduced entirely to the "anthropological" or the "anthropological" to "ontological." If we hold that the question of Being is basic for philosophy, this does not mean that other philosophical questions are unjustified. Even less can a philosophy be reduced to pure epistemology, anthropology or philosophy of nature. All who reduce philosophy to one of these "disciplines" or to a mixture of them, ignoring the essential philosophical question about Being, necessarily remain in the sphere of a noncritical, naïve way of thinking.

From this position I criticize (in the fifth thesis) unsuccessful attempts at a refutation of the theory of reflection. I insist that, although questions about thinking, consciousness, knowledge and truth are dependent on anthropological and ontological questions, one cannot simply refuse to ask them as relatively independent questions. One should try to see what these questions ask, and how the theory of reflection answers them.

There are two basic variants of the theory of reflection. According to one, which we find in Lenin and Todor Pavlov, our entire spiritual life is in essence reflection, and all forms of our consciousness are just different forms of the subjective reflection of objective reality. But it is not consciousness alone that is a reflection: matter, too, possesses a property akin to sensation, the property of reflection. Reflection is a general property of the material world, a property that in its higher form makes up the essence of our entire spiritual life.

In this version then, this is a theory of consciousness or thinking that does not aspire to solve the problem of knowledge and truth by itself, and so introduces a supplementary theory for the solution of this problem. In Engels, Plekhanov and Lenin this is what is called the correspondence theory of truth, a theory according to which our reflections are true when they correspond to reality. Thus in Lenin's interpretation of the theory of reflection, every consciousness is reflection, and reflection can, although it need not, correspond to what it reflects. If there is correspondence, agreement, between reflection and reality, the reflection is true.

According to the second version of the theory of reflection, it is reflection that is the very essence of truth and knowledge. The theory of reflection need not be "supplemented" by any theory of adequation or correspondence. To say that a proposition is true simply means that it reflects reality. This version is in fact encountered more frequently among those who oppose the theory of reflection than among its advocates.

When one says against the theory of reflection that truth is not the reflection of reality but rather praxis, this is a refutation of the theory of reflection that does not attain its goal, a refutation that fails to hit the interpretation according to which consciousness (and not truth) is reflection. The thesis that every consciousness is reflection and the thesis that truth is not reflection need not be in conflict. Conflict arises only if one assumes that truth is a kind, form or quality of consciousness. Those who maintain that truth is praxis refuse without reservation, however, the assumption that truth is a quality of consciousness, or thinking.

Therefore, such a refutation of the theory of reflection does not refute even that version of the theory according to which truth is reflection. It cannot refute it because it in advance takes upon itself another task.

If we say that praxis is man's truth, or that the true life is life in the revolutionary transformation of the world, then we speak of the truth that is a quality of man, not of thinking or of proposition. And it is with precisely this second truth that the theory of reflection and the theory of correspondence are concerned. Accordingly, the theory of truth as praxis is not another theory about the same question, but another theory about another question.

I am perhaps a little incautious when I say without

qualification that "a theory cannot be refuted by another theory about another question." On the basis of this someone might come to think that one theory can be refuted only by another theory about exactly the same question. Different theories about an identical question, at least when complex scientific and philosophical questions are at stake, are not possible, however. The question is not something external to the answer. Consequently, the thesis is a little exaggerated, but it is intended to provide the warning that only those theories that aim at answering "nearly identical," i.e., very similar and closely connected, questions can find themselves in mutual competition.

The theory of truth-praxis and the theory of truth-reflection attempt to solve basically different questions. Therefore, the theory of truth-praxis does not directly refute the theory of reflection, but only partly delimits its validity, leaving to it the whole sphere of consciousness and knowledge and especially the sphere of true propositions.

In my sixth thesis I state the view that the theory of reflection is not tenable even in that narrowed-down field that the theory of truth-praxis leaves. This means that the theory of reflection is not successful, either as a theory of the truth of man's living, or as a theory about the essence of consciousness or as a theory about the truth of our thinking.

I argue that the theory of reflection taken literally is incompatible with Marx's view of man as a creative being of praxis. What is even more important, however, the theory cannot be reconciled with the phenomena of consciousness, knowledge and truth. It is irreconcilable with the phenomenon of consciousness because it cannot show and explain that, and how, all our conscious acts reflect reality. For what do the will and emotions reflect? Are love, hatred, envy and malice only different forms of the reflection of the external objects toward which they are directed?

The theory of reflection appears more acceptable if regarded only as a theory of knowledge and truth. But if we study it more carefully we will see that it is not satisfactory even as a theory of the true proposition. We all daily state true propositions, whose truth we do not doubt in the least, although it is impossible to say what they may reflect. A negative existential proposition, for instance, is true if what it denies does not exist. How can such a proposition be interpreted as the reflection of objective reality? The whole system of mathematical propositions is a system of true propositions, which it is difficult to maintain reflect something. And what is reflected by propositions about the past, the future, about possibilities or impossibilities? The theory of reflection seems to be unable to survive, even as a theory of the true proposition.

I have pointed out that the theory of reflection is irreconcilable with Marx's conception of man as a creative being of praxis. In saying so I do not maintain that this theory cannot be found in Engels and Lenin, or even in Marx. The theory of reflection appears partly even in Marx's eleventh thesis on Feuerbach. Let me here recall the well-known thesis: "The philosophers have only *interpreted* the world in various ways; the point, however, is to *change* it." Let us consider what this means.

The thesis has two parts. The first says what the philosophers have done so far. Consequently, this is a specific historical thesis about philosophers. The second part says: ". . . the point, however, is to *change* it." This, then, is a kind of program, something that should be done, in contradistinction to what the philosophers have done. I do not want to enter into discussion of this thesis as a whole—it contains many problems—but I would like to draw attention to its first part. What does it mean to say: "The philosophers have only interpreted the world in various ways"?

First of all, what is the meaning of "*only* interpreted"? This "only," as indicated by the second part, means: they have not changed it. There has been a great deal of discussion on whether this is a right historical evaluation and whether Marx is, here, just to other philosophers. Leaving aside the question of whether Marx is "just" or "unjust," what is the theoretical basis for such an historical evaluation, if we understand it literally? The assumption obviously is that it is possible to interpret the world without changing it.

In my opinion, this assumption contradicts the essence of Marx's philosophy. An interpretation of the world that does not change the world is both logically and empirically impossible. When man interprets the world, by this very fact he changes at least his conception of the world. In changing his conception of the world he cannot help changing his relationship to the world as well. And in changing his conception and his behavior, he influences the conception and actions of other people with whom he is in different relationships.

It is a special question how much and to what extent a given theory changes the world. In principle, however, it is impossible for a philosophical theory not to change the world at all. It is impossible because every philosophical theory and every interpretation of the world already *is* a specific changing and even creating of the world. Philosophers create different theories, different interpretations of the world. What about these interpretations? Are they something nonexistent, or do they exist somewhere outside the world? Or do they themselves form a newly created part of the world? We sometimes regard philosophical interpretations as something nonexistent. But have not people for centuries lived and died with, for and in such interpretations? Did not people live with Aristotle or Thomas Aquinas; do they not live today with Marx? Is Marx's interpretation of the world somewhere outside the world? Where could that be? Is man divided into two parts, one of which is in the world and the other somewhere outside? Is he in the world only when he eats, sleeps and carries out his animal functions, and outside the world when he thinks and interprets the world?

Elements of the theory of reflection are sometimes encountered even where one would not expect them, for instance, in the first part of Marx's eleventh thesis on Feuerbach viewed in isolation. But this theory contradicts Marx's entire conception of the world and man. According to

Marx, man is a being that has a certain specific mode of Being, and this mode is praxis, i.e., free creative activity. So if we accept the conception that man is a creative being of praxis, it is natural to ask how thinking—as one of the forms of man's free, creative activity—can be a mere reflection of reality.

In order to save the theory of reflection, certain Marxists have maintained that reflection is a creative act. The term "reflection" derives from the sphere of physics, however. It means the "throwing back by a surface of sound, light, heat, etc." *Odraz* (reflection) is a necessary and exactly foreseeable consequence of *sraz* (collision). There is nothing creative about it.

If, in contrast to the original meaning of the word, we interpret reflection as creation, we get what I called (in the sixth thesis) an "improved" variant of the theory of reflection. It is, however, a "theory of reflection" in name only. Such a seeming theory of reflection is probably of no use to anybody.

In his *Philosophical Notebooks,* Lenin writes: "Man's consciousness not only reflects the objective world but also creates it."[1] To a careless reader it may seem that he thus advocates the theory of creative reflection. In fact, when he states that man's consciousness *not only* reflects the world *but also* creates it, Lenin obviously does not identify reflection and creation, but distinguishes between them and even contrasts them.

But if the theory of reflection is untenable, in what direction should the Marxist theory of thinking and knowledge be developed? I think one should start from the conception of man as a being of praxis, viewing thinking as a form of man's practical activity.

Thinking is not something nonexistent, but one of the forms of man's Being, one of the ways of changing and creating the world. Let us add that this is not the "lowest" form of praxis, that in his spiritual creativity man is perhaps more creative than anywhere else. The products of

[1] Lenin, *Philosophical Notebooks,* p. 184.

spiritual creation are often more lasting than those of purely material activity. Aeschylus' and Sophocles' plays, Aristotle's and Plato's works continue to live, while many products of ancient material culture have disappeared without trace.

What is meaning?

Mihailo Marković was first not only among Yugoslav Marxists but also contemporary Marxists in general to study carefully the problem of meaning, which is one of the central problems of contemporary philosophy. In his book *Dialectical Theory of Meaning*[1] he provides an excellent review and critique of the most important modern theories of meaning and advances his own original conception of meaning. This conception, expounded systematically, explained in detail and strongly supported by argumentation, can bear comparison with most important contemporary theories of meaning. Regardless of whether we agree with it or not, we can neither circumvent it nor pass it by in silence.

Dialectical Theory of Meaning is one of the most important philosophical books to have been published in Yugoslavia in the postwar period. The aim of this essay is not, however, to assess the value of the book or to ponder its "positive" and "negative" sides. I would merely like to state my own views on some questions that are raised in it, on which a fruitful philosophical dialogue is possible.

The Problem of Meaning and the Theory of Meaning

In the introductory part of his book Marković remarks that the problem of meaning has "different levels of generality," depending upon whether we have in mind: 1.) "the meaning of symbols and signs in general"; 2.) "the meaning of those symbols which are of more immediate interest for philosophy (and these are the terms of ordinary and scientific language, art symbols, moral predicates)"; or

[1] M. Marković, *Dijalektička teorija značenja*, "Nolit" (Beograd, 1961), 542 pp.

3.) "the meaning of those symbols by the help of which philosophical theories (philosophical categories and principles) are expressed."

The concept of meaning in its broadest sense includes "all problems of human communication and interpretation" so that "its complex consideration surpasses the exclusive framework of philosophy." This is a "broad field for collective investigations by philosophers, sociologists, anthropologists, social psychologists, linguists, ethnologists, etc." Neither epistemology, nor logic, nor even ontology is broad enough for this. Cassirer's "philosophy of symbolic forms" can be conceived as "one of the new philosophical disciplines that attempt to overcome this defect," but "those who do not wish to increase the number of philosophical disciplines" ought to reserve a place for these problems "within so-called general philosophy, i.e., general philosophical theory and method."

On the second, more special level of generality we no longer meet all signs, but "*symbols* which have a more or less expressed rational character, subject to theoretical analysis, and which, because of that, are of more special importance for philosophy (for example, symbols of scientific language, art, moral life)." On this level we have to do "*with language in general, with science, arts and morals,* in other words, with objects that are studied in the first place by special scientists (linguists, historians and theorists of art, anthropologists, sociologists, etc.)." Philosophers (logicians, aestheticians, moralists) are concerned with these objects "only in so far as they give general theoretical and methodological foundations for the work of specialists."

Finally, the third, most special, "more narrowly philosophical" level on which the problem of meaning appears is that on which we are confronted with problems of the meaning of philosophical language. The investigation of these problems is the object of "logic in a sufficiently broad sense of the word." It is often considered that the province of logic comprises only problems about the meaning of one part of philosophical terms ("those that concern the processes of thinking and knowing"), while problems of meaning of all other categories belong to the corresponding philosophical disciplines (ontology, ethics, aesthetics) or to their metatheories. In the opinion of Marković, it is acceptable that problems about the meaning of terms of different philosophical disciplines are part of their metatheories, but as "all metatheories nevertheless fall in a certain sense under logic," i.e., as "every metatheory really is a special logic or a part of logic," this does not contradict the thesis that problems of meaning of all disciplines are part of logic.

In another section of his "Introduction" ("The place of the theory of meaning in logic") the author expresses the view that there are "three basic groups of conditions that one formulated thought (proposition) ought to satisfy in order to be accepted as objectively true." These are: "1.) social communicability; 2.) theoretical provability, i.e., justifiability; 3.) practical verifiability, i.e., successful practical applicability." In accordance with this, one can divide logic into three parts: the theory of meaning, the theory of proof and the theory of verification. Theory of meaning is the introductory part of logic, that part in which "conditions of communicability and analiticity of propositions, logical criteria of sense and nonsense, as well as all other problems about meaning on whose solution the establishing or truth depends" are studied.

It seems justifiable to distinguish between the "levels of generality" in the problem of meaning. But in connection with the three levels Marković distinguishes several questions arise.

I

Is that level of meaning really most general in which it is a question of the "meaning of symbols and signs in general," i.e., "all problems of human communication and interpretation"? Is not that level more general on which we discuss the meaning of man's meaningful acts in general, i.e., meaning as a component or aspect of every really human existence and activity?

In science and in everyday life people quarrel all the time, not only about the meaning of words and other signs, but also about the meaning of human deeds and historical events, about the meaning of single persons, of social groups, movements, organizations and institutions.

Historians not only describe historical events; they also quarrel about the meaning of the Crusades, of the discovery of America, of Humanism and the Renaissance, of Napoleon Bonaparte, of the October Revolution. Those who do not go further than the mere enumeration of historical data are considered poor historians. Does the word "meaning" have one meaning when we speak of the meaning of historical personalities and events, and quite a different meaning when we speak about the meaning of words or mythological symbols? Or are we in fact talking here about different forms or kinds of one and the same basic phenomenon?

Not only in history, sociology, economics and other social sciences are we concerned with meaning. A prime minister suddenly interrupts his holiday and returns to his capital; in a certain country the head of the general staff is deposed; a rebellion breaks out somewhere; one peaceful country has massed troops on the borders of another, equally peaceable country; not only politicians, but also ordinary people all around the world make guesses about the meaning of these events. A friend passes us without salutation; an enemy affectionately smiles at us; a well-known deceiver offers a favor; in these and in many other cases we ask the question: What does this mean?

Do we use "meaning" in these cases in some wrong way, or are we here considering only different modifications of one and the same basic phenomenon of meaning? What is the essence of meaning?

This question is not easy to answer. Nevertheless, as a stimulus for discussion we can formulate the following theses:

1. Meaning is a phenomenon tied to man. Phenomena

in nonhuman nature can be described, compared, classified; asking about their meaning makes no sense. Meaning is present only when man is an agent—not man as a physical object or biological being, but man as a being of *praxis*.

2. Meaning of one deed, act, event is not identical with the external existence, givenness, appearance, of this deed, act or event. Meaning is something internal, hidden, nonobvious, which has to be found out, discovered, revealed.

3. That internal, nonobvious quality, owing to which something is what it is, is usually called "essence." Meaning is not the same as essence. Meaning is that internal through which a thing is not only what it is but also something else. It is through meaning that a human deed is essentially connected with some other deed, included in a broader human meaningful whole.

4. The meaning of an act is not the same as its essence, but neither is it something to which a deed is related externally, superficially, inessentially. The meaning of a phenomenon is something with which it is essentially, internally connected.

5. It is an essential characteristic of every really human act that it is not only what it externally is, that it is a constituent part of man's active self-expression. Therefore, meaning is not something present *only* when man is in action; it is also *always* present when man as man is active.

II

The way in which Marković determines the second level of meaning suggests that one should distinguish between the two basic groups of symbols: those "that have a more or less expressed rational character, liable to theoretical analysis, and that are therefore of special importance for philosophy (for example, symbols of scientific language, arts, moral life)" and those that do not have "a more or less expressed rational character" so that they are not "liable to theoretical analysis," nor are they of special importance for philosophy. Such considerations invite a number of questions:

1. Is it possible to divide symbols into those that have a more or less expressed rational character and those that do not? If we accept that "every symbol is first of all a material object," then by dividing symbols into those that have and those that do not have a "rational character" we assume that single material objects may be rational and irrational. This assumption does not seem acceptable even if "material object" is interpreted very broadly as a "thing, word, picture, tone, movement." A word, for example, may serve to express, describe, justify, criticize, etc., rational or irrational beliefs, hopes, fears, actions, human deeds in general. But it seems strange to classify any single word, as such, as rational or irrational. The same seems to hold for other kinds of symbols. Indeed, what conditions should a symbol satisfy in order to be regarded as rational?

2. If we assume that symbols can be divided into rational and irrational, then the question arises: Can only that which has a "more or less expressed rational character" be liable to theoretical analysis? "Ritual, mythical and religious symbols" are listed by Marković among irrational symbols. Are they really "not liable to theoretical analysis"?

3. Finally, does a "special importance for philosophy" belong *only* to that and at the same time to *all* that which has a "more or less expressed rational character," i.e., to that which is "liable to theoretical analysis"?

III

Concerning the third level one might ask whether the singling out of the question about the meaning of philosophical terms into a separate "level" means that philosophical terms possess meaning in some other sense than the words of ordinary language and terms of science and art.

I am inclined to answer this question in the affirmative. Philosophy is a specific spiritual activity different from both science and the arts, and the criterion according to which we determine whether an expression has meaning cannot in philosophy be quite the same as in science or the arts.

I have the impression that Marković, however, by separating the problem of meaning of philosophical terms into a special "level of generality" does not think that we here have to do with a special way or kind of meaning. By the problem of meaning of philosophical terms he understands the question of how to define concretely all those single terms that are used in philosophy. If philosophical terms, however, do not mean in a special way but only mean something else, what reasons are there for speaking of the meaning of philosophical terms as a separate question?

Concerning the division of the problem of meaning into different levels of generality, the question naturally arises about the sciences or theoretical disciplines that study this problem at different levels. What can we say about these?

1. We can agree that certain problems of meaning are also found outside philosophy. But it does not seem useful to say that this is a field for "collective investigations by philosophers, sociologists, anthropologists, social psychologists, linguists, ethnologists, etc." When we discuss *philosophical* problems of meaning, when we speak, for example, about the meaning of meaning, no collective can help a philosopher: he has to formulate and solve his problems by himself.

We may agree that no traditional philosophical discipline can comprehend all philosophical problems of meaning. We must add only that no philosophical discipline can comprehend any real philosophical problem—without previously simplifying and narrowing it down. Therefore, it is unnecessary to create a new philosophical discipline that would investigate the problem of meaning. It is an acceptable suggestion that meaning may be discussed within the limits of "the so-called general philosophy, i.e., general philosophical theory and method."

To speak about meaning is to speak about one essential dimension of man's practical activity, and to speak of *praxis* means to speak of the most authentic form of the Being of the being. Therefore the question concerning meaning is at the same time "ontological," and "anthropological," and "epistemological" and "logical," consequently, in the full sense, philosophical.

2. Not only was the second level of the problem of meaning not clearly defined, it is equally unclear as to who is to study this level. To all appearances, the work should be divided between special scientists and philosophers, not general philosophers but philosophical specialists (logicians, aestheticians, moral philosophers). The author's conception is insufficiently clearly expressed on this point.

3. The author's view about the third level on which the problem of meaning appears was formulated much more clearly, but does not seem acceptable. His conception is that the problem of the "meaning of philosophical language" is to determine the meaning of basic philosophical categories, and that this task falls under logic. This conception, according to which logic determines the meaning of all philosophical categories, and other "philosophical disciplines" (ontology, ethics, aesthetics) take over from logic clearly defined categories and without discussing their "meaning" only *by the help of them* formulate their own theses, seems untenable to me.

The difference between (true or false) theses and (conventional) definitions often fails in philosophy. But even in those cases where we can differentiate between "definitions" and "theses," the defining of concepts, if we wish to obtain "usable" concepts, cannot be made entirely independently of the formulation of the theses that we wish to express "by the help of" them.

In the section concerning levels of generality of the problem of meaning, three levels have been distinguished; in the section about the place of the theory of meaning in logic, three main parts of logic have been discerned, and the theory of meaning has been characterized as the first, introductory part of it. The question naturally imposes itself: On which of the three "levels of generality" of the problem of meaning mentioned is the theory of meaning taken as one of the three parts of logic concerned?

The theory of meaning as a part of logic is obviously too narrow to comprehend the first, most general level of meaning, not only when this level is taken more broadly as we conceive it, but even when this level is taken more narrowly, as it is interpreted by Marković. In discussing the most general level, the author himself acknowledges that it is too broad for logic and for any other special philosophical discipline.

To all appearances, logic is also too narrow to comprehend the whole second level of meaning. From what was said about that level, it appears that not only logicians, but also aestheticians and other philosophical specialists, are concerned with it.

Finally, what was said about the third level of generality clearly does not agree with what was said about the threefold division of logic. In discussing the third level it was maintained that logic investigates the meanings of all philosophical terms; in the threefold division of logic there is no mention of the theory of meaning as a discipline that would investigate and determine the meanings of philosophical terms.

So far as I can see, the doctrine about the three levels of generality could be reconciled with the doctrine about the threefold division of logic only by saying that the theory of meaning as a part of logic studies one part of the problem of meaning on the "second level," and that one special branch of this theory investigates the problem of meaning on the third level. But in order to make this reconciliation more than merely formal, one should perhaps reformulate both the problem of meaning on the second and the third level and the task of the theory of meaning as a part of logic.

Taking into account all the difficulties mentioned, however, it is perhaps better to make a more profound change in determining the levels of generality of the problem of meaning.

If we grant that the problem of meaning in its most general form concerns the meaning of any human act, then the question of the transition to a more specific level of generality is a question of distinguishing between the kinds, forms or aspects of human activity. We may consequently say that the problem of meaning has as many different forms and subforms as there are forms and subforms of man's practical activity.

If this problem most frequently and most sharply arises in the form of the question about the meaning of *words*, this is not a matter of chance, nor is it anything deplorable. The word is the most powerful guardian and creator of meaning. It is not a mistake to discuss the meaning of words; but it is erroneous to think that only words mean something.

Meaning as a Complex of Relations, and Relations as Forms of Meaning

Marković regards the final goal of his book as "providing a general definition of meaning and establishing general conditions of effective communication among men." Leaving aside general conditions of effective communication, I shall discuss the general definition of meaning.

In trying to accomplish the task he has chosen, the author came to the conclusions: 1.) that "meaning is not only one separated relation but a complex of relations"; 2.) that "all existing modern theories of meaning are one-sided, because they separate only one relation from this complex"; 3.) that these one-sided theories "are not mutually exclusive but complementary"; and 4.) that a "synthetic, dialectical approach to the problem should lead to a complex truth whose special moments are particular truths of single existing theories."

In the "structure of relations which we call meaning" the author sees five "specific moments":

"1.) A relation of the sign toward a certain mental disposition of the subject (*mental meaning*).

2.) A relation of the sign toward a designated object (*objective meaning*).

3.) A relation of the sign toward other signs of the given system (*linguistic meaning* in so far as the given system of signs is a language).

4.) A relation between two or more subjects some of which use the sign, whereas others interpret it (*social meaning*).

5.) A relation of sign to certain practical actions of the subject (*practical meaning*)."

This conception of meaning as a complex of five relations according to the author's view does not contradict Peirce's view about meaning as a triadic relation. Meaning can be conceived as "in the *last analysis* a triadic relation between the sign, 'the interpretant' and the designated object," but as the "interpretant" can be analyzed into four elements (mental, linguistic, practical and social) it is more correct to say that meaning "in fact is a six-termed relation."

In his book, Marković studied separately and in detail all "components" of meaning except the social one. In agreement with that he at some places characterizes the meaning as a complex of four (not five) relations (social meaning is not mentioned as a separate relation).

Defending his thesis of meaning as a complex of four relations, Marković also discusses the question: "Is the merging of two elements possible (in other words, must all four elements always be given distinctly as a condition for saying that one sign has a definite meaning)?"

Answering this question, he concedes that "in many cases the meaning of one sign cannot be distinctly analyzed into all four components" and that symbols even exist in which "all components of meaning are merged into one." But despite that he believes that "in so far as conditions are at all imaginable under which the meaning of a symbol represents the whole whose content is difficult to analyze into special components, the fact remains that the same content nevertheless has its different aspects: mental, linguistic, objective and practical."

But according to Marković, the definition of meaning cannot stop at the enumeration of basic components of meaning; it must also precisely state their "mutual structure." Such a definition is what in ordinary language (the author expresses it also by means of a formula) says:

"Symbol S_i is meaningful = Df an object exists that is the consequence of a set of practical operations; and to this object a disposition of mental reaction corresponds proper to the set of subjects X, which appears as a consequence of the symbol S_i and is symbolically expressed through the relation S_i toward the set of symbols S."

This definition seems to be expressed even more precisely in the summaries in foreign languages where it says:

"The symbol S_i is meaningful = Df the symbol S_i is associated (i) with an object O which is designated by it, (ii), a set of practical operations P, which are both determined by O and constitutive for it, (iii) a disposition of mental reaction M, which corresponds to the features of O and P and (iv) a system of symbols S such that S_i is a member of S and the relations of S_i toward other members of S express M, describe O and indicate possibilities of P."

In this briefly summarized theory one may perhaps notice first that the author vacillates on whether to acknowledge social meaning as a separate component of meaning or not, and that in accord with this he sometimes speaks of five and sometimes (more often) of four component relations of meaning. The question whether social meaning is a separate component of meaning might be very interesting, but it presupposes the general conception of meaning as a complex of relations. Therefore, until we have considered this conception, we may leave the question aside.

One is also struck by the fact that, according to Marković, the thesis about meaning as a complex of four (or five) two-termed relations with one common term is identical with his thesis about meaning as a five-termed (or six-termed) relation. This is not acceptable because no true polyadic relation can be analyzed into a number of relations with a smaller number of members. "Peter and Paul are taller than John" can be analyzed into "Peter is taller than John" and "Paul is taller than John," but "Peter gives a book to Paul" cannot be analyzed into "Peter gives a book" and "Peter gives to Paul," nor to "Peter gives a book" and "Paul receives a book," nor in any other way. The reason is simply that in the first case we had a conjunction of two two-termed relations expressed in an abbreviated way whereas in the second case we have a real three-termed relation.

It is, however, certainly not essential for Marković whether his conception contradicts Peirce's or not. Let us look, consequently, at his conception in itself.

What about the theory that meaning is a complex of four or five relations (mental, objective, linguistic, practical and maybe social)? If the theory is conceived so that a word has meaning only when it possesses all four or five relations, then it meets many more difficulties than any of the "one-sided" theories of meaning.

The basic difficulty of the realistic theory of the meaning of words is that there are plenty of words that, as it seems, have a meaning, but do not denote any *res*. In order to avoid this difficulty, the adherents of the realistic theory of meaning must resort to some auxiliary hypothesis, such as the theory about irreal objects (Meinong), the theory of autosemantic and synsemantic words (the later Brentano) or the theory of descriptions (Russell). Each of these theories seems clear and obvious to its originator, but unconvincing to the majority of other philosophers.

The greatest difficulty with different mentalistic theories of meaning is that there are many words to which, as it seems, we cannot deny a meaning, although they do not either denote or create mental pictures or any other mental experience. The most serious difficulty of the pragmatic theory of meaning is that some words that have no practical consequences obviously have some meaning.

This applies to all other "one-sided" theories of meaning. We usually reject a "one-sided" theory of meaning because there are words to which we attribute meaning although they do not possess the relation that the theory requires from meaning. In order to remove this difficulty, the theory usually has recourse to some auxiliary hypothesis, which seems acceptable to the adherents of the theory and artificial to others.

If we replace "one-sided" theories of meaning by some "complex" theory, which proposes, as the necessary condition of meaning, the sum of all conditions put forward by "one-sided" theories, it is obvious that this new theory will be richer in requirements, and, consequently, in difficulties and auxiliary hypotheses than those "one-sided" theories—simply because it includes *all* of their requirements, difficulties and auxiliary hypotheses.

This is a point that was partly noticed by Knjazeva. In her review of Marković's book she agrees with the conception of meaning as a complex of relations, but raises the question of whether a greater flexibility would not ensure the conception broader applicability and remove objections that could otherwise be made to it. "Why *must* a symbol have all dimensions of meaning (mental, objective, linguistic, practical, social)? Would it not be sufficient for a theory of meaning to define meaning as a complex of those relations that a symbol has, to consider what all those relations are, and to investigate for every category of symbols what kind of a symbol, of what dimensions of meaning, belong to it?"[2]

If I understand this correctly, she agrees with the thesis about meaning as a "complex of relations," and also with the view that there are five possible different "dimensions" of meaning. But she does not hold that the possession of all five is a necessary condition for possessing meaning. She did not, however, make clear how many

[2] S. Knjazeva, "Neki problemi epistemologije i teorije značenja" ("Some Problems of Epistemology and Theory of Meaning"), *Filozofija*, no. 3, 1962, pp. 56–57.

"dimensions" a "complex of relations" should have in order to be recognized as meaning. The definition of meaning as a *complex* of relations seems to preclude the possibility of reducing meaning to only one relation and suggests that we may speak of meaning only when at least two relations are present.

But regardless of whether we take two, three or four relations as a minimum condition of meaning, this "more flexible" variant of the "dialectical" theory of meaning assumes that none of the five relations is present (or absent) in all cases in which we talk of meaning. If she believed that only some of the five relations are a necessary condition for possessing meaning, whereas others are not, Knjazeva would probably propose introducing into the definition only those relations that characterize every meaning and exclude others from it.

Since she does not do this, and retains all five "dimensions" of meaning, but suggests conceiving meaning as the complex of those dimensions that are given in a certain case, she differs from Marković, not only in her definition of the concept "meaning," but also in her view about the concepts "concept" and "definition."

Whereas Marković accepts the traditional logical view that the definition of a concept should express its essential characteristics and only those characteristics can be essential that are common to all objects (without exception) to which that concept can be applied, Knjazeva obviously leans to a newer view of the concept, which is related to some views of the later Wittgenstein.

According to these views, in order to denote a set of objects or phenomena by the help of a word, it is not necessary that all these objects or phenomena have a common quality, which would be their essence. It is enough that they display what Wittgenstein calls "family resemblances." Wittgenstein's well-known example of this is those activities we call "games." There is nothing common to all games. But if we compare them carefully, we see "a complicated network of similarities overlapping and crisscrossing: sometimes over-all similarities, sometimes similarities of detail." These similarities can be called "family resemblances"; for the various resemblances between members of a family "overlap and crisscross in the same way."[3]

If I understand Knjazeva rightly, the essence of her correction of Marković's theory of meaning is in the suggestion that meaning, like games, should be conceived as a "family," i.e., that the word "meaning" should be given a "flexible" meaning.

We may agree with her that, not only in everyday life, but also in science, we often use words that have a "complex" or "flexible" meaning, words that, as it seems, do not have a quite "precise" meaning but are nevertheless not strictly "ambiguous." Although we cannot find any "characteristics" we always think of when we meaningfully use the word, we apparently do not use it in several different meanings. We are therefore inclined to say that the word has one meaning, which is, however, not "simple" and "crude," but "complex" or "flexible."

Words with such a "flexible" meaning are welcome not only in everyday life but also in science and philosophy; we often need them much more than words whose meaning is "exact," "precise," "not-volatilized." But this is not to say that the meaning of words with a "flexible" meaning cannot be further analyzed. In my view, words with a "flexible" meaning are as a rule ambiguous words with several related meanings.

Tennis and soccer are two different kinds of play in the same basic meaning of the word "play." When two checkmatists *play* a match for the world championship and when a child *plays* by throwing a ball against a wall, these are, on the contrary, two kinds of play, which are subsumed under two different, although in some points related, general concepts of play. I am consequently inclined to regard the word "play" as a word with several

---

[3] Ludwig Wittgenstein, *Philosophische Untersuchungen* (*Philosophical Investigations*), Basil Blackwell (Oxford, 1953), p. 32.

related basic meanings, each of which has a number of submeanings.

Something similar might hold for the word "meaning." Nevertheless, I am inclined to think that the word "meaning," even in ordinary language, nearly always has one and the same basic meaning, but this meaning has a lot of submeanings. Empirical investigation could establish whether this assumption is right or not. But I do not think that such an investigation is indispensable for philosophy.

Asking about meaning is not asking about the word "meaning," but about meaning itself. The actual use of the word "meaning" indicates the essence of the phenomenon of meaning, but it cannot be the decisive criterion for judging whether our definition of meaning is "good" or "bad." On the contrary, the very nature of the phenomenon of meaning is the "criterion" for adequacy or inadequacy of our use of the word "meaning."

Just because the phenomenon of meaning is a general phenomenon, capable of many different modifications, our language is "in order" only if the word "meaning" appears in a variety of modifications with the same general meaning.

I seem to be in agreement with Marković when I maintain that meaning is a very general phenomenon, which is differentiated in many ways. The main difference between the two of us is that, among the most general determinations of meaning, he includes the so-called mental, objective, practical and maybe social meaning, whereas I think that none of these specific relations is the constitutive element of meaning. In my opinion these special relations are determinations only of single specific forms of meaning.

Such a conception of meaning contradicts Marković's explicitly stated theory, but is in accord with the terminology he uses. The four relations he regards as necessary conditions for any sign to have meaning are called by him "mental *meaning*," "objective *meaning*," "linguistic *meaning*" and "practical *meaning*."

If the "relation of a sign toward a certain mental disposition of the subject" is not sufficient to allow meaning to a sign, it is strange to call this relation "mental meaning." It would be more logical to call it the "mental component or mental condition of meaning."

The name "mental meaning" suggests that the "relation of the sign toward a certain mental disposition of the subject" is not one of the conditions of meaning in general, but one of the special forms or kinds of meaning. Something similar holds for names' "objective meaning," "linguistic meaning," "practical meaning." These implicit suggestions of Marković's terminology are more acceptable to me than his explicit theories.

It is my opinion, consequently, that a general definition of meaning should correspond approximately to what was said in the first section of this paper (see theses 1 to 5 on pp. 202–3), and that basic forms of meaning should be determined in approximately the way in which Marković defines basic "moments" or "elements" of meaning.

Marković's rich and detailed analyses of different "dimensions" of meaning basically solve, I think, the question about different kinds of meaning. Even here supplements and corrections are possible, however. Certain distinctions that were made by Marković at one point in his book, but not developed later, could also serve this purpose. Without entering into details (which would mean writing one more book, about meaning) I will only mention:

1.) I agree with Marković when he does not make social meaning parallel to mental, objective and linguistic meaning. It is extraordinarily important to distinguish between the personal and the social meaning (or individual, group and social meaning), but this should not be confused with the difference, which is based on another principle, between the objective, mental and linguistic meaning.

2.) I think that "practical" meaning cannot be made parallel with mental, objective and linguistic. If *praxis* is conceived in a broader sense (as in Marx), all meanings are practical. And if it is conceived in a more narrow way, it is possible to place the practical meaning into some other division.

3.) Parallel to mental, objective and linguistic meaning

one should add conceptual. This is perhaps the most important, but also the most "mysterious," form of meaning. Where "mysteries" begin this paper must end. But discussion should continue.

Logic and mathematics

The relationship between logic and mathematics can be discussed in various ways. The most ideal approach might seem to be first to define both, then to explain these definitions in detail, and, finally, on the basis of definitions, to determine their mutual relationship.

There are various difficulties in the way of this "ideal" procedure, however. It is not so easy to give "good" definitions of logic and mathematics. Many have tried to do it, but we still do not have generally accepted or predominating definitions.

In one of his writings, Bertrand Russell remarks that "mathematics may be defined as the subject in which we never know what we are talking about, nor whether what we are saying is true."[1] This is probably one of the best definitions of mathematics, but it is equally probable that most mathematicians would strongly disagree with it.

The situation is no "better" when we turn to logic. There are a variety of mutually conflicting views concerning the nature of logic: it is difficult to say which is comparatively most widespread, and which most acceptable.

This does not, of course, mean that it is impossible to determine successfully the nature of mathematics and logic and their mutual relationship. But the limits of this exposition are too narrow for a systematic and complex analysis of the question. Instead of starting from definitions of mathematics and logic, I will start from a question suggested by the development of logic and mathematics in the course of the last 120 years.

The history of the relations between logic and mathe-

[1] B. Russell, *Mysticism and Logic* (first published 1918), Penguin Books (1953), p. 75.

matics is well known. May I nevertheless mention that we can divide this history into two main epochs: from the beginning of mathematics and logic until the middle of the nineteenth century, and from then until today.

Logic and mathematics originated independently of each other and up to the middle of the nineteenth century developed independently. Logic first separated itself into a specific theoretical field in the works of Aristotle. When we read the father of European logic, however, we see how his logic grew out of his metaphysics. The basic concepts of Aristotle's logic have their root in metaphysics, but the strong influence of grammar is also visible. Logical and grammatical analyses often intertwine and merge.

In the course of the centuries that followed, logic developed in close connection with metaphysics and other branches of philosophy, but also with grammar and rhetoric. Thus, in the medieval educational system logic, grammar and rhetoric made one educational whole (*trivium*), and arithmetics, geometry, astronomy and music the other (*quadrivium*). In the modern world logic is most frequently found in connection with and merged into the theory of knowledge, but it also approaches and is subsumed under ontology, psychology, anthropology, ethics, axiology.

Whereas logic originated and developed in company with other philosophical disciplines, and also with psychology, grammar and rhetoric, mathematics began and largely developed in connection with natural sciences and practical skills. Its development was in the early days mostly stimulated by the development of astronomy, geometry and mechanics, and later by the growth of other branches of physics and the natural sciences in general. No wonder that some have even directly reckoned mathematics among the natural sciences.

Pythagoras, Plato, Descartes and many other great philosophers were also great mathematicians. But even philosopher-mathematicians did not for centuries think of connecting logic and mathematics. This idea first gained definite shape with Leibniz, but after him immediately fell into oblivion again.

In the course of the last 120 years the situation has fundamentally changed. The notion of the closeness, similarity and even identity of logic and mathematics was formulated clearly and developed in detail in the middle of the last century, and it was soon widely accepted among logicians and mathematicians.

Boole declared in 1847 that logic is not a part of philosophy, that according to the principle of right classification "we have to combine not logic and metaphysics, but logic and mathematics."[2] Logic, according to Boole and other adherents of the algebra of logic, is only a branch of mathematics.

Frege, Russell and other representatives of logistics developed the contrary thesis that mathematics can be deduced from logic. Frege thought that there is no sharp borderline between logic and arithmetic; both make one single science. What was traditionally called arithmetic can be deduced from what was called logic, however; and in this sense we may say that arithmetic is a "branch of logic." Russell developed in detail the more general thesis that *all* mathematics can be deduced from logic. "The fact is that, when once the apparatus of logic has been accepted, all mathematics necessarily follows."[3]

The idea of founding mathematics with the help of logic was energetically opposed by Brouwer, Heyting and other representatives of intuitionism in mathematics. "A mathematical construction," writes Heyting, "ought to be so immediate to the mind, and its result so clear that it needs no foundation whatsoever." But this is not to say that logic and mathematics are essentially different. If we consider logical theorems carefully, we shall see that they are only more general than mathematical theorems. "This

[2] G. Boole, *The Mathematical Analysis of Logic* (Cambridge, 1847; reprinted Oxford, 1951), p. 13.

[3] B. Russell, *The Principles of Mathematics* (first published 1903, second edition 1937, reprinted London, 1951), p. 8.

is the case for every logical theorem: it is but a mathematical theorem of extreme generality; that is to say, logic is a part of mathematics, and can by no means serve as a foundation for it."[4]

The adherents of formalism in contemporary mathematics and logic, Hilbert and his followers, also emphatically reject the idea of deducing mathematics from logic. But they do not insist that logic is a part of mathematics, although they maintain that symbolic logic is "an extension of the formal method of mathematics to the field of logic."[5] It is essential for them to construct both logic and mathematics as formal deductive systems in which the question of the interpretation of symbols has no importance.

In contemporary logic and mathematics there are, consequently, three basic views concerning their mutual relationship: according to one, mathematics is a part of logic; according to the second, logic is a part of mathematics; according to the third, they are two complementary parts of the same science. All of these three opinions have many variants.

All the variants have in common, however, the belief that in our time logic and mathematics have come so close that it is, strictly speaking, impossible to distinguish between them: "Logic has become more mathematical, and mathematics has become more logical. The consequence is that it has now become wholly impossible to draw a line between the two; in fact, the two are one. They differ as boy and man: logic is the youth of mathematics and mathematics is the manhood of logic."[6]

One aspect of the thesis about the merging of logic and mathematics is the assertion that logic, which previously was a philosophical discipline, has now become science.

---

[4] A. Heyting, *Intuitionism* (Amsterdam, 1956), p. 6.

[5] D. Hilbert und W. Ackermann, *Grundrisse der theoretischen Logik* (Berlin, 1928), s. 1; cf. *Principles of Mathematical Logic* (New York, 1950), p. 1.

[6] B. Russell, *Introduction to Mathematical Philosophy* (first published in 1919, eighth impression 1953), p. 194.

And this emancipation of logic from philosophy is regarded as a part of a long and progressive process, a process in which new scientific fields continually secede from philosophy, always leaving it poorer, with a smaller field of action and a diminishing right to mingle with science.

This is the view I would like to comment upon. Has logic really been so fundamentally transformed because of its newly established connection with mathematics that from a speculative philosophical discipline full of unprovable and uncertain assumptions it has become a precise and certain science free from doubts and controversies?

II

If we carefully consider the content of traditional logic, we will notice an internal dualism in it. In addition to certain doctrines that were never contested by anybody who managed to grasp them, we will also find a number of theories and hypotheses over which there is constant conflict and contention without any of them being definitively "established" or "refuted."

The traditional logicians agree on, for example, which are valid forms of the so-called immediate inferences by opposition, subalternation, equipollence, conversion, contraposition; or which are valid modes of categorical, hypothetic and disjunctive syllogism, polisyllogism, etc. But they differ on questions such as: Is the "immediate inference" really an inference or a transformation of the proposition? From which source do valid syllogistic modes derive their validity? What is the cognitive value of single valid modes of syllogism and of syllogism in general? What, in fact, are the syllogism and its elements, concepts and propositions: Are they real mental experiences, linguistic and grammatical creations or ideal structures? Where is the source of the validity of logical principles and rules: In experience, intuition, thought, or convention? Does logic study thinking, thought, language or symbols? Forms, laws, principles, rules or norms? Traditional logic is full of such questions.

In addition to questions on which there is nearly full agreement and those on which almost nobody agrees with anybody else, traditional logic also includes questions that are somehow "in the middle": agreement is widespread but by no means complete. One such question, for example, is the doctrine about the kinds of propositions. The division of propositions developed by Aristotle and Teophrastus and symmetrically rounded up by Kant was basically accepted by the majority of traditional logicians after Kant, although nearly all of them introduced certain corrections in detail.

The existence of such "middle" questions need not contradict the general picture concerning the inner division of logic. It is possible that they are only "complex" questions, which can be analyzed in their "solvable" and "insolvable" parts.

The more carefully we study traditional logic, the more we come to see that theses that remind us of "$2 + 2 = 4$" are intertwined here with those that remind us of those "metaphysical," eternally controversial theses, such as "All is the Absolute Idea" and "All is matter." Nevertheless, these two types of theses cannot be separated; without "metaphysical" theses the "mathematical" ones lose their meaning and interest; without "mathematical" theses, the "metaphysical" remain empty.

Traditional logic was consequently split into a part that was "certain," in the sense in which people think mathematics is, and another part that is as controversial as metaphysics, the part in which it was impossible to achieve any unity and agreement.

But it is an illusion to think that by a synthesis or unification of logic and mathematics this dualism disappeared. Contemporary logic in its symbolic form contains a number of formulas, schemes, rules, principles or laws that are disputed by nobody, although they are differently expressed or systematized by different individuals. Just, however, as in traditional logic, so, too, in modern logic there are controversies about essential questions, often even sharper and more profound.

Look at the simplest part of contemporary logic, the "calculus of propositions." Modern logicians by and large agree on which "formulas" of the calculus of propositions are valid and which are not, and at first it might seem that all differences among them are reduced to how these formulas are systematized, and specifically in which of them are taken, in the axiomatic development of the calculus, as primitive propositions, and which are deduced as theorems. But if we consider the matter more carefully we will see here, too, many other controversial questions. Single contemporary logicians differ even in what they call this part of logic. For some of them, it is the "propositional calculus"; for others "sentential calculus." And some do not like to speak of "calculus," so that they refer simply to the "logic of propositions" or "sentential logic." Behind these different names are hidden not only different stylistic preferences, but also different logical conceptions—for example, disagreement on the question of what the element of this "calculus" is: proposition, statement or sentence.

There is no less disagreement over the logic of predicates, logic of relations, logic of identity and other parts of contemporary logic. And these disagreements are widest not in what concerns this or that special part of contemporary logic, but in questions that concern all of its parts: what logic really is, the nature of its theses, its relationship to other philosophical and scientific disciplines, its value for science and life.

Traditional logic contained some "neutral" doctrines, but it also included questions that were neither "neutral" nor purely logical, questions that were equally epistemological and ontological, hence in a full sense philosophical. Modern logic is not in this respect different in principle from traditional; in addition to many "neutral" formulas it includes a number of discussions that are basically metaphysical and epistemological.

I would not like to maintain that there is no essential difference between traditional, "nonsymbolic" and contemporary, "symbolic" logic. Very great and real differ-

ences exist. But if we were to consider carefully some of
the specific characteristics of contemporary symbolic logic,
characteristics such as the universal use of ideographic
symbols, a consistent formalism and the use of the axiomatic method, we would see that they are not entirely
new. Both the use of ideographic symbols and the view
that logical principles and forms are valid regardless of
content, and even the beginnings of the axiomatic construction of logic, are found in Aristotle.

Without disputing the difference, I insist that there is
a continuity between traditional and contemporary logic,
a continuity greater that has sometimes been assumed,
and especially greater than some ardent adherents of contemporary logic are ready to acknowledge.

This continuity is manifested by the fact that, among
other things, modern logic, like traditional, is "crucified"
between metaphysics and mathematics; it includes fundamental philosophical questions, which always were and
will always remain controversial (which does not mean
that all answers to them are equally good), and also questions it is possible to "solve" (which means to make them
theoretically uninteresting and put them at disposition to
"application").

But the continuity lies not only in "dualism" or "duality,"
but also in the content of the "uncontestable," as well as
in the content of the "controversial" part of logic. In its
"noncontroversial," "precise" and "certain" part, contemporary logic includes the "precise" and "certain" parts of
traditional logic, but also many other things. The "definitive" part of contemporary logic is much richer than the
"definitive" part of traditional logic.

Modern logic's "nondefinitive," "controversial," "discus-
sible" part is also not "poorer," but "richer," than traditional logic's. Many new problems have arisen (for example, problems about the relationship between natural
and artificial languages, problems connected with the construction of axiomatic systems, etc.). But traditional
philosophico-logical problems have not disappeared. Many

controversies in contemporary symbolic logic are only a continuation of controversies in traditional logic, and trends or fighting parties, although they carry new names, are often old and well known.

The eminent American logician W. V. O. Quine believes, for example, that three contemporary doctrines that clash on basic questions of philosophy, mathematics and logic (logicism, intuitionism and formalism) are only new forms of the three medieval views about the nature of universals: realism, conceptualism and nominalism. Logicism, which is represented by Frege, Russell, Whitehead, Church and Carnap, is only a new form of medieval realism; the intuitionism of Poincaré, Brouwer and Weyl represents a new form of conceptualism; and Hilbert's formalism corresponds to medieval nominalism.[7]

What Quine says here also holds for many other contemporary logical problems, trends, doctrines and conceptions—although at first they seem to have nothing in common with those older trends, actually they represent their new forms.

III

The coming together of logic and mathematics in the course of the last 120 years is an uncontestable fact, and the aim of the above exposition was not to dispute it. On the contrary, I partly wanted to explain it, by a reminder that traditional logic also, though formally unconnected with mathematics, contained theses akin to mathematical ones. But I have tried to show that the fact that logic and mathematics are coming closer to each other does not "free" logic from philosophy, or logicians from the obligation to think.

Leibniz dreamed of a universal scientific language (*characteristica universalis*) in which all scientific concepts would be represented as combinations of basic ideograms,

[7] W. V. O. Quine, *From a Logical Point of View* (Cambridge, Mass., 1953), pp. 14–15.

and of a universal logical calculus (*calculus ratiocinator*) by whose help all problems expressed in the universal language could be automatically solved. *Ars combinatoria,* which would comprehend such a universal language and the logical calculus, would enable philosophers to solve their controversies by calculation. Instead of engaging in long discussions, it would be sufficient to take pens, to sit at the abacus and say to each other: "Let us calculate!"

The closing of the gap between logic and mathematics in the course of the last 120 years has not justified these hopes of Leibniz. Even logic, not to speak of other branches of philosophy, has not been reduced to calculation.

The question about the meaning and result of coming together of logic and mathematics can also be approached from another angle, however—the angle of mathematics. One can ask what this process has contributed to mathematics. If mathematics did not bring that precision and clarity into logic which would enable it to calculate instead of discussing, perhaps logic brought something to mathematics?

We can answer this question in the affirmative. Logic gave such "firm foundations" to mathematics that it shook it to its very foundations. Logic helped mathematics to see better those most fundamental questions about which mathematicians did not previously think enough. By the help of logic all those divisions, discussions, controversies, which throughout centuries were part of logic, epistemology, metaphysics and philosophy in general, now flourish in mathematics. Calculating has not eliminated discussion from philosophy, but discussion has pushed calculation in mathematics into second place.

Many still think that mathematics is predominantly concerned with the discovery of "unshakable" truths such as "$2 + 2 = 4$." But this is less and less true. Discussions concerning the nature and the methods of founding mathematical theses are more and more taking central place in contemporary mathematics. And these discussions are in essence philosophical. Philosophy has penetrated into the center of mathematics and threatens to swallow it—from within.

Of course, there are still many mathematicians who try to close their eyes to the philosophical problems of mathematics: "at all crossroads of his activity the mathematician can try to escape roads that would lead him to philosophical questions." But, "the attitude of one who, out of concern for exactness, vigilantly tries not to engage in any philosophical reflection, is not an aphilosophical attitude. Even if it is inspired by care for exactness, it is an attitude that does not offer any guarantee of exactness. It can be compared to the attitude of a man who, in fear of losing his way, vigilantly does not light his lantern."[8]

Contemporary mathematics, despite the antiphilosophic inclination of individual mathematicians, is split into conflicting schools and trends: formalists, intuitionists and others. Just as in philosophy, it is difficult to enumerate all the basic trends that contend within it; not only is there no generally accepted standard for deciding which trend is right, there is no generally accepted criterion of classification that would make possible the compilation of a generally acceptable list of "main trends."

Whether and how philosophical controversies can be "solved" is very much in question; they certainly cannot be solved by calculation. Similarly, no calculation can help to settle basic controversies among contemporary mathematical trends. Indeed, by what kind of imaginable calculation could basic theses of intuitionist mathematics be proved or disproved, as, for example, the thesis that "a mathematical theorem expresses a purely empirical fact, namely the success of a certain construction,"[9] or that mathematical theories can be arranged according to descending degrees of self-evidence, so that "the difference

[8] F. Gonseth, "Des Mathématiques à la Philosophie," *Dialectica*, no. 35–36, 1955, pp. 22, 226.

[9] Heyting, *Intuitionism*, p. 8.

between 1.000 and 1.001 is less clear than that between 3 and 4."[10]

The intuitionist Heyting, whose "mathematical" theses have been quoted here, is not an adherent of introducing metaphysics into mathematics. On the contrary, he pleads for "Brouwer's program," which requires "that we study mathematics as something simpler, more immediate than metaphysics."[11] But despite such "antimetaphysical" statements, he "intuitively" sees that such theses cannot be proved by any calculation, and he tries to justify them by essentially philosophical, "metaphysical" reasoning. He wrote the book from which we quoted above, in the form of a dialogue, i.e., in the form of a philosophical symposium, in which six persons with characteristic names take part: Class (the adherent of the classical mathematics), Form (formalist), Int (intuitionist), Letter (conventionalist), Prag (pragmatist) and Sign (significist).

Thus among mathematicians the awareness is developing that what they do or should do is not merely calculation; that the horizon for what is more narrowly "mathematical" can be opened up only by reasonings that are not purely mathematical; and that mathematics like every other theoretical "discipline" can investigate and secure its foundations only by transcending itself as a closed "special" discipline.

Contemporary mathematics is discovering itself as an integral part of man's creative spiritual activity, and although such a discovery can be painful for those who adapted themselves to a life of speciality, it does not imply anything bad about mathematics. It simply shows that the process of self-knowledge in mathematics has gone further than in many other "special" sciences and disciplines.

My answer to the question of what the development of logic and mathematics in the course of the last hundred

---

[10] A. Heyting, "Intuitionism in Mathematics," *Philosophy in the Mid-Century*, edited by R. Klibansky (Firenze, 1958), vol. I, p. 103.

[11] Heyting, *Intuitionism*, p. 2.

or so years has meant is consequently as follows: logic
has not emancipated itself from philosophy and become
a branch of mathematics, but mathematics, by forming
closer ties with logic, has come to realize better than ever
before (or at least to "feel") that it rests on assumptions
that are not purely mathematical.

Index

Action. *See* Praxis

Aeschylus, 198

Aesthetic phenomena, 22

Alienated Labor, 83, 88–89, 142

Alienation, 5, 48, 135–37, 144; application, 139; approaches, 139–40, 141; causes, 88–89; characteristics, 83–84; concepts, 86, origin, 135–36; de-alienation, 135–37; definitions of term, 135, 140–41; end, 150–51; forms, 141–43, 145; individual-social distinction, 144; nature of, 108; progress-regression, 149–50; psychology, 135, 136, 138, 139–40; revival of interest in, 138–39; theory, 32, 81–83. *See* Self-alienation

Anomie, 140

Anti-Dürhing, 33

Aquinas, Thomas, 196

Aristotle, 15, 171, 196, 198, 225; disciplines, 55; logic, 219; man, defined, 77; philosophy, 54–55; propositions, 223

Atheism, 160, 161, 162

Atomic bomb, 134

Bauer, Edgar, 182

Being: defined, 172–75; essence, relationship, 180–82; explanations by delimitation, 185–86; materiality, 178, 179; meaning, 65, 183; non-Being, 177; praxis, 171 ff., 183, 186, 189; proof, 177; space-time, 178–79, 186–88; thinking, 182, 191–92; unity, 188

Bentham, Jeremy, 73–74

Bernstein, E., 52

Biological factor, 105

Biologists, 71–72

Bloch, J., 12, 13, 91

Böhme, Jakob, 189

Bolsheviks, 18

Boltzmann, Ludwig, 14

Boole, G., 220 and n

Bourgeois society, 48, 74, 96

Brouwer, 220, 226, 229

Bukharin, N., 24

Calvez, Jean-Yves, 141

Capital, 13, 15, 26, 32, 37–42, 49–51, 113–14; alienation, 81; date written, 37, 38 n; fundamental idea, 42–43; labor, 73, 111; on man, 73–74, 77; nature, 73; philosophical phraseology, 41, 53; subtitle, 42

Capitalism, 74, 88; criticism, 133; freedom, 119, 133; socialism, 155, 156–57, 159

Carnap, 226

Cassirer, 200

Chevalier, M. Michel, 108

Church, 226

Classless society, 97, 98–100; determining factors, 109–11; freedom, 130; labor, 111–12

Class society, 23, 32, 100; factuality, 108–9; freedom, 130; "spheres," 159

Class struggle, 130, 131

Communication: in concept of meaning, 200; mass, 119, 133; technology, 133, 134

Communism: alienation, 87–88, 148; etymology of word, 160; followers, 161; humanism, 57–58, 161–62, 163; Marx, 160–64; phases, 155–60, 163; philosophy and politics, 166–69; socialism, 155–56; Stalin, 155–57, 159; "transitory period," 162–63

Communist party, 18–19, 52, 121

Concept(s): defined, 206, 213; praxis, 117 (see Praxis)

Consciousness, 22, 194

Continuity thesis, 25–51; interpretations, 36; key ideas, 37

Contribution to the Critique of Hegel's Philosophy of Right, 53

Contribution to the Critique of Political Economy, 91, 96

Correspondence theory of truth, 192–93

Creativity: freedom, 127, 128; spiritual, 116, 197–98

Critique of the Gotha Program, 156, 157

Croatian Philosophical Society, 9 n

Cuvier, G., 71

Darwin, Charles, 91

De-alienation, 5, 138, 139, 150–51; alienation, 135–53; progress, 149

Dehumanization, 32

Descartes, 219

Dialectical materialism, 58, 59, 62–66; spirit (God), 61; Stalinists, 18, 21–22

Dialectics, 14, 24, 25, 27; negation, 24; Stalinism, 24–28

Dictators, 118, 127

"Dictatorship of the proletariat," 155–57

Distribution principle, 157–58

Dühring, Karl, 178

Economic(s), 91, 92, 94; de-alienation, 152, 153; determinism, 151; materialism; 102–3, 105; terminology, 43–45

Economic and Philosophical Manuscripts, 32, 37–42, 49–51, 53, 163; alienation, 81, 82, 88, 138, 142, 148; date written, 37–38 and n; fundamental idea, 41–43; on man, 73, 78, 79; preface, 41, 42; wealth, 49

Economic animal, man as, 112–14, 159

"Economic factor," 98, 99–100, 101–2, 105

Engels, Friedrich, 6, 9, 10–13, 30, 33, 34, 100, 195; alienation, 81–82, 86; on Being, 178; classless society, 109; class society, 100; dialectics, 21–22, 24, 27, 58–61, 64; *Dialectics of Nature,* 14, 25, 27, 33; economics, 92, 102; freedom, 122; history, 91–92, 94, 97–98; on man, 14, 79; Marx, 14, 24–25, 38 n, 39, 91; *Origin of the Family, Private Property and the State,* 86–87, 97–99; philosophy, 15, 63; Plekhanov, 30; production, 93, 103–4; reflection, 63; self-alienation, 148; truth, 192–93

Enlightenment, 55

Essence, 65, 75–76

Ethics, 5, 22. See Morality

Existence, 177–78

Existentialism, 17, 138, 147
Exploitation, 32

Factors theory, 101–9
Family, 49–50, 109–10
Fascism, 118
Feudalism, 88
Feuer, Lewis, 142
Feuerbach, Ludwig, 15, 16, 29, 31, 36; alienation, 136, 137, 142; on Being, 175–76, 177, 178, 180, 181; Marx, 195, 196; philosophy, 142
France, 16, 71, 107–8
Franklin, Benjamin, 77
Freedom, 5, 71, 88, 118–34; aspects, 131; burden of, 118–19; degrees, 127–28, 129; escape from, 118–19; essence, 120, 128, 131–32; forms, 119–20, 131–32; philosophy, 31; praxis, 118 ff.; problem, 133–35; relativity, 127; Stalinists, 31; theories, 120–27; unfreedom, 119. See Unfreedom
Free society, 128–30, 133
Frege, G., 220, 226
French Revolution, 16
Fromm, Erich, 141, 148–49

"Games," 213–14
German Ideology, 32, 33, 39, 53, 180; alienation, 81, 88; on man, 73
Germany, 71
God, 61; concept of, 172–74; negation (see Atheism)
Gorki, Maxim, 19
Greeks, Ancient, 122, 198

Hegel, G. W. F., 12, 13, 15, 20, 22, 31, 35, 55, 77, 136, 171; alienation, 135–37, 142; on Being, 117, 173–75, 176, 178; dialectics, 24, 25, 26, 27, 41; essence, 75; freedom, 122; Logic, 16, 75, 174; on man, 80; Marx, 17, 80, 137; Nature, 136; self-alienation, 141, 144–45; Stalinism, 16–17
Heidegger, Martin, 17, 185–87; alienation, 86; on Being, 183–84; essence, 76; Introduction to Metaphysics, 184, 185, 187; nihilism, 187; Sein und Zeit, 76, 86, 183, 184, 187
Heyting, A., 220, 229
Hilbert, D., 221, 226
Historical materialism, 21, 22, 94–96
History, 79–80, 91, 127, 136; completed, 54; concepts, 105, 106; factors, 91–92, 98–99, 103–4; Marx, 17, 91–92, 94; self-alienation, 148–49
History of C.P.S.U., 18 n, 19
Hobbes, Thomas, 121
Holy Family, The, 39, 53
Humanism, 5, 9 and n, 161–62; concept, 163–64; Marx, 23; philosophy and politics, 166–69; revolutionary, 37
Human nature, 74, 81

Idealism, 28, 60–61
Idolatry, 136
Isolation, 143

James, William, 171
Jews, 43
Josephson, Eric, 140, 143
Josephson, Mary, 140, 143

Kant, Immanuel, 125, 171, 187, 223; on Being, 172–73; on God, 172–74
Kautsky, K., 52
Knjazeva, S., 212–13, 214

Labor, 73, 111–12; alienation, 88–89; object, 79

Labriola, 92, 94

Lacombe, P., 102–3

Lassalle, 39–40, 42

Law, 135

Leader, 118

Lefebvre, H., 87

Leibniz, Gottfried, 220, 226–27

Lenin, Nikolai, 6, 9, 10–13, 15–16, 19, 22, 28–29, 94, 195; on Being, 178–79; dialectics, 24, 25, 26, 27, 33, 34, 58, 64; Engels 14; essence, 75–76; Marx, 14; *Materialism and Empirio-Criticism*, 13, 14, 19, 28, 33–34, 60, 63, 178–79; *Philosophical Notebooks*, 12, 13, 14, 24, 25, 28–29, 34, 191, 197; Plekhanov, 13, 14; production, 93; reflection, 63, 191, 192, 193; truth, 11, 191–93

Leske, C. W., 39

Levin, Murray, 140

Logic, 5, 18, 22, 201, 206–7; contemporary, 223–26; mathematics, 218 ff., 226–30; nature of, 218, 225; object, 200–1; origin, 219; philosophy, 226; propositions, 223; as science, 222; traditional, 222–24

Love, 177–78

Lukacs, G., 12, 13, 138; *History and Class Consciousness*, 14–15, 138

Man, 5, 14, 17, 71–75, 79, 105, 111, 115–16; animal, differences, 74–75; Being (*see* Being); conceptions, 77; defined, 67–68; dehumanization, 67; economic animal, 77, 90–91, 94, 112–14; end of production, 45–48; essence, 23, 73, 75–76, 80, 83–85, 120, 146–47; etymology of word, 69–71; as future, 80; Hegel-Marx differences, 80–81; history, 79–80; multimeanings of term, 68 and n–70; nonalienated, 138; object of philosophy, 62; praxis, 32, 116; primitive, 87; rational animal, 115, 116; social animal, 106–7, 115–16; social history concept, 79; "spheres," 77–78, 90, 94, 95; as spirit, 71; toolmaking animal, 77, 90, 92, 94, 112, 116; working animal, 116. *See also* Alienation *and under* Marx *and* Stalinism

Manifesto of the Communist Party, 32

Marković, Mihailo, 199, 201, 203, 204, 205, 207, 208, 209, 212, 213, 215, 216; *Dialectical Theory of Meaning*, 216

Marx, Karl, 9, 11–13, 22, 29, 39–40, 53, 71, 72–76, 87–88, 160–61, 167; alienation, 136–38; on Being, 180–83, 186; continuity of thought, 35–51; dialectics, 24–25, 27–28; economics, 77, 102; health, 39–40; history, 94; on man, 14, 22–24, 28, 63, 64, 65, 73 ff., 77–78, 80–81, 191, 194, 196–97, defined, 116 (*see* Praxis); philosophy, 15, 19, 20, 52 ff., 55, 155; self-alienation, 23, 141, 144–45, 148; "young" and "old," 13, 14, 29, 31–37, 41

Marx-Engels-Lenin Institute, 38 n

Marxism, 52; authentic, 9–11; "classics of," 11, 12, 14; creative, 5, 10, 34; existentialism, 17; freedom, 31; humanistic problems, 9 and n; pragmatism, 17–18; Stalinism, 9 ff., 11–18

Materialism, 28–30, 60–61

Mathematics, 5, 228–29; defined, 218; intuitionism, 220; logic and, 218 ff., 226–30; origin, 219; philosophy, 219, 227–28

Matter, 22, 63, 64

Meaning, 5, 203–5, 208–17; concept, 200, 217; definition, 208–11; dimensions, 216; essence, 202–3; objective, 209, 211, 215, 216; proof, 201; theories, 199 ff., 201, 211–12; of words, 208, 211, 214–15

Meaninglessness, 142–43

Medicine, 135

Mehring, F., 52

Metaphysics, 219

Metatheories, 201

Method, conception of, 22

Moore, Stanley, 140–41

Morality, 107–8

Naturalism-humanism, 57–58, 62, 64–66

Natural sciences, 26–27

Nature, 22, 61, 73, 91, 136; dialectics, 25, 27–28; self-alienation, 145

Nazism, 118, 150

Nettler, Gwynn, 140

Nietzsche, Friedrich, 54–55

Nihilism, 11, 12, 187

Normlessness, 143

nth hour of work, 107–8

Old Testament, 136

Ontology, 34

"Original sin," 135

Party-character principle, 19

Pavlov, Todor, 192; *Theory of Reflection*, 63

Peirce, C. S., 209, 211

Personality, 129–31, 140

Philosophers, 60–61, 195–96, 219

Philosophy, 5, 15–16, 22–23, 54, 59–62, 75, 195–96; alienation, 135, 136, 138, 139, 148; basic question, 59–62; under communism, 166; defined, 164; disciplines, 54–55, 192, 201, 206; essence, 54–55; of history, 5; under humanism, 166; logic, 221–22, 226; Marx, 5, 15–16, 52 ff.; mathematics, 227–28; politics, 19–20, 154–69; science, 20; terms, 204–5

Plato, 54–55, 136, 154, 171, 198, 219

Plekhanov, George, 12, 13, 14, 29, 34, 60, 92–93, 94, 100–1, 103, 106, 107, 109, 192–93; dialectics, 25, 58, 64

Poincaré, M., 226

Political economy, 36, 41, 42, 108, 112

Politics, 19–20, 154–69; defined, 164–65

Poverty, 49

Powerlessness, 142

Pragmatism, 17–18

Praxis, 5, 9 and n, 29, 32, 193–94; and Being, 171 ff., 183, 186, 189; characteristics, 118, 186; defined, 78–81, 117–18, 171–72; man as, 23, 63, 112–14, 116; meanings, 111 n, 203, 206, 216; philosophy of, 56–58 (*see* Naturalism-humanism)

Private property, 110, 152, 153, 160, 163; origin, 88–89

Production, 50–51, 83, 91, 93, 158, 163; as determining factor in history, 90, 93, 98, 99, 103; end of, 43–46, 47–48; man-animal differences, 79

Proletariat, 54, 112, 155–57

Propagation of species, 97–99

Prostitution, 107–8

Psychology, 135, 136, 138–40

Pythagoras, 219

Quine, W. V. O., 226

"Redemption," 135

Reflection, 9 and n; theory, 29, 62–63, 190–98; truth, 190–98

"Reification," 135, 138

Religion, 109–10, 160

Responsibility, of freedom, 118

Revisionists, 12, 13, 52

Ricardo, 108

Russell, Bertrand, 218, 220, 226

Sartre, J. P., 17, 125

Schachtel, Ernest, 142

Scheler, Max, 77

Science, 20

Seeman, Melvin, 142–43

Self-alienation, 23, 32, 42–43, 82–84, 108–10, 135, 141, 143–45; defined, 145–47; development, 147–48; essence, 151; forms, 137–38; freedom, 119

Self-determination theory of freedom, 125–27

Sex, 98

Sketches for the Critique of Political Economy, 37–42, 49–51; date written, 37, 38 n; fundamental idea, 42–43; philosophical terminology, 41

Slavery, 88, 128

Social consciousness, 90

Social development, 100–2, 105, 113

Social groups, 144, 165

Socialism, 5, 67, 150–51, 154, 155–57, 160, 163; concepts, 154; defined, 155; freedom, 119, 133; philosophy and politics, 154–69; Stalin, 155–57, 159

Social orders, sequence, 155–56

Social sciences, 106, 202

Society, 22, 33, 67, 97, 118–19, 144, 162; essence, 128–29; self-alienated, 146, 152

Sociology, 135, 136, 138, 139, 148

Somerville, John, 121, 122

Sophocles, 198

"Spheres," 77–78, 90, 94, 95, 110, 113; economic, 116, 164

Spinoza, Benedict, 122

Spirit, 61

Stalin, Josef, 11, 63, 93, 94, 155, 156; dialectics, 19, 24, 58; philosophy, 10–11, 19, 22. See Stalinism

Stalinism, 9–11, 12, 14, 15–18, 18–24, 24–30, 155–57, 159; criticism, 6, 10; essence, 11

Stalinists, 18, 21–22, 24–28, 31; freedom, 31; idealism, 28; "old" Marx, 31, 32, 35

State, the, 95, 98–99, 109–10

Symbols, 203–4

Technology, 67; freedom, 133–34

Temporality-praxis, 186

Teophrastus, 223

Thermonuclear war, 54
Thinking, 191
Time-Being relationship, 186–88
Truth, 5; correspondence theory, 192–93; multimeaningness, 190; pragmatic theory, 17; praxis, 193–94; reflection, 190–98; Stalin, 11
Two Marxs thesis, 38–39

Unalienated man, 111
Unfreedom, 119, 132; degrees, 127–28; Stalinists, 31
Utility, principle of, 73–74

Vasiljev, D., 67

Wealth, 43, 45, 46, 47–49
Weiss, Frederick A., 142
Whitehead, A. N., 226
Wittgenstein, Ludwig, 213–14 and n
World, 18–21; interpretation-change, 55, 56–57, 195–96; old-modern, 48; unity, 178
World War II, 138

"Young" and "old" Marx, 9 and n, 31–34, 35, 36–37, 41, 86, 139
Yugoslavia, 169; Marxism, 6, 9 n; Stalinism, 30

ANCHOR BOOKS

PHILOSOPHY

AESTHETICS AND HISTORY—Bernard Berenson, A36

THE AMERICAN TRANSCENDENTALISTS: THEIR PROSE AND POETRY—
Perry Miller, ed., A119

* ARISTOTLE—ed. by Julius Moravcsik, AP1

BASIC WRITINGS ON POLITICS AND PHILOSOPHY—Karl Marx and
Friedrich Engels; Lewis Feuer, ed., A185

BERDYAEV'S PHILOSOPHY: The Existential Paradox of Freedom and
Necessity—Fuad Nucho, Introduction by Richard Kroner, A539

THE BIRTH OF TRAGEDY AND THE GENEALOGY OF MORALS—Friedrich
Nietzsche, A81

THE BROKEN IMAGE: MAN, SCIENCE, AND SOCIETY—Floyd W. Matson, A506

THE COSMOLOGICAL ARGUMENTS—A Spectrum of Opinion—Donald
R. Burrill, ed., A586

CRITIQUE OF PURE REASON—Immanuel Kant, trans. by F. Max
Müller, A551

CRITIQUE OF RELIGION AND PHILOSOPHY—Walter Kaufmann, A252

* DESCARTES: A Collection of Critical Essays—Willis Doney, ed.,
AP5

EITHER/OR, Vol. I—Soren Kierkegaard, A181a

EITHER/OR, Vol. II—Soren Kierkegaard, A181b

ESSAYS ON POLITICS AND CULTURE—John Stuart Mill; Gertrude
Himmelfarb, ed., A373

ESSAYS IN PHILOSOPHICAL PSYCHOLOGY—Donald F. Gustafson, ed.,
A417

ETHICS AND SOCIETY: Original Essays on Contemporary Moral
Problems—Richard T. DeGeorge, A512

THE FAITH OF A HERETIC—Walter Kaufmann, A336

FEAR AND TREMBLING AND THE SICKNESS UNTO DEATH—Soren
Kierkegaard, A30

FIVE STAGES OF GREEK RELIGION—Gilbert Murray, A51

FOUR EXISTENTIALIST THEOLOGIANS—Will Herberg, A141

FROM HEGEL TO NIETZSCHE—The Revolution in Nineteenth-
Century Thought—Karl Löwith; trans. by David E. Green,
A553

FROM SHAKESPEARE TO EXISTENTIALISM—Walter Kaufmann, A213

FROM THE STONE AGE TO CHRISTIANITY—W. F. Albright, A100

* Modern Studies in Philosophy Series

Philosophy (continued)

THE GENESIS OF TWENTIETH CENTURY PHILOSOPHY: The Evolution of Thought from Copernicus to the Present—Harry Prosch, A536

HEGEL: A Reinterpretation—Walter Kaufmann, A528a

HEGEL: Texts and Commentary—Walter Kaufmann, A528b

THE HUMAN CONDITION—Hannah Arendt, A182

* HUME—ed. by V. C. Chappell, AP2

INDIVIDUALS—P. F. Strawson, A364

THE INTELLECTUAL HISTORY OF EUROPE, Vol. I: The Beginnings of Western Civilization to Luther—Friedrich Heer, A610a

THE INTELLECTUAL HISTORY OF EUROPE, Vol. II: The Counter-Reformation to the 20th Century—Friedrich Heer, A610b

IRRATIONAL MAN—William Barrett, A321

* KANT: A Collection of Critical Essays—Robert Paul Wolff, ed., AP4

* LOCKE AND BERKELEY: A Collection of Critical Essays—David M. Armstrong and C. B. Martin, AP6

LOGIC AND LANGUAGE—Antony Flew, ed., A449

MAN IN MODERN AGE—Karl Jaspers, A101

MARX IN THE MID-TWENTIETH CENTURY: A Yugoslav Philosopher Reconsiders Karl Marx's Writings—Gajo Petrović, A584

MARXISM AND EXISTENTIALISM—Walter Odajnyk, A443

THE MARXISM OF JEAN-PAUL SARTRE—Wilfrid Desan, A507

THE METAPHYSICAL FOUNDATIONS OF MODERN SCIENCE—Edwin Arthur Burtt, A41

MODERN SCIENCE AND MODERN MAN—James B. Conant, A10

MYSTICISM AND LOGIC—Bertrand Russell, A104

THE ONTOLOGICAL ARGUMENT—Alvin Plantinga, ed., A435

PATTERNS OF ANARCHY—Leonard I. Krimerman and Lewis Perry, eds., A501

PERCEIVING, SENSING AND KNOWING—Robert J. Swartz, ed., A460

THE PHILOSOPHY OF HISTORY IN OUR TIME—Hans Meyerhoff, ed., A164

PHILOSOPHIES OF JUDAISM—Julius Guttman, A509

THE PHILOSOPHY OF TIME—Richard Gale, ed., A573

PRAGMATIC PHILOSOPHY—ed. by Amelie Rorty, A538

PSYCHE AND SYMBOL—C. G. Jung, A136

SELECTIONS FROM THE WRITINGS OF KIERKEGAARD—Lee M. Hollander, ed. and trans., A210

SOCIALIST HUMANISM: An International Symposium—ed. by Erich Fromm, A529

* Modern Studies in Philosophy Series

SOCIAL AND POLITICAL PHILOSOPHY: Readings from Plato to Gandhi—John Somerville and Ronald Santoni, eds., A370

SOCRATES—A. E. Taylor, A9

THE SPIRITUAL HERITAGE OF INDIA—Swami Prabhavananda with Frederick Manchester, A419

THE TACIT DIMENSION—Michael Polanyi, A540

THREE WAYS OF THOUGHT IN ANCIENT CHINA—Arthur Waley, A75

WHAT IS PHENOMENOLOGY?—Joseph J. Kockelmans, ed., A585

WITTGENSTEIN AND MODERN PHILOSOPHY—Justus Hartnack, A469

* WITTGENSTEIN: The Philosophical Investigations—ed. by George Pitcher, AP3

WRITINGS OF THE YOUNG MARX ON PHILOSOPHY AND SOCIETY—Loyd D. Easton and Kurt H. Guddat, trans. and eds., A583

ZEN BUDDHISM—D. T. Suzuki, A90

ZEN FLESH, ZEN BONES—Paul Reps, ed., A233

ZEN: Poems, Prayers, Sermons, Anecdotes, Interviews—Lucien Stryk and Takashi Ikemoto, eds., A485

* Modern Studies in Philosophy Series